Urban Life and Urban Landscape Series

Merchant of Illusion

JAMES ROUSE, AMERICA'S SALESMAN OF THE BUSINESSMAN'S UTOPIA

NICHOLAS DAGEN BLOOM

The Ohio State University Press
Columbus

Library of Congress Cataloging-in-Publication Data

Bloom, Nicholas Dagen, 1969-
   Merchant of illusion : James Rouse, America's salesman of the
businessman's utopia / Nicholas Dagen Bloom.
      p. cm. — (Urban life and urban landscape series)
Includes bibliographical references and index.
   ISBN 0-8142-0953-X (cloth : alk. paper) — 0-8142-9026-4 (CD-ROM)
   1. Rouse, James W. 2. — Urban renewal — United States — History
— 20th century. 3. City planning — United States — History — 20th
century. 4. Real estate developers—United States—Biography. I. Title. II.
Series.

   HT175 .B54 2004
   307.76'0973'0904—dc22
                                                     2003018245

Cover design by Dan O'Dair
Type set in Goudy
Printed by Thomson-Shore, Inc.

9 8 7 6 5 4 3 2 1

Contents

James Wilson Rouse Timeline

1914   James Rouse is born in Easton, Maryland.

1939   Moss-Rouse (Mortgage) Company is founded in Baltimore, Maryland.

1951   Rouse leads Mayor's Advisory Council on Housing Law Enforcement, part of "The Baltimore Plan" neighborhood renewal project.

1953   *Encyclopedia Britannica* releases the film *The Baltimore Plan* to a national audience.

1954   Rouse serves on Eisenhower's Advisory Committee that designs the Housing Act of 1954.
        Rouse is a founding member of ACTION, the American Council to Improve Our Neighborhoods.

1955   Rouse becomes a founding member of the Greater Baltimore Committee.

1958   Rouse is elected president of ACTION.
        The Rouse Company opens Harundale Mall, the second enclosed shopping center in the United States.

1959   Charles Center plan is unveiled in Baltimore, Maryland.
        Plan is generated from action of the Greater Baltimore Committee.

1963   Rouse announces Columbia, Maryland, a fifteen-thousand-acre new town project.

1969   Hartford Process, a nationally known plan of urban transformation led by Rouse's American City Corporation, is launched.

1970   Title VII, a $500 million federal new town program is created.

1976   The Rouse Company opens Faneuil Hall "Festival Marketplace."

1979   Rouse retires from The Rouse Company at age sixty-five.

1980   Rouse opens Harborplace "Festival Marketplace."

1982   Enterprise Foundation is founded.

1995   Rouse is awarded the Presidential Medal of Freedom.

1996   James Rouse dies in Columbia, Maryland.

Introduction

So here this great nation, the leader of Western civilization, at the peak
of its economic prosperity, is piling its people into cities which are rotting away at the core, infested with slums, and with the slums spreading
out into the middle-aged areas beyond. It's not a pretty picture.

James Rouse,1960

Mr. Rouse says the [Enterprise] Foundation stems, in part, from his belief
that the United States has fallen behind the Soviet Union in meeting the
"human needs" of its poorest citizens. "The free enterprise system—our
system—just doesn't do it at all . . . But it can."

Paul Engelmayer, "Developer of Festival Marketplaces Sets Up
Foundation to Renovate InnerCity Homes," 1983

A worldwide outbreak of "creeping socialism" after the Second World
War was more than just the fevered imaginings of the most rabid anticommunist crusaders. The Soviet Union's extension of power over
Eastern Europe, the replacement of European empires in the Third World
with socialist or left-friendly home rule, and the unexpected strength of
labor and social democratic parties in Western Europe augured a future world
more socialist than capitalist. Even within the United States many conservative Americans had watched uneasily as the federal government massively expanded, to their minds, its role in social policy during the New
Deal. Domestic blacklisting, direct and covert military intervention, and
the Marshall Plan are the most potent symbols of the American battle against
the spread of world socialism. Not every response to the socialist challenge,
however, was so blatant or violent.

For many Americans the superiority of democratic capitalism could best
be demonstrated by developing the ability of the free enterprise system to deliver
the good life to burgeoning urban populations. The notion that capitalism
had the ability to compete in the realm of social improvement proved something of a novelty, but the concept of market solutions to public needs gained
rapid favor among businessmen, politicians, and a large part of the American
population uncomfortable with state solutions. A spirited competition in urban

policy ensued between socialism, both Soviet Communism and European social democracy,[1] and powerful antisocialist "free enterprise" forces in the United States. In Europe and the Soviet Union, cities were rebuilt as part of diverse socialist plans to initiate a new era in human social relations. In the United States, aging industrial cities were rebuilt and reconceived to match the demands of progressive capitalism and the socialist challenge.[2] The race between the diverse forms of socialism and the free enterprise system thus transformed urban civilization on a global scale.

The United States, most notably, could no longer turn a blind eye to the blighted state of its many cities. Since at least the late nineteenth century America's urban affairs had been shocking to visitors. The contrast between the tenements and the Gold Coasts, the skyscrapers and the meat-packing districts, the lush suburbs and the grimy central cities could rarely be overlooked. The disordered although vibrant state of America's cities had been a real but much less pressing issue when America was merely a leading industrial power in a world of capitalist nations; American cities seemed no less unappealing and unjust than those in any other country. The steady rise of communist and social democratic urban planning, however, cast America's ramshackle cities in a darker shadow. According to retired American propagandist Alvin A. Snyder, by the 1960s, "The America portrayed abroad through TV shows, news broadcasts, and movies was violent and racist. Images of America's ghettos dispelled those of the American people as generous and open-minded."[3]

In an era when socialist and social democratic nations were undergoing what appeared to be breathtaking improvements in urban affairs through housing programs, national health care, comprehensive planning, full employment policies, and planned new towns, the seeming failure of U.S. cities to keep pace bespoke something unnerving about the ability of capitalism, even with its abundant consumer society, to create a good society for all. An urban civilization like the United States had to demonstrate that it could create great cities on largely capitalist models; to fail to do so posed a threat not only to domestic tranquility but also to the expansion of American power and influence abroad.

As a leading voice of progressive business interests and great propagandist for American city rebuilding, James Rouse often spoke of the miserable state of American cities in a comparative context, gaining a great deal of rhetorical punch by asking his listeners to imagine the foreign, and particularly communist, response to America's urban shame. In 1960 he enlightened a group of shopping center developers to the dangers of ignoring America's urban crisis: "When Khrushchev came to Washington, it seemed particularly appropriate that the President should have shown him Washington in a helicopter. This is the way it looked the best. If he [the

President] had taken him on the ground and through the middle ring that surrounded the Capitol district of Washington it would have been a squalid, dirty, filthy mess that we [the United States] would have been showing the head of the Communist nation." This middle ring, growing larger after the war, undermined familiar, and more upbeat, images of American affluence projected around the world. Rouse explained in the same speech that others shared his embarrassment: "I made this statement once in a talk in Washington and a fellow came up to me afterwards and said, 'You know, I work in the Pan American Union. . . . I have to keep them [important foreign visitors] away from the center of American cities in order to have them understand America. There's no way that I can adequately explain how a nation with this enormous capacity can allow these conditions of deterioration to exist, where its people live.'"[4]

Improvements in the backward state of American cities over the decades came slowly. After a visit to the Soviet Union in 1985 where he encountered what he considered to be unimpressive housing projects, Rouse still admitted, "I don't believe there could be a South Bronx in Russia, nor a Harlem, nor the slums of most American cities. How could it be that a Communist tyranny could provide so well for its potentially poor but that our vigorous, productive, free enterprise system could provide so badly?"[5] No one could deny American affluence, but as evident to sensitive observers like Rouse was the degree to which this abundance did not reach to the lower levels of American urban society.

These concerns could, on occasion, be echoed at the highest political levels. President Harry Truman, during his hard fight for reelection in 1948, asked a crowd of supporters in Wisconsin to consider the public relations danger posed by American slums: "How can we expect to sell democracy to Europe until we prove that within the democratic system we can provide decent homes for our people ?"[6] Adlai Stevenson, the leading voice of 1950s liberalism and ambassador to the United Nations under Presidents John F. Kennedy and Lyndon B. Johnson, lamented to urban leaders in 1959 that "In distant places, I have, like you, often thought that in spite of our standard of living, in spite of amenities that exceed the grasp, even the imagination of most people, we in America have still fallen far short of even arresting the spread of blight and decay in our cities." This urban disorder, a black spot on America's global image, damaged the nation's ability to keep pace with the communists: "Like you I have often wondered how we can hope to solve the problems of maintaining our alliances, of meeting the communist economic offensive, of extending a helping hand to the peoples now searching for national identity and independence, of standing firm against aggression anywhere, if we can't mobilize our domestic resources to meet the needs of day-to-day work and living."[7]

A modern reader, familiar with the demise of the Soviet empire, will likely attach little significance to the concerns of Rouse, Truman, or Stevenson. What we now know about the actual realities of life in the Soviet Union should not, however, allow us to forget that before the 1980s, and particularly after Stalin died in 1953, the USSR looked impressive and had made actual progress in addressing urban problems through national health care, massive housing projects, universal education, and national employment schemes, even though resources committed to urban improvements likely exceeded reasonable expenditures for a comparatively poor country such as the USSR. The positive appearance of Soviet urban progress over the decades was greatly enhanced by government censorship of its national media. Although American failings in civil rights, and in eliminating urban blight and poverty were well publicized both in the United States and other nations, the Soviet Union projected a utopian image of its urban affairs.[8]

The Soviet Union's growing reputation for urban progress allowed people around the world, particularly many left-sympathetic political leaders, to overlook the Soviet's stolid and unimaginative centralized planning, harsh repression of dissent, and the absence of a vibrant private sector. Our lack of memory should not distort the facts of the past—communism, in the minds of many influential Americans, appeared to be outpacing the United States in creating an appealing (if to their minds entirely illusory) version of the good life. In the race to convert countries around the globe, the United States had to demonstrate, particularly within its own borders, that its economic and political system could deliver the good life to urban majorities.

⌒

Although allied militarily to Canada, Great Britain, and numerous Western and Northern European nations, no less threatening to conservatives in the United States were social democratic governments in these countries that combined extensive social welfare with private enterprise and democratic practices. American conservatives frequently called social democracy "creeping socialism," and they disliked the massive public housing programs, national insurance, family allowances, and nationalization efforts that they saw as a first step toward a totalitarian communist system. Henry Hazlitt, a famous free-market advocate and frequent contributor to *Newsweek,* made the connection between the diverse forms of world socialism in 1951: "Russia is the ghastly symbol of what happens to human liberty when Socialism becomes complete, instead of merely partial as in England, France, or Sweden."[9] To men like Hazlitt, democratic socialism was just as great a threat as Soviet Communism; the two systems were distinct only in the degree of adherence to socialist principles.

For many conservatives, the legacy of the New Deal posed as serious an internal threat as socialism abroad. Postwar urban policy would not continue the expansion of the New Deal welfare state (as embodied, for instance, in Truman's Fair Deal), much loathed by many businessmen and considered to be a part of the worldwide spread of socialism. Local business elites across America despised the New Deal because it had, in their minds, massively expanded the role of government in everything from social welfare to regional planning.[10] Conservative forces greatly exaggerated the radical aspects of the New Deal, but it is true that the American response to the Depression had been impressive and had even made the United States a world leader in social welfare. The patchwork Depression era programs had given the United States, according to political scientist Edwin Amenta, the lead position in the percentage of the Gross Domestic Product devoted to social spending; nearly 30 percent of national government spending flowed to social programs. Indeed, "on the eve of the Second World War the United States pledged more of its national product to security in this larger sense than any major industrial nation."[12] Wartime mobilization massively increased the power of the federal government in areas such as industrial production, transportation, and employment. Truman's Fair Deal also envisioned a significant expansion of the welfare state. The hasty retreat from this increasingly state-oriented system in the late 1940s and 1950s, engineered by conservative forces both political and financial, and well-documented elsewhere, was just as notable.[13]

The socialist and New Deal challenge was answered in this country not only with the repudiation of the national activist state at the federal level, but also with the greatest flurry of idealistic planning, propaganda, and reconstruction ever undertaken in American cities. Although much has been written on the content and course of urban renewal,[12] the growth of world socialism, I believe, partly answers the question of why urban renewal, and other forms of business-led planning from the 1940s to the 1990s, suddenly became so popular and powerful. Many of the projects promoted by progressive businessmen in this period, including reconstruction of whole city centers, housing code creation and enforcement, and planned new towns, had generated in an earlier time and place alternating bouts of fierce opposition and apathy from other businessmen and property owners. But in the postwar period these efforts suddenly found solid backing from even conservative political and business interests. Why the sudden change?

The identification of reform with business interests partially allowed this shift to more aggressive programs, but just as important in buttressing these new policies were far more radical social policies brewing in Europe. A worldwide socialist constellation providing varying degrees of centralized planning, universal health care, housing, and full employment to its citizens, and the legacy of growing state intervention of the New and Fair Deal, fore-closed certain radical policy options but simultaneously, and almost imperceptibly, expanded the acceptable boundaries of urban policy in the United States.

A probusiness vision offering a series of business-friendly solutions to America's urban crisis, devised by businessmen like James Rouse, entirely filled the space created by the growing scale and scope of international urban policy. Business ideology, with its emphasis on cutthroat management, profit creation, self-help, and low taxation, gained remarkable strength exclusively in the United States as the best approach to a variety of long-standing and complex urban problems. Business leaders acknowledged that in propor-tion to American wealth, American city centers appeared particularly unim-pressive. They did not, however, share the European belief that massive national resources would necessarily help urban conditions. Businessmen, or at least the most idealistic among them, like Rouse, sought a perfectly managed version of capitalism that could, with only a delicate amount of government money, create a uniformly impressive urban civilization.

A variety of different groups allied with conservative political forces thus not only successfully beat back social spending, but also mounted national public relations campaigns to promote business leadership as the solution to both economic and social problems in American cities. These businessmen did accept federal and local dollars, but only to the degree that this money supported local projects they had generated. Direct social spending or gov-ernmental leadership remained more suspect. William Zeckendorf, for instance, the dynamic head of a New York development company, wrote regularly on urban affairs for the *Atlantic Monthly* during the 1940s and 1950s. Although he called for strenuous incorporation of areas surrounding inner cities, expan-sion of local government powers of condemnation, and the use of con-demnation to replace inner-city slums with office towers, he prized private enterprise as the most important force in making redevelopment work: "To have private capital develop or redevelop the urban areas is vital and essential. I do not believe a bureaucratic, city-wide, state-wide or national planning or executive commission could possibly accomplish the actual work." He lauded "the hard, cold analysis that venture capital will give everything that it goes into. Success of individual enterprise is the only true test."[14]

Yet James Rouse—more than Zeckendorf, Paul Mellon, Donald Trump, John Portman, or any other single urban business figure in the second half of the twentieth century—shifted this battle for private sector leadership to American cities.[15] An opponent of "big" government programs, Rouse found ways throughout his long career to make the point that the private sector—including both corporations and nonprofit organizations—should take the lead role in reform of the urban order. He was a master builder not only of unique places but an appealing cultural and intellectual vision of private sector leadership for urban America. As *Newsweek* noted in his obituary in 1996, "he became one of the most influential (and most imitated) social engineers of his time."[16] In 1995, a year before his death, President Bill Clinton awarded Rouse the Presidential Medal of Freedom; Rouse deserved this great honor because his direct impact on cities and urban ideals spanned both decades and national borders.

Rouse may be best remembered for his festival marketplaces, but for decades he was the leading propagandist for a business program of urban reform. He was not only an eloquent speaker and savvy marketer, but also a living, breathing embodiment of the promise of the American free enterprise system. Born in 1914 to an established family on Maryland's Eastern Shore, he lost both parents at age sixteen and subsequently supported himself through law school in Baltimore by working as a parking lot attendant for sixteen hours a day. With a friend, Hunter Moss, he created a profitable mortgage business in Baltimore in 1939 that during the 1940s and 1950s made money by arranging commercial and residential properties; by 1953, his company was Maryland's largest mortgage broker. During the 1950s he gained fame as a pioneer of some of the first enclosed shopping malls. The Rouse Company (based in Columbia, Maryland, the new town he founded in 1963), which grew from his many efforts, remains one of America's leading land development and management companies. He became a wealthy businessman but never seemed to lose the common touch; he sported worn, mismatched suits and lived modestly in a small suburban house.

Another major ingredient of Rouse's national success derived from his pragmatic political outlook that allowed him to work with both liberal and conservative politicians. Private sector idealism on urban issues and modest government expenditures on social programs proved equally appealing to both leading American political parties. While Rouse strongly supported moderate conservative candidates at the national level, such as Wendell Wilkie, Dwight D. Eisenhower, and Senator Charles "Mac" Mathias, politicians skeptical of both social programs and foreign military adventures, he associated with a wide range of national politicians at different moments, including Lyndon Johnson, Richard Nixon, Jimmy Carter, Ronald Reagan, George Bush Sr., and Bill Clinton. Strategic alliances throughout his career allowed him to cross party lines and pursue his urban agenda.

Finally, and of no less importance, Rouse remained throughout his life a liberal Christian who often sounded more like an adherent of the Social Gospel than a builder of shopping malls and suburban planned communities. His belief in the utility of Christian beliefs in social reform understandably attracted quite a bit of attention from national politicians. This winning combination of self-improvement, moderate conservatism admixed with pragmatism, and Christian beliefs made him a formidable presence on the national scene. His affable smile, lively sense of humor, and upbeat proclamations sealed his fame and popularity.

Delivering hundreds of speeches before business groups, major conventions, mayors, planners, architects, and others throughout his life, he repeated key elements of his program to near universal acclaim. He believed, in sum, that there was hope for the capitalist city and that the ideal city could be realized by partnerships between enlightened business interests and local governments. Businessmen were hungry for this optimistic propaganda from one of their own and rewarded him with money and national media attention.

Rouse's upbeat message was integrated into the philosophies of the different organizations he helped to create, including ACTION (American Council to Improve Our Neighborhoods), The Rouse Company, the American City Corporation, and the Enterprise Foundation. These organizations held conferences, created publications, planned whole cities, and created built environments as demonstrations of the diverse potential of private enterprise—some of the most effective cultural and intellectual propaganda ever conceived, and more than a match for Rouse's socialist and communist rivals.

The built projects, and most of Rouse's social vision, did not originate with his own creative process. From an existing tradition of urban social reform he borrowed housing code reform, neighborhood unit planning, and regional planning concepts. Rouse possessed a great talent for adapting high culture and often left-wing ideals for private sector application. In the built environment, the same adaptation of high culture on a sound business basis held true. Rouse found the money to bankroll architects and planners willing to adapt "high urbanism" for profit and the businessman's utopia. The urban renewal projects in which he was involved came indirectly from the folios of Le Corbusier, Walter Gropius, and Mies van der Rohe, his new towns were strongly influenced by Northern European models of new town and garden city development, his malls took cues from Milan's Galleria and Paris's Arcades, and his festival marketplaces capitalized on the growing, and primarily elite, passion for historic preservation. Rouse was not a truly original thinker, but he became a patron with the ability to find designers such as Victor Gruen, David Wallace, Morton Hoppenfeld, Pietro Belluschi, Benjamin Thompson, and Frank Gehry, willing and eager to adapt culturally sophisticated projects for a mass audience.

What Rouse lacked in originality he more than made up in unorthodox application. He overlaid sophisticated management concepts, borrowed from the American corporation, on innovative social planning and modernist designs. Neighborhood improvement projects in which he was involved called for streamlining of city departments, housing code enforcement, and affordable housing construction along a business model. New modernist designs for downtown were paired to private redevelopment corporations; suburban pedestrian malls were strictly managed by private businesses and lacked public services; renovated public markets became models of corporate management; and new towns ran smoothly under the direction of a corporation and a private community association. The forms were often avant-garde, but the businessman was in the saddle.

What Was the Businessman's Utopia?

The businessman's utopia was an elastic cultural and intellectual framework, encompassing both actual places and ideas about the city, that held together the many disparate projects Rouse promoted. Where some had pinned all of their hopes on one type of project or a particular brand of design, Rouse created a constellation of new urban forms and ideas that came, through his efforts and those of like-minded supporters, to define the postwar landscape. Most observers have seen the utopian tone only at Columbia, Maryland, his new town—a direct and clear descendent of the garden city tradition. This focus on Columbia as Rouse's sole utopia is a common error. Rouse could be found on the road in the 1950s, for instance, advocating the creation of "slumless" cities and towns through urban renewal and housing code enforcement. He offered his malls as ideal public spaces on the new suburban fringe. His festival marketplaces were self-conscious attempts to restore human connections and small-scale capitalism in the modern metropolis. The Enterprise Foundation promised to eliminate all blighted housing and create a private sector social welfare system in American cities during the 1980s and 1990s.

This composite utopian vision, although rooted in the operation of the free market and local government, proved to be remarkably close in goals to the utopian vision pursued in the Soviet Union and social democratic Europe. His counterparts in Europe and the USSR primarily engaged public powers to create an impressive urban lifestyle. Family allowances, national health care systems, macroeconomic policies designed to maintain full employment, and massive public housing and new town projects affected rural areas, too, but more dramatically revolutionized life for urban populations across Europe and the Soviet Union.

Rouse put little store in such government-led utopianism and created a unique and ideologically cohesive formula for his competing vision. His belief that in the United States uniformly healthy and beautiful cities could be created through minimal federal government interference (except for limited financial support), local governmental participation, high standards of design, and maximum private sector leadership—what has come to be called the "private/public partnership"—allowed him to advocate comparatively radical notions, in the American context, such as massive condemnation downtown, slumless cities, and planned new towns, without appearing to be a dangerous leftist.

There is a delicious irony to this ideological flip. Compared to communist and social democratic methods, Rouse was conservative, but advocacy of the "private-public" partnership in another age had once appeared as a challenge to the status quo. Late-nineteenth- and early-twentieth-century reformers such as Daniel Burnham faced much more resistance to these partnerships, and their more ambitious plans sank in the sea of laissez-faire ideology. American planners failed to gain the massive condemnation of urban real estate that made possible ambitious schemes by Baron Georges Eugène Haussmann and other city planners in Europe: "In the contest between property rights and planning, the odds were loaded differently in the United States than Paris. The city that had been mortgaged to private land investments was not, in practice, easily remade as a symbol of civic unity."[17]

The battle against creeping socialism, as discussed above, put condemnation of urban property, and other extensions of municipal power, in a new context. Rouse, and many others during the 1950s and 1960s, could advocate significant changes in cities in part because "radical" in the urban context had shifted in other countries (and during the New Deal) to the left. Rouse may have been calling for a dramatic change in business practices, massive condemnation, and expansion of local governmental powers, but he was never advocating the creation of a welfare state, centralized planning, or collectivization.

The reliance on local government proved central in Rouse's seemingly contradictory advocacy of activist government; local government could be trusted to avoid the radical activities of federal actors, because local government was so closely tuned to business elites. Rouse argued in front of business groups many times that "it's conservative to give power to local government. It's the way to solve problems that makes it unnecessary for the federal government to intervene. We can control local government."[18] The businessman's utopia had to be built out of reach of liberal national politicians bent on sweeping redistribution of wealth or centralized planning.

The places businessmen built interlocked nicely with changing expectations of public space and city services after the war. The businessman's utopia was characterized by greater attention to systems of urban management. The old models of urban life had not worked particularly well to create an attractive environment. In certain respects, many practices seemed decidedly opposed to creating the city beautiful or efficient. Business development and social policy had to be entirely reconceived. In the era of The Organization Man and new suburbs, cities as a whole had to be reinvented.

Although the traditional downtown was losing its allure before World War II, the search for a safe, clean, well-managed, and auto-friendly city that had started in the 1920s took on new urgency. The cult of the new, of science, and of high technology made older downtowns, declining slums, and even old main streets appear as tired relics concealing a dangerous, seamy underside. The disorganized webs of ownership and management threatened imminent collapse or growing disorder in both old cities and new suburbs. The individual pieces of Rouse's utopia matched ambitious new expectations of street life in this era at his shopping malls, urban renewal projects, new town of Columbia, the festival marketplaces, and the Enterprise Foundation's community redevelopment projects. These projects ideally replaced decentralized, chaotic management with perfectly tuned, well-designed spaces that concealed any rough edges. According to Rouse, even blighted neighborhoods could be transformed into smoothly regulated places without dispossessing slum landlords.

The reinvented places James Rouse was promoting ran smoothly and gleamed in the sunlight of a new middle-class America: "We, as a people, have demonstrated throughout the country how we want to live, to work and to shop," Rouse proclaimed. "Fresh, green, open residential communities overwhelm the countryside outside the cities along with neat, attractive industrial plants with lawns and gardens and new office buildings in campus-like settings." He was convinced that Americans had to "make the central city fit for modern living, working, [and] shopping" by essentially duplicating these conditions in the city center as best as possible. This would mean major and painful reconstructive surgery for America's central cities, but the process would potentially yield great benefits.[19] The web of the businessman's utopia promised, and partly achieved, a new era in urban life for the nation.

Rouse's face graced national magazine covers, his projects received flattering attention in magazines and on television, and he gave hundreds of speeches to the most influential people in the country from the 1950s to the 1990s. This rhetoric, paired to appealing projects, had a cumulative effect. His outlook influenced the work of numerous politicians, planners, and the general public. Rouse was at the leading edge of the triumph of privatization, particularly on urban issues, that helped steer America away from the creation of a comprehensive urban social welfare state after the New Deal by offering a compelling alternative to leftist planning and progress. Rouse's genuinely friendly demeanor, his belief in the beneficial power of private enterprise in urban affairs, and his demonstrated success in creating unconventional projects made him the ideal spokesperson for conservative forces determined to show the superiority of the free enterprise model in urban public policy without appearing coldhearted.

Up until now, Rouse has been largely overlooked in scholarly research, because his efforts do not fit into the familiar framework of urban policy history, with its emphasis on government policy and lobbying by national associations; individuals like Rouse fade into the background of bureaucratic histories. Nor does recent urban history devote much attention to the effects of serious ideas translated through popular culture, an arena in which Rouse proved particularly able. Rouse may not have been personally responsible for all of modern urban policy, but the appealing cultural and intellectual style he pioneered helped sell private sector public policy to the general public. Finally, because Rouse was an honest businessman, a philanthropist of note, and a truly decent human being, he has not attracted any critical or serious work up until this time (as compared to notorious figures such as Robert Moses and Richard J. Daley). That Rouse has been heretofore ignored in scholarly literature does not in any way diminish his importance. Nor should the fact that he had good intentions allow him to forever elude critical analysis.

To fully understand his national influence, one need only imagine for a moment postwar urbanism without his presence and projects. Like few others, he responded over the decades to the statist challenge, stringing together a grand series of idealistic and experimental private sector projects. For every challenge from the socialist and social democratic worlds, and domestic New Deal, Fair Deal, and Great Society programs, there emerged projects and propaganda that claimed an equal standing and effectiveness for the free enterprise system. That many of these projects failed to gain their lofty aims, even according to Rouse, should not lead us into the error of believing that they had no effect or that Rouse was a failure. The power of his creativity can be read in the mammoth amount of attention paid to these projects by politicians, the general public, and the media over so many decades. Each of the chapters of *Merchant of Illusion* frames an urban challenge Rouse hoped to address, summarizes the effects of the different projects he initiated, and considers the role that these projects played in constructing a compelling national private sector urban ideology.

As the different chapters demonstrate, Rouse deserved much of the positive press showered upon him. In many cases Rouse and those around him commissioned better planning than the communists and social democrats who had staked their entire reputations on superb planning. Columbia is more attractive and livable than many socialist new towns (if also more elite); modernist urban renewal in cities was occasionally more impressive and lively than much urban reconstruction in Europe (if more narrowly

focused on business interests); the festival marketplaces helped many suburban Americans rediscover the pleasures of downtown; and even the affordable housing projects of the non-profit Enterprise Foundation seemed like
a plausible and successful response to problems of the inner city and low-
cost housing (if limited in extent). In the end, the businessman's utopia
hastened the fall of the Soviet Union; images of America's consumer society played a role in Soviet discontent—and those images were primarily
urban. Through the efforts of Rouse and others, from the 1950s to the 1990s,
the image and appearance of American cities was partly remade to fit this
image of an abundant and uniformly wealthy society.

In retrospect, however, the businessman's utopia proved to be equal parts
of reality and ideology. The stubborn persistence abroad of America's
unenviable reputation for slums and urban violence during the Cold War
and after can in part be accounted to this partial success. The innovation
and transformation in American urban affairs in the postwar period, and
that sense of optimism for which Rouse is rightly famous, did give businessmen
and politicians much to hold up to the world. Industrial nightmares like Baltimore
were not terribly impressive in the 1940s and 1950s. Baltimore, Pittsburgh,
Boston, or Chicago as reconceived during this era, with delightful water-
fronts, green suburbs, massive highways, shiny office buildings, and slick shopping malls, looked very good. The businessman's utopia, however,
concealed flaws, and suffering—massive slums, unmatched violence, widespread homelessness, and environmental destruction—continued on a
grand scale, even as private sector urbanism won in the battle for the hearts
and minds of citizens around the globe.

Future Prospects

Rouse and his generation set the tone for a distinct type of urban policy in
the postwar period, and in many cases we are better off for their efforts. This
legacy, however, strategically limited the boundaries of American urban policy within the context of antistatism and probusiness ideologies. *Merchant of
Illusion* offers, I hope, a rising generation some breathing space to reconsider
the private sector approach to urban issues. Could we strike a better balance
between private and public action in cities and metropolitan areas without
turning to discredited socialist policies? Perhaps. As anyone who reads this
book will learn, even Rouse often envisaged a far more capacious role for public forces, particularly after his more idealistic projects faltered in practice.

Those of us who have grown up in the postwar era have forgotten that
business leaders like Rouse created the modern city to fit their personal vision
of an ideal city. This vision was profoundly shaped by a worldwide struggle

against socialist movements that undermined state action of many kinds. Now that communism, and even much of social democracy, has retreated around the world, it is time to consider the role of the state "after ideology." Broad-ranging public sector leadership, offering creative and nondoctrinaire approaches to existing problems, needs to balance private sector initiatives.

The reluctance of intellectuals and public leaders to question business leadership and to propose an alternative vision has had serious results, beyond the low esteem in which public service is held in this country. Businesses can provide many wonderful goods and services, but an urbanized society has needs and expectations—in affordable housing, education, environmental conservation, mass transit, welfare, recreation, child care, and health care—that will rarely be placed on a sound for-profit basis. The notion that profit should guide public policy, that non-profit organizations have the resources to address urban problems on a large scale, or that we need more "miracle workers" from the private sector, has been inflated far beyond its usefulness, particularly in urban affairs.

In tandem with his network of conservative (and sometimes liberal) allies, Rouse labored successfully to make private sector ideals appear to be the most logical answers to urban needs and essential to urban health. Alternatives fell by the wayside not because they had no merit at all, but because private sector advocates proved to be such gifted promoters of the businessman's utopia. Magnificent propaganda—spoken, textual, visual, and built—crowded out other visions. There may have been nothing inherently logical about these goals and efforts, but to reject them became impossible. The notion that businesspeople understand the wider needs of modern society is rarely questioned as closely as it should be. Even failure by Rouse and others was defined not as their failure, but reflective of an urban crisis so complex that both private and governmental interests could have little effect. This vision, so carefully created, merits deconstruction.

CHAPTER 1

Diverging Paths to Urban Social Welfare

It is curious that we Americans, people of good-will, should continue to let our actions deny our ideals. Why are we fighting this war? Are we eager to rescue the people of other countries from intolerance and persecution but entirely willing to disregard what is happening to millions on our own soil?
Dorothy Baruch, "Sleep Comes Hard"

While we are genuinely concerned about the threat of communism, and are spending billions abroad to enable other countries to earn a standard of living which will make them prefer it to the false promises of communism, let us not overlook a weakness in our own nation.
Representative Thomas Lane,
"Americans Demand Low Rent, Public Housing—Action!"

Cities became ideological weapons when the Second World War ended. Politicians in the USSR and Western Europe devoted considerable national resources to urban rebuilding for more than humanitarian reasons; they aimed to create, in record time, convincing urban demonstrations of socialist ideology. Leftists across Europe were determined to show that their growing global power could correct the defects of capitalist cities they had catalogued and criticized since the nineteenth century. Even the Soviets, who had a head start on Western Europe, indulged in an unparalleled era of city reconstruction.

The dominance of the public sector generated by these ambitious goals undercut economic efficiency and often stymied creativity and personal liberty in many countries, but from the 1940s to the 1970s, when Rouse was moving into a position of influence and power, such a clear, if frequently overstated, connection between state power and national malaise remained purely theoretical. To many people around the world, particularly those who had lived through the darkest days of the Depression, the violent swings of the capitalist system and horrors of the capitalist city seemed a far more frightening prospect than state bureaucracy. Businessmen faced

1

an uphill battle when it came to demonstrating their ability to create an attractive urban society.

It is easy to forget that the United States, Western Europe, and the Soviet Union all achieved unparalleled growth after World War II even though they diverged in urban social policy. Massive social spending in Western Europe and the Soviet Bloc helped rebuild broken economies and created new city centers and suburbs that, for a time, *solely* seemed to reflect the benefits of social democratic and communist ideals. In Europe and the Soviet Union, government spending created a more uniform but also less affluent society; social redistribution eliminated the more jarring contrasts between the poor and rich (and the Soviets eliminated personal wealth entirely). The problems that would plague this urban ambition failed to be identified fully until the 1980s; by that time, however, most of these societies had been dramatically reshaped through substantial application of national resources.

Private enterprise advocates in the United States restricted the development of a social welfare state but nevertheless created a booming consumer economy for a growing suburban middle class that in time posed its own significant ideological challenge to social democracy and communism. Although the United States government played a major role in bankrolling postwar metropolitan prosperity, antistatist ideology overrode social welfare and led to the dominance of private sector–led policy, for both better and worse, in the United States.

American urban policy helped rebuild commercial downtowns and created affordable and spacious new suburbs, but it also encouraged a two-tiered urban system of prosperous suburbs and slum neighborhoods of shocking contrasts. Very few national resources flowed to the poor neighborhoods of cities, and it showed; some federal programs restricted the flow of private capital to urban neighborhoods, others paid for highway and urban renewal programs that further destabilized poor neighborhoods. Rouse contributed to the creation of this antistatist system and benefited from government policy as a mortgage banker, advocate of urban renewal, and mall developer, while over the decades developing a parallel set of private sector solutions that he thought could make up for the glaring deficiencies in the American approach to urban affairs.

Ideal Housing and New Towns for Old Cities

Frank Fisher, a New York economist writing in a 1945 issue of *The Nation*, held up Europe's rapid plans for rebuilding as a model to be imitated in the United States: "The Germans had hardly been driven from Russian soil before the rebuilding of Stalingrad and other devastated areas was undertaken. In England, at the height of buzz-bomb blitz, Parliament found time for an extensive debate on the question of compensation for land to be taken over for reconstruction purposes. The smaller countries, too, are perfecting their plans." Even more notable than reconstruction was that this activity was "designed to provide [Europe's] inhabitants with few gadgets but all the necessities for healthful life which good planning can produce." Indeed, all of Europe committed itself to a frenzy of construction and planning designed to create an ideal society.[1]

The Soviets, in particular, made the most of their heroic urban efforts. *Soviet Life*, the propaganda magazine distributed in the United States by the communists during the Cold War, reported the shocking facts of wartime destruction in 1959 that made their postwar achievement even more impressive: "The Nazi armies destroyed, either totally or partially, 1,710 cities and towns and more than 70 thousand villages. Twenty-five million people were left homeless." Destruction, however, meant the possibility that new types of cities could rise from the ashes, cities that better reflected utopian communist aspirations: "Minsk, Kiev, Stalingrad and many other large cities had literally to be rebuilt from ruins. They have all been restored now with wide and spacious avenues, parks and modern apartment buildings."[2] For decades, communists had matched utopian architectural and planning visions to their political efforts; now utopia seemed close to realization.

Soviet propaganda made a habit of overstating progress, but these rebuilding cities looked much improved from a distance. The country may have faced severe housing shortages and cramped conditions even before WWII, but it was during the postwar period (and the late 1950s, in particular under Khrushchev) when the Soviets seemed to have found solutions to problems that had bedeviled modern cities for centuries. Whole districts were rebuilt and new ones created on the principles of modern planning, including separation of industry and housing, high-rise housing amid planned park areas, and new highways and subways.

In *Soviet Life* and at exhibitions in Brussels, the New York Coliseum, and Montreal, among others, the communists put on an impressive show of their urban progress. At New York in 1958 they boasted, "Foreign tourists to the Soviet Union invariably comment on the enormous amount of construction going on." Massive construction changed the entire mode of urban life, offering a progressive contrast to the capitalist city suitable for framing: "The Exhibit will show in graphic form the vast improvements in living conditions, the new apartment buildings designed for comfort, air, light and convenience . . . the well-planned residential garden districts that are becoming a familiar feature of Soviet urban living."[3]

Another article in *Soviet Life* from the period explained the ambitions of the communists when it came to housing: "New housing for 75 million

Figure 1. Cheremushki Project, Moscow in the 1950s. The Soviet Union embarked on
the construction of vast districts of planned social housing that heralded the arrival of a
left-wing utopia. National resources devoted to urban reconstruction made large Soviet
cities impressive propaganda tools during the 1950s and 1960s. Tulane University School
of Architecture Slide Collection.

people, almost a third of the population of the Soviet Union—that is the
staggering goal projected by the seven-year plan for 1959–1965. The target figure calls for the construction of fifteen million apartments in urban
communities and seven million cottages in rural areas."[4] As this quotation
indicates, cities overwhelmingly reaped the rewards of this national effort.

To a great degree *Soviet Life* and the exhibitions of Soviet housing represented more than idle boasts. The communist government indeed committed itself to rehousing its population, and construction became highly
mechanized, plans repetitive, and many of the apartment buildings partly
prefabricated in order to speed delivery to a mass audience. The Soviets
built fast, if not well: "The massive housing construction program
launched by Nikita Khrushchev during the late 1950s succeeded in turning over nearly 70 million apartments to just under 300 million Soviet citizens by the late 1980s."[5] Average living space doubled between 1956 and
1989, and 90 percent of urban residences had running water, central heat-
ing, and indoor plumbing by the 1980s.

Compared to middle-class American standards of living, the new apartments were primitive and cramped; only compared to pre–WWII conditions (and American slums) did they represent a great leap forward.
Long-term maintenance problems have made life difficult in many of these

complexes; Soviet cities were "surrounded by massive apartment blocks clustered in bleak mega-districts." Soviet planners took a particular interest in the modernist Superblock, with "towers in the park," that looked good on paper and could be easily duplicated.[6] The lack of private sector construction (that might have created a higher standard for those with better salaries) made these apartments and achievements less impressive in the long term.

These negative long-term results of government housing programs would become more obvious later, but during most of the Cold War the Soviet housing program gleamed from distant shores. Soviet approaches to planning were widely adopted in Eastern Europe, leading to a great many planned districts of similar design in East Germany, Poland, Hungary, and a number of countries behind the Iron Curtain.

The communist nations, however, were not alone in their ambition to create urban embodiments of leftist ideology. Britain's labor government pursued social democratic policies; one of the most ambitious and famous new town programs emerged amid this spirit of reform. Although the garden city concept had been born in Britain, and the country housed two leading examples of the new town ideal created by private interests—Letchworth (1902) and Welwyn (1920)—a number of government committees had promoted new towns to little effect during the 1920s and 1930s. It was only during the Second World War that the new town concept became national policy. Lord (John) Reith led a newly created Ministry of Town and Country Planning (created in 1943) with an eye to population decentralization in the future. Spurred in part by fears of social disorder created by returning servicemen without housing, Reith and others successfully gained the New Towns Act of 1946, an ambitious large-scale new town program. Many quite similar towns flowed from this legislation, as all shared the aim of balancing industry and residence and featured modern styles of housing, highways, mass transit connections, extensive open space, and pedestrian-oriented town centers with both commercial and civic functions (that looked superficially a great deal like American shopping centers). Between 1946 and 1950 the government started fourteen towns, and by 1971 there were twenty-nine under development with total projected populations of between three and four million by the 1990s. According to reputable figures, these new towns absorbed "12 percent of national population increase between 1951 and 1970."[7]

The individual new towns had some unique features, and planning practices changed over time, but all of the towns were strongly controlled by national government authorities. The British secretary of state designated the areas for new towns, consulted with local officials, created development corporations, approved master plans, attained long-term loans, and used compulsory purchase to grab large areas. "New towns in Britain are the creation of central government. It is the Government which decides when, where and for what purpose a new town is to be built; and having done so sees the job through." The new towns combined social idealism (residents of different classes rented at both market and subsidized rents) with environmental, industrial, and commercial planning.[8] Although Labor initiated these projects, Conservative governments continued these new town policies during the 1950s and 1960s, substituting more private housing for public housing in each town.

Perhaps even more important than new towns was the continuing commitment of British politicians to building public housing around major cities and clearing out slum legacies of the industrial revolution. Beginning in the 1920s, housing authorities throughout Britain created a great many "council estates" of public housing. Nearly two million houses were built in these estates before World War II, and another four million units were added after the war. A wide variety of architectural and planning styles can be found in these estates, including historically inspired terrace housing and steely modernist high-rises. The postwar building boom in public housing, and an emphasis on maximizing numbers through prefabrication and high-rise development, ultimately undercut political support for the program by the 1970s. As in the Soviet Union, some of these estates have deteriorated, many towers have been demolished, other estates have been renovated and rebuilt, and a surprising amount of the housing in the more popular estates has been entirely privatized and sold to residents. During the era of public housing construction, private sector housing continued to be constructed for more affluent sections of the British population.[9]

Northern European housing and new town programs became even more famous than those in Britain. Stockholm "in the late 1950s and early 1960s . . . became known worldwide as the quintessence of a social philosophy, realized on the ground. Its apartment towers, grouped around its new subway stations and shopping centers, impeccably designed and landscaped, became an object of pilgrimage for informed visitors from all over the world." The nonprofit and public sector dominated Sweden's "housing industrial complex" with nonprofit housing corporations and cooperatives taking up 20 percent and public housing another 45 percent of all urban construction. Although criticized for poor construction and the small size of apartments, the Swedish government created 650,000 units nationally during 1956–1965 and over a million units from 1965–1974. These were significant numbers for such a small country and alone dwarf American efforts in state-sponsored housing. As in Britain, during the last two decades Sweden's private sector housing industry has grown in popularity as some of the public housing projects have declined. Public housing remains important but is no longer the focus of the society as a whole.

Figure 2. Two views of Vallingby, Sweden, a leading 1950s new town. The figure above illustrates residential areas; below is a photograph of the town center shopping/civic district. New towns such as Vallingby organized urban growth into comprehensively planned and landscaped districts. The creation of new towns, linked to an expansion in government and labor union power, further reflected the ambitions of social democratic politicians. Rouse, in time, built Columbia, Maryland, his private sector version of social democratic new towns. Tulane University School of Architecture Slide Collection.

Sweden and the rest of Northern Europe also gained notice during this time for progressive urban planning. A series of new towns in Sweden combining industry, culture, and residence with abundant natural areas drew worldwide attention. Vallingby and Farsta were the most famous, and Rouse made visits to both during the 1960s.[10]

Other European countries such as Finland, France, Germany, and Holland also committed to impressive public building programs, and many built extensive new towns. Tapiola, Finland, a modern but comfortable planned community, constructed by a group of trade unions during the 1950s,

Figure 3. Allied and Axis warfare did the initial work of clearance and condemnation in cities such as Rotterdam. American businessmen had to invent the means of "creative destruction" after the war. Photo by KLM Airways. Printed in Martin Meyerson, *Face of the Metropolis* (1963).

became a particularly fashionable stop for planners in the period. Attractive clusters of multifamily housing, high-rises, thick plantings, and water features made Tapiola the poster child of new town design (and clearly influenced Rouse's Columbia project).

Social democrats and communists around the world in the postwar period seemed, at first, to be achieving the long held but never realized ambitions of socialist, utopian thinkers. The Soviet Union and Europe were quickly beginning to "look" socialist on a massive urban scale. There were, of course, major differences between Soviet Communism and the social democratic or "sewer socialism" complemented by private sector activity pursued in much of Western Europe, but these differences were lost on conservatives in the United States fighting state activism of any kind. In the long term European and Soviet efforts revealed serious flaws, but during the era of the Cold War leftist cities luxuriated in national resources with a political purpose.

The United States government refused to decline a role in urban housing but took a distinct path from Europe that took longer to coalesce into a distinct vision. The specter of Britain's new town and public housing programs, in particular, frightened conservative interests who lumped all new towns and social democratic planning with communism as represented in the Soviet Union. That the British, close cousins of Americans, should pursue social democratic policies with such fervor merely illustrated once again the pernicious seductiveness of worldwide communist ideals.

Distinctions between versions of socialism rarely emerged, even though British new towns, for instance, included private homes one would never find in Soviet-planned towns. These major differences meant little to American conservatives.

In 1946 Henry Luce's *Time* portrayed British Labor politicians as radical socialists bent on undermining Anglo-Saxon freedoms. The minister of Town and Country Planning, Lewis Silkin, called "Socialist Silkin" by *Time*, "smoothly explained" to residents of the little country town of Stevenage, designated as a new town site, that because London was "smothering in its own amorphous bulk," their town, among others, would be ruthlessly urbanized. Local residents demanded, "Why pick on Stevenage?" and cursed him with terms such as "Gestapo." *Time* also heralded a "Basic Revolution" in 1947 that in theory threatened free enterprise and private property in Britain: "Britain's Labor government this week proposed a revolutionary act—in its implications the most sweeping act since the Soviet government's decree of forced collectivization of the peasants (1929). It was the 'Town and Country Planning Bill, 1947.'" These laws did in fact give tremendous powers over land regulation to government officials and planners so that they could carry out the new town projects. Although a truly foreign concept to the United States during this period, and even today, British planning was in no way equivalent to forced collectivization in the Soviet Union, where millions perished in concentration camps and the entire system of rural property was dramatically overthrown. The *Time* article even claimed: "planners had captured the Englishman's castle."[11] These statements may have been dramatic, but they were not true; nevertheless, they aided the widespread goal of conflating social democracy with communism.

The United States, like Britain, faced a serious urban housing shortage both during and after the war. Demobilization, massive movement of rural people to urban areas during both the Depression and war years, and the growing baby boom contributed to the American housing crisis and exacerbated slum conditions. *The Nation* described poor workers living on the streets in 1945, sleeping "on benches, on floors, in washrooms; in alleys and on sidewalks." Thousands had moved west for work, creating huge demand in cities such as Los Angeles, and wartime housing construction met only a small part of need, particularly for growing urban black populations: "children lived in windowless rooms, amid peeling plaster, rats, and the flies that gathered thick around food . . . ordinarily there was no bathtub . . . Sometimes as many as forty people shared one toilet." Public housing units barely made a dent in a city like Los Angeles, and any private construction during the war years went to whites. Conditions were similar across the country, if not worse.[12] Rouse himself acknowledged in 1945 that Baltimore was experiencing "an unbelievable shortage of housing in all price ranges."[13]

One might expect this kind of hand-wringing from liberals at *The Nation*, but *Fortune* repeatedly described similar conditions, including "the fuselages of unfinished bombers" that had "been pressed into service as stopgap housing." Near San Antonio "tourist camps and motor courts are no longer accepting transients," and in Norwood, Ohio, "within twenty-four hours after the arrest of a man who strangled his wife, police received five telephone calls from people who wanted his house."[14] *Fortune* magazine's editors in 1947 worried that the housing shortage reflected a "failure by capitalism" that "will do more to undermine free institutions than ten thousand Union Square orators."[15]

Although the crisis was well documented in national media outlets, only in magazines like *The Nation* and the labor press would one find proposals for public housing or new towns. While *Life* magazine, for instance, "visualized the housing shortage . . . the only solution the magazine showed was the single-family house." *Life*, and other mainstream magazines, "promoted a vision of the United States as a nation of middle-class homeowners." The single-family home certainly was not a difficult sell to the American public and was well established as the most desirable style of housing, but other housing options struggled for any serious recognition.[16]

The housing industry, notoriously disorganized, small-scale, and conservative, failed to respond quickly to demand. Some materials remained in short supply after the war, but many other builders used the crisis to jack up already high prices or continued to build comparatively expensive houses for those least in need.[17] Local governments also ignored the housing crisis. Although many city governments stepped up planning efforts during the war and immediately after, housing code creation rather than public housing dominated the housing component of city plans.[18]

In 1946 there had existed strong public American sentiment for federal action. According to a *Fortune* public opinion poll, "nearly half of those who were polled went so far as advocating government construction of homes on a large scale."[19] Most Americans may have desired single-family homes, but they obviously were not optimistic that private developers would deliver for the average or poor household. Such clear public support for government action paralleled the situation in Europe and reflects the lingering popularity of the New Deal, with its work projects, public housing, and social security systems. Americans wanted action, and a majority seemed ready to have the national government play a direct role in remedying the crisis. These sentiments represented a genuine threat to the free enterprise system; after all, the government, rather than businessmen, could have built single-family homes. The United States government might have become at that moment a leading force in housing construction, but under the direction of well-organized business interests diverged from the social democratic route.

During the 1940s and 1950s the federal government took a complex approach to the problem of housing that minimized national government direction and spending and laid the groundwork for the businessman's utopia: initial centralized regulation of private builders, expansion of federal insurance of the private mortgage industry, private/public reconstruction of existing neighborhoods, and public housing on a small scale. Rouse left his mark on many of these approaches (and benefited extensively from government policies), as will be described in more detail later in this book, but it is worth summarizing the broad outlines of the American approach to housing that not only eluded the creation of a large social housing program, but also set the framework for idealist private sector urban efforts in which Rouse was involved.

In 1946 the federal government placed price controls on certain essential housing materials, set restrictions on commercial building, and provided subsidies to those promising prefabrication on a large scale. Although this process created a brief upswing in housing starts in 1946, it also led to unfinished houses, lack of significant progress on prefabrication, public anger, and business opposition to centralized policies. The National Housing Administrator, and the designated "housing expeditor," Wilson Wyatt, "probably the last authentic New Dealer" in a top Washington job, resigned in frustration in 1947 as his program faltered.[20] It should be noted that the programs Wyatt instituted relied almost entirely on federal *direction* rather than federal *action* or direct spending.

The federal government's system of government insurance for long-term financing for home mortgages proved far more successful in meeting housing needs and gave far more leeway to private builders. This system, "called mad spending of taxpayers' money and socialism by Republicans in 1934,"[21] had begun during the New Deal as a controversial way to pump the economy and stall foreclosures, but it came into its own in the postwar period. Private bankers and developers leveraged an expanding consumer demand to build suburban housing for not only middle-class people, but for many working-class citizens as well. Mortgage insurance combined with veteran's benefits and mortgage tax deductions in the postwar period to widen the class of homeowners. Although FHA (Federal Housing Administration) and veteran's loans and mortgage tax credits are not generally seen as forms of big government, they did reflect the national government's concern for housing issues and spurred the construction of millions of comparatively affordable houses.

Because mortgage insurance flowed from private banks to private developers, the program was not in any way socialistic, did not demand social experimentation, and proved moderate in cost to the government; nor were mortgage insurance or tax deductions likely to create a large central government apparatus bent on regulation. Small- and large-scale planned "community builder" suburbs were leveraged on federal mortgage guarantees (and eventually interstate highways) but were constructed by red-blooded American developers on a for-profit basis. Rouse was one of the first mortgage bankers in Maryland to deal in FHA-insured mortgages and did very well by them.

The private housing market in time ended the housing crisis of the white middle and working classes. Innovative community developers like William Levitt built new subdivisions at a record pace by adapting assembly line techniques for housing construction. While preserving the essential elements of the suburban lifestyle—freestanding homes with space for expansion and gently curving streets—these developers used this newfound efficiency to make suburban homeownership affordable to average Americans. America's suburban frontier emerged as the most potent statement of the private sector's ability to create the good life for urban populations. The government and mass media exported the image of the commodious suburban house to great effect. In contrast to the cramped apartments of the communist east and much of social democratic Western Europe, new suburban subdivisions were well-built, spacious, flexible, and attractive. In spite of this clear progress, a growing urban housing crisis still gripped Cold War America.

The federal insurance programs gave with one hand to white suburban Americans and took with the other by speeding up central city housing decline. Older cities found themselves with residential neighborhoods cut off from mortgage money because of restrictive standards set by the FHA in terms of race, ethnicity, and housing quality or types. A significant stock of existing housing had been opened to poor people as a result of the creation of new suburbs, but the steep decline in many urban neighborhoods due to national mortgage policies and highways undercut many of the potential benefits of neighborhood succession.[22] New highway projects moved suburbanites from center to periphery but also cut mercilessly through vibrant African American neighborhoods. American politicians acknowledged the problems, but they responded slowly to these glaring deficiencies.

Public housing, which might have played an immediate role in changing urban conditions, faltered on antistatist and anticommunist concerns. During the 1930s the New Deal funded public housing on a small scale with the goal of making work for the unemployed and improving dangerous urban conditions. Some of these early projects have been noted for their high-quality design and were influenced by European prototypes.[23] During the war temporary housing was also constructed for many war workers. Public housing supporters tried unsuccessfully to use the example of defense housing to make the case for public housing immediately after the war. Charles Abrams, the famed housing advocate, reminded readers in *The Nation* in 1947 that during the war "no one considered [government construction of housing using private contractors] a challenge to our way of life. Is the logic that dictates government building in a war emergency less forceful in a post-war emergency?"[24] In contrast to the massive public housing programs of Europe after the war, public housing in America remained a minor part of the national or local agenda and was stalled at the federal level until 1949 by well-organized homebuilders, mortgage bankers, and conservative politicians from both major parties.[25]

Rouse and many other businessmen viewed public housing as essentially anathema to the free enterprise system. As chairman of the Legislative Committee of the Mortgage Bankers Association (MBA), in testimony to Congress in 1949, he promoted the idea that subsidizing real estate interests was palatable, while public housing was not: "As a representative for the MBA, I was automatically cast as a member of the real estate lobby and did, in fact, oppose the public housing legislation, but supported the redevelopment law which passed that year."[26] Rouse may not have been a vociferous foe of public housing, but he remained safely in the mainstream of business opinion. Daniel Seligman, in *Fortune* magazine, summarized the business position on public housing: "From its inception in 1937, the federal program was subjected to a fusillade of abuse from real-estate groups: public housing was 'socialistic': it was unfair competition to private enterprise."[27]

The chairman of the Home Builder's Association of metropolitan Washington, for instance, warned in 1948, "America will never go down the road of state socialism through the government ownership of the homes of the people if they are told the facts of what state socialism is. They must learn that the TEW [Taft-Ellender-Wagner] bill . . . employs the same fundamental procedures employed by Berlin, London, Paris, or Moscow." This unlikely group of capital cities, cutting across Cold War alliances, reflects conservative awareness of similarities between social democratic and communist housing policies, and also the deliberate and successful strategy of merging social democracy with communism. Statism, after all, was the true enemy and had to be defeated at all costs.[28]

Republican Congressman Ralph Gwinn (New York) in 1948 suggested the specter of public housing residents voting for the socialistic parties that delivered the housing—"Congress has before it a proposal to corrupt permanently our free political system with all the evils in subsidized housing inherited from the New Deal"—and reported ominously that "word comes from England that the Socialist Parliament came to power partly through socialized housing."[29] These were not fringe voices, but represented a common view during debates about public housing during the 1940s and 1950s. "This [1949] bill plainly, openly and boldly declares socialism to be our new national policy," declared Democratic Congressman E. E. Cox (Georgia), for instance, among many others.[30] Conservative interests wanted to let the private housing market meet the crisis, if they were even convinced that a housing crisis existed at all.

Some public housing supporters tried to stake out more ambitious goals for public housing, viewing public housing as a bulwark against communism rather than a first step toward it. Democratic Senator Scott Lucas (Illinois), during debates in 1948, argued boldly that public housing "is a challenge to the menace of communism which breeds easily in some of the slum-blighted areas throughout the country . . . Make no mistake about it. The communist groups are working 24 hours a day in attempting to carry on and achieve their ultimate objective."[31] Legislators listening to Democratic Congressman Ray Madden (Indiana) were reminded that "we are spending billions across the water to curtail the spread of communism; this legislation will be of untold value in curtailing the communistic agitators in the industrial centers throughout America."[32] Liberals promoting public housing faced a great challenge in distinguishing between social housing in America and that in socialist and communist countries. Their conservative opposition would in time carry the day in policy, debates, and public relations.

The leading and unexpected proponent of public housing, and of the Taft-Ellender-Wagner bill that after years of wrangling became the Housing Act of 1949, Republican Senator Robert Taft (Ohio), argued persuasively that "there was nothing to show that private building in the future, any more than private building in the past, would ever eliminate the slums."[33] Taft had once been an outspoken opponent of public housing, but he changed his mind after close study of the housing problem and made startling statements such as, "You can't get decent housing from the free enterprise system."[34] Taft envisioned public housing as providing a minimum standard for housing for the working poor, addressing the housing needs of those the market had barely served.

The Housing Act of 1949 championed by Taft passed because of strong presidential support and lingering liberal sentiment in Congress. Approximately 135,000 units per year over a six-year period represented the most ambitious housing effort of the postwar era and would have led to 810,000 units by 1955. In fact, only about 84,000 federally sponsored units had been constructed by 1954 because of effective conservative opposition and new spending priorities for the Korean War. The 1954 Act itself approved only 20,000 units of public housing, and subsequent years saw approval of similarly low numbers of units. Public housing had few powerful advocates and survived almost solely on the notion that it was necessary as a result of displacement that resulted from business-oriented urban redevelopment. Many housing advocates even turned against public housing by the late 1950s when confronted with the sterile, poorly constructed "towers in the park" that had been hastily constructed in already segregated black neighborhoods.

During the 1960s and 1970s the small numbers of new public housing shifted to serving elderly Americans, rightly considered better tenants. By 1972, 800,000 public housing units had been built in the United States (a mixture of local and federal efforts). A number of other mortgage and rent subsidy programs, including Section 235 (that helped low-income people buy houses) and Section 236 (that subsidized rental housing constructed by private interests), initiated during the 1960s did yield hundreds of thousands of affordable housing units, but a variety of factors—including widespread corruption, foreclosures, and substandard construction—undermined support for these programs. Section 8, a form of rent assistance to low-income renters, grew strongly during the 1970s under Richard M. Nixon and succeeding presidents. It too, however, was scaled back during the Reagan and subsequent administrations.[35] Even considered as a whole, the diverse forms of housing subsidy in the United States paled in comparison to the massive housing efforts in Europe and the Soviet Union.

The United States government's refusal to invest massively in urban public housing in the long term may not seem like such a terrible choice now. Many of the public housing projects have been badly built, poorly maintained, and have over time become warehouses for the poorest of the poor. The problems in both American and European public housing reflect common (but not necessarily intractable) problems in the management of state-sponsored housing, but public housing problems both here and abroad have been grossly overstated. The implosion of mammoth concrete towers made good footage but did not represent the majority of ordinary, if not particularly attractive, public housing projects in either Europe or the United States. Housing for the very poor, and their attendant dreary and threatening social environments, have never been terribly enticing, even under state subsidy. The number of truly distressed public housing units in the United States, for instance, has been overstated (10–20 percent is a more accurate figure) even though the best American public housing, and even that in Europe, might not be "an environment which many middle-class persons would find desirable."[36]

Setting aside the mixed long-term results of public housing around the globe, the unwillingness of the United States government during the Cold War to take a proactive role in urban housing (on a comparable scale to that in left-leaning countries) did create a starker contrast in the United States between the luxury suburbs and poor central city districts. Compared to countries like Sweden or Britain, a small amount of social housing had been built over such a long period of time. By 2000 the diverse forms of "fedrally assisted housing for the poor total[ed] only slightly more than 4 million units . . . the smallest proportion among western democracies."[37] It was in the declining central city residential slums that Rouse would consistently find an opening for his private sector housing alternatives; solutions that promised social improvement without extensive state intervention. (Extensive coverage of public housing, Cold War ideology, and the Housing Act of 1954—and Rouse's role in housing policy—can be found in chapter 3.)

Public housing played a minor influence in central cities compared to new legislation endorsing private sector rebuilding of urban neighborhoods. The redevelopment sections of the Housing Acts of 1949 and 1954 proved more popular than public housing, but not because redevelopment built much housing or made a greater impact on housing problems in urban neighborhoods. Run-down, blighted areas under these acts would be condemned, and in their place would rise modern urban neighborhoods meeting the contemporary standards of hygiene and design. The federal government paid two-thirds of the cost of land acquisition and clearance, allowing local planning agencies to sell the land to private developers at reduced cost. Although public housing authorities could apply for land cleared using funds provided by the federal legislation, it was considered at the time more desirable to sell these lands to private interests for housing developments for a middle-income audience. According to the December 1957 issue of *Fortune*, Title I was seen by some as the equivalent to massive urban reconstruction in Europe: "cities were going to demolish large tracts of decayed housing and, in a massive redevelopment program, private capital would put up vast new housing estates." The scale of urban redevelopment, outside of New York City, under Title I was not the "blitzkrieg" many had hoped for, but Title I did set certain important precedents.[38] Historian Roger Biles notes that, although packaged and sold as part of a comprehensive attack on the problems of urban housing, Title I became "largely a vehicle for constructing office buildings, parking garages, swank apartment complexes, and shopping centers" because federal and local officials loosely interpreted the legislation's call for "predominantly residential" projects—developers built comparatively little housing as part of these commercial developments.[39]

The Housing Act of 1954, while paying more lip service to neighborhood preservation, massively expanded the feeding frenzy of local redevelopment agencies. Through Rouse's efforts the term "urban renewal"–referring to a more comprehensive approach to replanning neighborhoods—came into more common usage in 1954 but had little noticeable effect. By 1962 a city like New York had received nearly $75 million in urban renewal capital grants, and little Baltimore a whopping $18 million. According to urbanist Jon Teaford, "whereas the earliest projects had provided moderate- or middle-income housing, now local planners sought to apply federal dollars to more glamorous schemes . . . Amendments to the federal urban renewal law in 1959 and 1961 gave cities greater leeway in spending renewal funds for commercial projects."

Cities like Pittsburgh and Baltimore that had started projects with local bond issues and private financing now expanded their projects with the help of federal money: "Baltimore was implementing its Charles Center project of offices, stores, apartments, and theaters, relying now on federal funds rather than relying solely on local government and private initiative."[40]

What began as a postwar housing and neighborhood program had become a financial opportunity for downtown elites. Transformation resulted from the legislation, but humanitarian improvements—ending blight and inadequate housing in urban areas—did not emerge from these housing bills. These programs simply moved poor people and their problems from one area to another, many times worsening the situation by removing the social and commercial networks of poor neighborhoods. (Rouse's leading role in redevelopment and federal policy is discussed in chapter 2.)

Although mostly forgotten now, the United States made a small but high publicity effort to duplicate the European new town experience without direct government construction and supervision. The New Deal Greenbelt towns of the 1930s had adapted garden city ideals for the United States but were viewed by many as socialistic because of the leading role played by the federal government in their creation (as well as the unfamiliar cooperative aspects integrated in their designs).[41] During the 1940s and 1950s little attention was given to the creation of large new planned communities as had been undertaken in Europe. Some builders, like William Levitt and Phil Klutznick, mixed watered-down garden city planning concepts into their for-profit suburban developments, but these were the exception rather than the rule during the suburban boom. During the 1960s, as a result of the growing environmental and social justice movements, certain congressmen, President Johnson, and businessmen like Rouse began to push for American new towns. The Title VII program from 1970, modeled loosely on Columbia, became the federal government's leading attempt at new town legislation during the postwar period. Unlike its counterparts in Europe, the legislation subsidized private interests in the hopes of gaining environmental, social, and design innovation in large new suburban communities. (This program succeeded in attracting interest but failed to sustain participating developers and is discussed in chapter 6.)

As the new town experience indicates, the American path of urban rebuilding was not taken in ignorance of European models; American businessmen and politicians self-consciously chose an alternative route to urban reform. Rouse, for instance, had traveled to Europe and knew well the statist approach undertaken there. ACTION's research unit, under the direction of planner Martin Meyerson, published a major work on modern cities in 1963, *Face of the Metropolis*, that positively featured reconstructed cities, experimental public housing estates, and new towns from Europe.

A 1960 letter to Rouse from an administrator at ACTION reflects, too, that Rouse and those around him were aware of Soviet examples. James Lash wrote to Rouse when ACTION was planning its own exhibition on planning for the New York World's Fair of 1964 that "The Russian exhibit on modern city building at Brussels was well attended and very attractive because of its extreme orderliness. The Russians made a great point of how industry was located first, then living and other facilities provided according to the needs of people in that industry. An American exhibit on the city should include a strong statement of the democratic processes by which our city planning, renewal and development is done."[42] Americans planners disliked communist policies but understood the challenge they posed to the American system.

Rouse had a particular fascination for social democratic efforts. He owned a number of scholarly books on new towns in his collection, and he visited European new towns while planning Columbia, Maryland. Rouse's admiration for social democratic activities is also evident in his ambitious affordable housing projects developed by the Enterprise Foundation. Through the expansion of these projects he promised to eliminate slums and poverty in American cities and create affordable housing on a similar scale (hundreds of thousands of units a year) to that undertaken in Europe and the Soviet Union. Rouse believed that careful planning, housing for the poor, and abundant social services should be the goal of any society, but he believed equally that these goals could be achieved without major state action. Not surprisingly, he was constantly frustrated that such change in the direction of social justice was not faster in coming to the United States.

In 1979, Rouse, then a leading voice in American urbanism, made a trip to the Soviet Union. Although he was impressed with the people he met and the talent of many local architects, he commented on "the dull, monolithic high rise buildings of their new communities, the poor construction and poor maintenance." He asked his hosts, "How could [they] explain this gap between their capability and their performance?" One of them replied, "'You are right. All the incentives have been stripped from our system. Each Russian is born with a silver spoon in his mouth. We know from birth that we will be educated, our health will be cared for as will our old age. We will have jobs. And furthermore we know there is nothing much we can do about it. This removes the incentives.' And then he said, 'But we don't have your poor and we don't have your slums. As a society, we are prepared to make that trade.'"[43] As Rouse himself said, "However plain, dull and limited life may be, the disparities are minimal. There is no 'gold coast.'"[44] He also found that, according to what he could determine during his trip, "everyone is receiving the opportunity for decent housing at very low rent. Education, recreation, health care are available to all. Public transportation is good and cheap."[45] Indeed, Rouse and his allies had to contend not only with housing and new towns, but also with a comprehensive social welfare state in both Soviet and Western European cities that compensated for some of the dreariness of the massive state housing complexes.

Two Paths to Social Welfare: One Path to Urban Peace

National social welfare programs that flowed to cities further distinguished Europe and the USSR from the United States. Foundations of the social welfare state had been laid during the 1920s and 1930s, but the tabula rasa of postwar Europe created a vacuum into which flowed formerly marginal leftist sentiments. The right, in many countries, had been at least partly discredited. The capitalist classes had devoted their industrial might to the production of goods for governments, and most everyone had served the government in one manner or another. Statism had become a cultural habit even outside the Soviet Union; and the Soviet Union's expansive social welfare promises put Western elites under pressure to improve human welfare: "The reconstruction of Europe after the war required parties committed to a fair measure of state intervention aimed at achieving social equality and redistribution of wealth."[46] What is most overlooked when discussing the European and Soviet social welfare state is the extent to which it was an *urban welfare state* that created dramatic and rapid effects upon urban conditions throughout Europe. Politicians aimed to use the urban welfare state, in tandem with housing and new town programs, to create a potent symbol of the promise of world socialism.

The Soviet Union boasted of great improvement in urban social welfare through their communist methods. By nationalizing all property, industry, and labor, the state had tremendous resources at its disposal; intimidation and unspeakable crimes ensured unanimity. Nikita Khrushchev in 1959 explained, "We take care of our people's health . . . Every industrial and office worker and professional has an annual holiday with pay from the state. The finest sanatoriums, health resorts and rest homes have been turned over for the people to rest in. Everyone in the country gets free medical treatment." Educational provisions were no less generous: "All our children study. Not only a high school, but college education as well is free in the Soviet Union," and he boasted of more engineers than the United States. Soviet citizens could count on lifelong employment (in state industries), health care, retirement, and vacations as rights of citizenship. Many of these systems did not meet the standards of the West, but the rapid progress of the Soviet Union, a comparatively poor, rural nation, certainly cast richer, capitalist nations in an unfavorable light.[47] Moreover, the success of the Soviet space program and atom bomb allowed "Western experts to give credence to other Soviet claims of achievements in welfare, education and the economy."[48] The Soviets exported their model, flawed as it was, to other countries under their sphere of influence.

Those countries outside the Iron Curtain took a moderate path known as social democracy. Although the progress toward social improvement had been evident even before the war, the real progress and the "golden age" of social democracy came only after 1945. Even though electoral victories of social democratic and labor parties proved uneven postwar, the expansion of social democratic policies was not. Social democrats developed a complex system to further their socialist ends. Although they preserved the majority of private property and upheld democratic processes, they did experiment with nationalization of certain large industries such as coal and steel. Social democratic governments primarily adapted macroeconomic policy as best they could to maintain full employment and high wages. They also employed a variety of progressive taxation schemes to redistribute national wealth through social welfare programs, including national health insurance, social insurance, and minimum family allowances.[49] Unlike the situation in the United States, where business interests cast government action in dark shadows, in Europe "there was a widespread belief that public administration would also yield greater efficiency and uniformity of provision (compared with the patchy and disorderly regime of semivoluntary services)." From a United States perspective, even more remarkable was that many "social democrats believed that in time the quality of public services would render private and market-determined alternatives irrelevant."[50]

Most famous were the Northern European countries. One of the leading experts on the Scandinavian social welfare state, John Logue, explains that "the long post-war economic boom expansion, assisted by government policies both orthodox and innovative, provided the wherewithal for transforming what had been among the poorer and more backward countries of Europe into the richest and most progressive in the last quarter of the twentieth century."[51] Progress on social welfare in Sweden started long before the Second World War, but during the period from 1946–1950 the government created the groundwork for universal old age pensions, national health insurance (based on mandatory employer contributions), child care and child allowances, and a massive expansion in education. Labor and capital worked together for full employment, and there were few strikes; government provided training to workers, and subsidies and tax shelters to industries. The public sector expanded to keep unemployment low, and personal income taxes were kept high to redistribute income and support a high level of services.[52] *Time* reported in 1960 that "despite the cost of the most imposing set of welfare services in the world, Swedes are rich and getting richer"[53] The result of so much social spending in countries like Sweden, Norway, and Finland became clear even to opponents of social welfare spending: "Although the Scandinavian countries are not the social paradises sometimes imagined by their less realistic admirers, they have used the public sector to abolish the kind of abject poverty and economic insecurity that continue to characterize life for significant minorities in other advanced industrialized democracies."[54]

Other Western European nations pursued less ambitious but still impressive urban social welfare policies. Immediately after the war, Holland elected "sewer socialists" who provided children's allowances, homes for the elderly, and employment for disabled workers.[55] In West Germany a generous social welfare program included a national health care system, unemployment insurance, and family allowances. Trade unions were active in Germany and gained improved wages and conditions for workers. Near full employment during the postwar period allowed labor and capital relations to remain amicable.[56] The French also created national health care, unemployment, and retirement systems. The United States helped fuel this sewer socialism across Europe; social democratic governments were not above using Marshall Plan monies to create a social democratic infrastructure that would have proved controversial in the United States.

The most surprising addition to the urban social welfare family, from the American perspective, was Great Britain. The British, under Labor leadership, quickly and alarmingly jumped fully on the social welfare bandwagon. The war years had mobilized all of British society and, according to economic historian Nicholas Barr, "forced the British government to adopt powers (e.g. rationing and the direction of labour) on a scale hitherto unknown. It also reduced social distinctions . . . the pressure of common problems prompted the adoption of common solutions." Social class mixture became common in the army; the evacuation of urban children helped the public see common interests; and school meals, relief, and health care were expanded and reorganized. The Beveridge Report of 1942 envisioned a future of family allowances, comprehensive health care service and provisions for full employment. The National Insurance Act of 1946, closely based on the 1942 report, indeed allowed employee benefits for flat-rate contributions in new, national systems related to unemployment, maternity, sickness, widowhood, and retirement. In 1948 progress included the founding of a national health department, welfare for the elderly, and the outline of a child care system. During the 1940s and 1950s the national health care system grew and included an ever increasing proportion of the population (and influenced the creation of a similar health and welfare system in Canada).[57]

Even conservatives such as Churchill endorsed, or at least did not openly attack, the fundamental elements of the social welfare state after the war. Henry Hazlitt in 1956 noted with chagrin that "the Conservatives in Britain have not dared to repeal most of Labour's socialist and welfare planning."[58]

Average educated Americans knew about British experiments with national insurance and social welfare. *Time* and *Newsweek*, for instance, reported both the skyrocketing costs of the welfare state and the general satisfaction numerous times. A Tory soapboxer in London, colorfully described in *Time*, asked his listeners in 1949, "What's left in your wage packet after this government has taken its share of taxes and national insurance?" A heckler yelled "'Stuff a sock in it' and launched into a speech of his own. He had spent six months in a hospital, his wife had a baby, his mother got spectacles and new dentures, his brother got a long needed truss, and 'all under this labor government.'"[59] Even *Time* had to admit that even though the British welfare state was eating up 40 percent of national income and tilting the country toward serious economic problems, "by standards of social justice and decency, the rise in working class incomes may be approved— certainly the majority of Britons approve it."[60]

Social democratic and labor parties failed to hold control of governments on a regular basis outside of Sweden, but even conservative parties in much of Europe stayed the course on the urban welfare state until the 1970s. Built on the back of record growth, social welfare faltered as government revenues failed to cover increasing unemployment and other social welfare costs during the 1970s, but "the principle of universalism" has been maintained even with cuts in services and new fees. "Europe's postwar welfare state retired class conflict from a continent where it had been rife," writes Robert Kuttner, who notes that these systems "also helped lay to rest the economic hardship and ultra-nationalism that had fed on each other for a century."[61] This social peace manifested itself in comparatively calm and prosperous urban centers where the majority of citizens lived, although Rouse and other businessmen never made the connection. Social welfare meant urban welfare in modern, industrialized societies.

The United States government developed a more restrained and uneven social welfare system that did less to preserve the peace in American cities. Most notable in immediate postwar American social welfare policies were generous programs for veterans. The G.I. Bill provided mortgage assistance (which overwhelmingly favored suburbs) and education aid to veterans; in time veterans gained a national system of state-run hospitals. Veterans' benefits remained the generous exception in social policy. The New Deal precedents did not provide the clear leadership of the Beveridge Report or other 1940s social democratic plans in Europe.[62]

Most Americans have forgotten that both Presidents Franklin

Roosevelt and Harry Truman, caught up in the statist spirit of the time, attempted to create national health insurance systems. Roosevelt in 1944 "proposed a greatly expanded post-war New Deal which would guarantee nothing less than economic and social security for all Americans" to no effect, and Truman pushed his health plan in 1949–1950, as part of his Fair Deal initiatives, with similarly desultory results.[63] Truman made appeals to national wealth and dignity in his call for national health care: "In a nation as rich as ours, it is a shocking fact that tens of millions lack adequate medical care . . . We need—and we must have . . . a system of prepaid medical insurance." Truman proposed a flat payroll tax on all workers in the area of 3–4 percent and his secretary of the Federal Security Administration, Oscar Ewing (a former Wall Street investment banker), proposed to expand Social Security to include health care and expand the number of Social Security recipients so that 85 percent of the nation would be covered. Ewing had to be careful to distinguish his plan from European models and explained to the media "especially since his recent visit to Britain, that his plan is not 'socialized medicine.' [Ewing] reserves that term for systems like the British, in which hospitals have been nationalized. His plan would leave them as at present under private or local control." Leading Americans were thus well aware of the social democratic challenge, and press coverage of the British system was extensive. The American Medical Association did not as carefully parse the American and European efforts and fought Truman's proposal hard, spending millions over a number of years (with insurance companies) to stop the effort: "Each month, meetings of many county medical societies hear denunciations of the Ewing plan. The societies have organized speakers' bureaus and they stage exhibits at state and county fairs. In most areas, the battle cry is 'socialized medicine.'"[64] Truman's belief that "medical care is needed as a right, not as a medical dole" was not shared by the AMA, Congressional Republicans, and southern Democrats who effectively blocked his program.[65]

Social Security did grow during the 1950s and 1960s to become a universal system of old age insurance and distributed aid primarily based upon contribution rather than need, making it popular with America's broad middle class. Medicare, offering health benefits to a wide group of retirees, initiated in 1965 during Johnson's Great Society legislation, also expanded mightily because of its large middle-class constituency but did benefit many poor, retired Americans.

Social welfare exclusively for the poor under retirement age grew far more unsteadily and even penalized the working poor. The unsteady development of this side of the welfare state is directly related to the massive urbanization of southern populations: "More than any other single development in the late 1950s and early 1960s the massive migration of southern blacks to northern cities framed the formulation of both urban and antipoverty programs."[66] Federal officials had to demonstrate concern with urban conditions and riots in America, but could not be too generous or they would alienate their majority white, middle-class constituency. Aid to Families with Dependent Children (AFDC), within Social Security, expanded during the 1960s, but benefits remained small compared to European counterparts and were not indexed to inflation. Unlike the European systems of family allowances, participants were penalized or dropped from rolls for working even minimum wage jobs. Medicaid, created in 1965, offered minimal, primarily emergency, health services for the poorest citizens through a mixture of state and federal funding, but also dropped poor people willing to work low-wage jobs. Nor did Medicaid offer the generous (and preventive) care provided by national health systems in Europe.[67]

Social spending in America thus increased enormously, but most of this money was funneled through the Social Security retirement system (in 1984, for instance, Social Security distributed approximately $180 billion in benefits to retirees, whereas AFDC distributed $8 billion) and most benefited middle-class populations living increasingly outside traditional city centers. High social spending for the middle classes masked the comparatively low levels of social welfare in poverty-stricken cities, even after the Great Society programs, that contributed to dangerous conditions found nowhere else in the industrialized world—and certainly was more shocking in the world's richest country.[68]

Parallel to these governmental efforts, and slowing social welfare expansion, was an impressive expansion of corporate welfare programs (health care and pensions) and nonprofit social welfare services, including charity hospitals, clinics, food kitchens, and shelters. By 1950, too, 40 percent of all Americans were in private health plans (about 60 percent in 2003), including those offered by private insurance companies and Blue Cross. Because of the generosity of corporate health and pension benefits during the 1950s and 1960s, and high-visibility nonprofit social services, most middle-class Americans did not mourn the absence of generous national systems. As corporate welfare programs have withered since the 1970s and health care costs have skyrocketed for those even in the private plans, the lack of universal systems for health care has become a mainstream issue. During the entire postwar period, however, cities found themselves with growing numbers of poor, uninsured citizens who lacked access to quality health care or generous state social welfare.

The form, scale, and scope of America's urban social welfare programs placed it far outside the European and Soviet systems. Aggressive corporate welfare programs combined with political action by private insurers, urban political bosses, and conservative white southerners to maintain this distinctive path; comparatively few national resources flowed to cities. The lack of radical labor ideology and the disappearance of American labor parties in the United States also removed a spur to reform for the mainstream political parties:[69] those who would propose expansive social welfare schemes, in fact, had to be prepared to defend themselves against the charge of socialism. "To those fearful of the social power of the state," writes Daniel Rodgers, "the Cold War added a tactical advantage."[70]

The lack of urban social welfare systems during the postwar period compounded the lack of major housing programs and made Rouse's private sector urban solutions both more challenging and more appealing. Planning and housing programs of the East and Western Europe were buttressed by social welfare spending that cooled social conflict and improved urban life. By no means were these systems perfect, and they likely bankrupted many poorer countries, but social spending had benefits as well as costs. On the whole, communist and social democratic cities during much of the Cold War appeared to have achieved superior conditions in comparison to America's less regulated and subsidized urban centers.

American cities suffered not only from substandard housing conditions and redlining, but also from dire poverty that compounded physical decline. American urban riots beginning in the 1960s, and the massive slums where these riots rumbled, best reflected the growing distance between America and the rest of the industrialized urban nations. Nowhere else in the industrialized world experienced such violent and destructive uprisings of poor, angry people; American slums seemed more on a par with those found in the Third World than developed nations. The lack of protest and disorder in Soviet cities was easy to explain away by repression and pure collectivization. America, however, a country that bragged constantly about its national wealth, stood out even among Western industrialized nations for its embarrassing urban conditions.

Rouse did not disagree that something had gone wrong in the United States. He lamented as late as 1989, for instance, "No other free, democratic, industrialized country—no country in Western Europe, the United Kingdom, Japan—has these physically deteriorated, dehumanizing, disgraceful conditions."[71] Although he grudgingly acknowledged Soviet concern for the poor (with an equal and justifiable amount of disdain for Soviet politics), he was never able to acknowledge that forty years of social spending in Western Europe and Japan might have had any effect upon urban conditions in a democratic context. Rouse never made any connections in speeches or letters between generous European welfare and housing programs and urban improvement. Obviously, something miraculous and inexplicable had transformed European cities for the better and left America with the worst conditions in the industrialized world.

Rouse even argued many times that America's comparatively small welfare state had actually created dire conditions in American cities by encouraging dependency and disorder among the poor. Like most Americans, he failed to distinguish between total social spending on programs like Social Security and smaller programs specifically designed for urban poverty. As a businessman, Rouse's assessments of America's dismal urban conditions may have been rare, but his belief in creative, antistatist solutions to social welfare placed him safely in the mainstream of American social policy. His unique combination of frank social criticism with private sector solutions made him a leader among his peers.

CHAPTER TWO

Reinventing the Capitalist City

The products of our creative genius are evident on every hand and nowhere so extensively as on our own shelves. But, so far, we have failed to apply this same creative vitality to bringing the physical city in which we live up-to-date with our knowledge and our hopes of how to live. The American people have learned how to live better, work better, shop better, than the central city can provide, and they will desert it in increasing numbers as better alternatives are made available to them.

James Rouse

To hypothesize the working city, the city where people were employed, had incomes capable of coping, lived in communities where there was a delivery of health care, where people were well educated, moved about in reasonable systems of mass transportation, where there was beauty and community health and a city full of spirit: now, that's not beyond our capacity.

James Rouse, "Utopia: Limited or Unlimited"

Whole city blocks no more than piles of rubble proved a good match to the left-wing aspirations of postwar European planners. The massive destruction of the Second World War led, in much of Europe, to far more far-reaching urban reshaping than was possible in the United States, untouched by bombing or warfare and hampered by laissez-faire politics. American city centers remained layered, thickly built places comparatively free of central direction and planning. Those who would completely replan the cities of the United States for the modern age, and show that the leading Western democracy could create a modern image of the capitalist city, had to invent the means of large-scale destruction in peacetime, as well as create the space for progressive planning in an atmosphere that distrusted centralization and leftist schemes.

A *Life* magazine reporter recorded one of Boston's leading architects, William Greeley, showing just such enthusiasm for creative destruction in 1945. Presiding over an unveiling of radical reconstruction plans for postwar Boston, Greeley argued that "since Boston presumably will not have the 'advantage' of being destroyed in the war like London, it is up to

Figure 4. Pittsburgh's "Golden Triangle" project, including the Renaissance I Center, from the 1950s made a splash where the Monongahela and Allegheny join to form the Ohio River. A leading example of the renewed urban landscape pioneered in this great industrial city, this project resulted from the efforts of the Allegheny Conference, a dynamic private sector civic improvement organization. Rouse and businessmen across America found inspiration in the total transformation achieved in Pittsburgh's central business district. Library and Archive Division, Historical Society of Western Pennsylvania.

Boston's citizens 'to destroy our own diseased tissues and by heroic will-power rebuild our community as a worthy competitor of the newer type of city.'"[1] Architects like Greeley knew well that America's oceans would not isolate the nation's cities from international comparisons.

Architects and planners donated the artistic vision, but in the end they were not the engines behind this transformation. Only through business-led planning did these planning powers emerge, and they likely could not have emerged from any other quarter in the increasingly para-noid politics of the postwar period. In a time when state power in the United States was held in low esteem, only businessmen had the freedom to propose sweeping changes to urban policy. James Rouse, and figures such as Richard Mellon and William Zeckendorf in other cities, stood at the forefront of this expansion. During the 1950s and 1960s American city centers and their surrounding regions transformed themselves under business leadership as the stumbling blocks to comprehensive planning dis-solved.[2]

What urban businessmen knew about cities of the 1940s and 1950s was fairly sobering. Dense urban centers constructed in the era of carriages and streetcars had failed to make an adequate adjustment to the mass popularity of the automobile in the 1920s. The lack of parking and fast roads gave advantages to emerging suburban areas, even by the 1920s. In a 1945 article in *The Nation*, Frank Fisher acknowledged that the United States had "escaped the more obvious destructive consequences of war. But the war has accentuated our long-standing housing shortage and accelerated the disintegration of many of our cities."[3] Much of the commercial real estate of cities in older buildings, although made up of a variety of impressive architectural styles, lacked the light and comfort that modern buildings possessed. Real estate owners did not necessarily update properties or were too busy in speculation schemes to concern themselves with property management.

City centers, mired in old ways, started to lose ground to the suburban edge. Older department stores in city centers, for instance, lost ground to new suburban branches. Between 1948 and 1954, retail trade in metropolitan Baltimore may have increased a strong 25 percent, but it sank nearly 2 percent in the downtown shopping district. Worse, "the assessed value of the central business district dropped from $175 million in 1931 to $128 million in 1947."[4] In 1946 *Life* found that "in the crowded center of car-conscious Detroit, property values have tumbled some 2,000,000 since 1930." Shoppers "frequently take their business to suburban centers where parking is not so difficult."[5] Less value in the center meant diminished tax revenues, and cities across the country experienced similar or worse declines. The power of American management skill needed to be focused on the moribund cities in order that they, too, would reflect the benefits of the free enterprise system.

Massive condemnation was the first and perhaps the most essential tool of urban redevelopment. What bombs and socialism had done in other countries, condemnation had to achieve in the American city. Speculators and recalcitrant owners could not stand in the way of the greater good. As Rouse explained, as important as zoning and other powers were, without condemnation there could be little in the way of *comprehensive* planning: "you must USE THE POWER OF CONDEMNATION. You can't flinch from it. Unless you declare the heart of the city a redevelopment area, unless you're willing to go in and take steps necessary to make it work, you might as well give up . . . Streets need to be widened, closed, changed—the whole character of your downtown community needs to be revised, if it's going to be workable." "Whole character" meant excess condemnation (the destruction not only of a few necessary buildings, but also of whole districts deemed necessary to new planning) on a scale never before witnessed in America. Rouse honestly believed that there was a greater injustice in not taking property for a greater civic good: "it's absolutely unfair to the city, it's unfair to the people who want to do the good things to say that the city doesn't have the courage to go in and use the power of condemnation."[6] Rouse's comment reflects a reversal in traditional thinking about the rights of urban property owners.

Rouse's philosophy paralleled and drew from changing ideas of local urban power around the country. Pittsburgh made great strides in condemnation, as did developers in New York during the 1940s and 1950s. New redevelopment authorities, many created to take advantage of provisions in the Housing Act of 1949, stepped up slum clearance projects adjoining central business districts, and the courts and state legislatures stood behind them. William Zeckendorf, one of New York's leading developers of the postwar years and a leader in Title I development across the United States, came down strongly for the expansion of this now controversial activity. American city government, he argued, "should be much more generous in its use of eminent domain for redevelopment purposes and it should also try to make a profit. This may be heresy, but I am against the windfall profit for the fellow who has nothing to do with the creation of increment through a communal development." This condemnation, as has been widely described by urban historians, almost always led to displacement of poor urban residents. Even Rouse's early projects (described in the following chapter) displaced a number of low-income black residents. Zeckendorf, too, unashamedly saw the destruction of slum areas as an excellent opportunity for both private profit and higher tax revenues: "But one of the worst tendencies in redevelopment throughout the United States is to demolish slums close to the central core after condemnation, and then to replace them with low-cost housing. The downtown area of the cities in the United States should not be used for housing but should be devoted to high tax producing sites."[7] Rouse differed from this view only in believing that upscale housing should be integrated into redevelopment plans as part of increasing urban tax revenues.

For those who questioned such a major expansion of government powers at the expense of private owners, Rouse had a ready response, which was repeated in many speeches during the 1950s and 1960s. Plans for condemnation were rightly the activities of local government, and local government, even if benefiting from federal largess, remained distinct in its goals and values from the federal state. "We have found it necessary to progressively enlarge the powers of municipal government in order to make our cities fit places in which to live," he explained to a national convention in 1957 and at many other times.[8]

In a speech to Baltimore real estate men in 1964, Rouse tried to explain away the apparent contradictions in his support for the expansion of local but not federal power: "I think that most of us tend to be conservative when we look at powers of government, and in our habit and tradition of conservatism we fail to distinguish between conservatism in the role of the federal government and conservatism in the role of local government. It's conservative to be radical in giving powers to local government. Unless we give the power to local government to take the action necessary to solve the problems, we are creating a demand for the power of federal government to—that gets beyond their control." Rouse in this quotation hints at both the New Deal and its more intrusive social programs as well as the leftist governments of Europe. Businessmen, however, need not fear local government, because "I don't believe anyone has ever seen any city in the United States in which there has been an abusive use of too much power." As evidence of the security businesspeople could feel in expanding local government, he asked his audiences to consider "cities like New Haven and Norfolk, which are conservative cities both of them, and look at the enormous pace of redevelopment in those cities . . . because they weren't afraid of their local government. They weren't afraid a bit, because they felt they controlled their local government—and we do." The "we" referred, quite obviously, to local business interests, which Rouse considered to be the guardians of civic virtue. Agents of local power, like redevelopment agencies or planning commissions, could be changed with ease if they got "very far off beat," and it wouldn't be "long before enough pressure can be brought on it to bring it back in line, or people get thrown out of office and new people elected."[9] Local government and local businessmen could be trusted to do right by the city and even recalcitrant property owners. The identity of the powerful was as important as the powers granted to them.[10]

The federal government did play an important role in the business vision of local government programs, and for this reason Rouse and others in development supported the creation of federal urban renewal and highway programs that subsidized local planning agencies. However, the provisions that federal money be distributed through local government and local redevelopment agencies carefully restricted the federal government's role. The Housing Acts of 1949 and 1954 made money and power available to urban leaders interested in redevelopment, but *no* provisions were made for national planning agencies as occurred during the New Deal.

Local businessmen and elected officials promoted federal highway programs, too, their routes determined more often than not by local rather than national considerations. Federal highway funding began to flow in large amounts to cities as early as 1944, but the Interstate Highway Act made billions available to city officials after 1956. Half of the $27 billion approved in the act "went to the fifty-five hundred miles of freeways that cut through urban areas."[11] Like most businessmen at the time, Rouse believed in urban highway expansion: "Major expressways must be ripped through to the central core and these expressways properly planned to give definition and boundaries to the residential neighborhoods surrounding downtown."[12] The Greater Baltimore Committee, of which he was a founding member, played a leading role in the creation of massive, and eventually controversial, urban highways through Baltimore city neighborhoods.

Rouse summarized the cumulative effects of these federal programs: "The Urban Renewal Program dates from 1954. We're now underway with a huge highway program. Ninety-eight billion dollars is scheduled to be spent in America on highways in the next twenty years . . . by the Federal Government, states, cities, and counties. A very large part of it will be spent within the central cities, tearing out old areas, giving new boundaries to neighborhoods, and new shape and formation to the city."[13]

At long last the businesspeople and the planners had the resources and powers to make their dreams a reality: "for the first time in the history of the American city, the people who live there have the tools, the capacity, the organization, to make their city into what they want it to be."[14] These enhanced local governments, running on a refined blend of federal funding and business leadership, then had to reshape the old city to suit modern suburban values.

Rouse himself was a leader in suburban development in Maryland and saw promise in the suburban lifestyle. He held a brief position as a clerk in the New Deal's Federal Housing Administration in 1935, where "one of my first jobs was to try to persuade Baltimore lending institutions to make an FHA loan."[15] One year later, in 1936, Rouse, then only twenty-two, "talked Baltimore's venerable Title Guarantee Company into letting him set up a mortgage department."[16] In 1939 Rouse started a small mortgage banking firm in Baltimore with a friend, Hunter Moss. The firm grew quickly but was disbanded during the war as most members of the firm went into the military, including Rouse. After military service, Rouse returned to Baltimore, and with Moss their "small, prewar mortgage banking business . . . turned into a booming postwar operation." Moss explained that "the housing market grew like the dickens," and the firm "represented life insurance companies, matching the firms' money with developers in need of loans." Rouse began a relationship with Connecticut General Life Insurance that would last his whole life and bring him to Hartford a number of times.[17]

In an important speech of the late 1950s on one of those visits to the high modernist corporate campus of Connecticut General designed by the leading architectural firm, Skidmore, Owings and Merrill in 1957, Rouse sketched what he considered to be the ideals for a capitalist urban society like the United States. The fact that Connecticut General had left the city center for a suburban campus was not a sign of urban decline per se, but of changing urban ideals that could in time act as a spur to further urban reimagination:

> A great insurance company has pulled up stakes and withdrawn from the central city. It has been willing to sacrifice the proximity to people who work for it and with it; the easy access to its many business associates and public officials; the convenience of hotels, railroad stations, taxicabs, in exchange for the efficiency, the peace, the beauty of this magnificent building at the center of a 265–acre farm. This is not a flight from the problems of the city; it is a forthright attack upon them . . . it is a bold step forward in expressing how we can and ought to live and work.

At the new campus, Rouse believed that a transformation in living had occurred, creating a more pleasant and amiable form of capitalism: "an insurance company reveals itself as an organization of people. Every clerk has been made important by the environment in which he has been put to work . . . The people have been made important by their association with each other, their building and the country about them." The campus, in Rouse's opinion, had taken on the better aspects of the American small town: "The corridors are a series of main streets. Watch the exchange of greetings, the faces, the conversations as the huge clerical staff and the executives too respond to the openness, the color, the gardens and, above all else, the obvious concern for their welfare."[18]

This new campus reflected the potential of corporate welfare—particularly, the ability of a transformed environment to reshape urban relationships from strictly competitive and grinding to nearly transcendent: "The magnificent mechanical efficiency and smooth flow of this building is economically important, but the lake, the swans in the lake, the green grass, the trees, and just plain space, lift the souls of the people who work here and the company for which they work. Somehow, this building expresses the best of our technical knowledge about how to work and our human aspirations too."[19]

The Connecticut General campus thus set a standard to which the rest of the city, even the city center, should aspire: "Compare it with the city which it leaves behind. Compare it with the steel and concrete, the grim, impersonal jam which represents the city." The pattern should be, then, of not shaping humans to fit a particular model, but reading the habits of Americans at their best, in suburbia, and projecting this vision back onto the city: "Station wagons, blue jeans, barbeques, give expression to the casual, mobile, outdoor family living that marks the American family. They seek space and they are finding it, in the scatteration around our cities." Even the malls he was building in this period fit in this new model. They were not harbingers of urban destruction, but a new vision of urban potential: "No longer blocks of stores piled into a maelstrom of people, automobiles, streetcars, buses, and traffic lights, noise and dirt, these new centers are convenient, gay and human. Ample parking and landscaped parking areas conveniently organized in relationship to the stores and their particular parking demands. The stores themselves face each other across landscaped malls . . . There are sidewalk cafes, exhibits and displays, families shopping together and music in the air." These new institutions of office parks, malls, and suburban subdivisions set the tone of modern American living, the best that capitalism could provide, and cities had to be massively reshaped to fit these expectations. It could not be the other way around.[20] Rouse was not alone in his celebration of sub-urban life, and dozens of urban redevelopment plans from the time reflected this thinking, but he developed the clearest vision of the impact of suburban innovation on urban centers, which contributed to his popularity as a public speaker.

When it came to specific reforms for urban areas that would match these expectations, Rouse promoted ideas that were not his own. He championed them so well, however, and for such a long period of time that he became strongly identified with this appealing vision of complete urban transformation. During the 1950s Rouse created a personal collage of concepts from different phases of American and European planning traditions. Because of his unwavering devotion to the free enterprise system, he was able to easily glide over the more complex social dimensions of some of the traditions from which he borrowed. All concepts were flattened into usable tools for an ambitious and idealistic businessman.

The American planning tradition was quite perfectly suited to his purposes in proposing dramatic transformations in American cities. In this case, however, Rouse made it clear that more dramatic action would be necessary to create a new city. The City Beautiful had offered the model of civic splendor and comprehensive regional planning that appealed to Rouse. He often quoted Daniel Burnham's famous dictum—"Make no little plans, they have no magic to stir men's blood"—and in practical terms was never afraid to cast his net over whole cities. Rouse knew that the power of certain private interests had stymied most idealistic planning in America before his era, but he still believed that the great plans had power to transform the city as a whole.

The notion of functional and efficient cities theorized and promulgated by planners since the turn of the century also appealed to a man who wanted cities with high-quality services, the end of so-called blight, and rapid transportation routes. Great strides had been made in highway design, zoning, traffic signals, and infrastructure by the time Rouse appeared on the urban scene in the 1930s. He stood for the extension of these innovations on a wider basis and worked hard to promote new highways, zoning regulations, housing code enforcement, and improved sanitation systems.[21]

The modernist movement appealed to Rouse for its fascination with clean edges and new materials. While uncomfortable with the more radical edge of modern design for mass residential design, throughout his career Rouse selected crisp modernist designs for his commercial and urban projects. He did not care for the socialist politics that accompanied much of the movement (particularly in Europe), but was a dependable modernist patron. The identification of modernism with corporate America was solidified in the postwar period, particularly in office parks and downtown districts, what has sometimes been classified as American Imperial Modern style, to distinguish it from the leftist politics that accompanied much of European modernism.[22]

Rouse may not have agreed with modernist politics, but he did share the modernist taste for comprehensive planning. Modernists, and Rouse, aimed to destroy old cities to fit a new conception of urban form. Congested streets were the enemy of modernists and businessmen alike. Modernists envisioned separation of pedestrians and autos, high-speed expressways, and superblocks protected from automobiles; businessmen like Rouse supported these same innovations for improvements in downtown business. Modernists envisaged a much tidier city, with exclusive zones of industry, commerce, residence, and recreation; many businessmen predicted greater efficiency and property value appreciation from careful zoning of the city into separate districts. Finally, "towers in parks," when divorced from social democracy, were efficient and profitable ways to house both the urban middle classes and poor people displaced by slum clearance.

In practical terms Rouse drew inspiration from business groups organizing around the country in the 1940s and 1950s to redevelop cities. Although Robert Moses of New York is most famously remembered for his role in transforming New York City during this period, businessmen were playing a more important role in urban form than public officials. In New York, for instance, William Zeckendorf and David Rockefeller were the outstanding examples of business leadership for civic renewal. Pittsburgh was particularly famous for its nearly complete transformation by business leaders. An *Atlantic Monthly* article of 1951 described the immediate postwar situation in Pittsburgh: "The decrepitude showed in its worn-out

Figure 5. The Connecticut General Life Insurance campus on Hartford's suburban edge reflected the suburban ideal toward which Rouse thought the entire city should aspire. G. E. Kidder Smith, courtesy of Kidder Smith Collection, Rotch Visual Collections, MIT.

office buildings, its degraded housing, its traffic-choked streets, its sordid alleys, its polluted and uncontrolled rivers, and, above all, in the dense, choking smoke that covered the city and the river valleys with gray despair." Business leaders like Richard (Dick) Mellon led the way in changing the city: "During the war many of Pittsburgh's leaders, men like Dick Mellon and others of his generation, were away in the service. When they returned they saw their home town in a different perspective. They were shocked and awakened." This may have been an old story in America, the shock engendered by returning to American cities after a European tour, but the results this time were different.

Infused with the generational energy that would fuel the postwar boom, Mellon and his associates joined together (in 1943) to create the Allegheny Conference, a voluntary organization with the goal of acting "as a catalytic agent in fusing old self-interests and a new feeling of social responsibility." After the war, in large measure due to the organized power of the Allegheny Conference, federal and local efforts brought highways, flood control, and a new airport. Most notably, a smoke ordinance for the first time drastically reduced contamination that had made some sunny days near pitch black; the combined strength and prestige of the conference members finally forced local industries to reduce their smoke emissions. An ambitious slum clearance program for what became known as Gateway Center, including new office towers and a park, replaced "an ancient slum on the site of birthplace of Pittsburgh";[23] corporate headquarters, garages, and parks sprouted on cleared downtown lots. This redeveloped land at the confluence of the Allegheny and Monongahela Rivers quickly came to be known as Pittsburgh's Golden Triangle.

Rouse admired the swiftness of urban change in Pittsburgh: "The Allegheny Conference in Pittsburgh represented an alarmed uprising by the business leadership of that City against its withering decay. The business community asserted the leadership which, working hand in hand with planners and enlightened public officials, resulted in the splendid Golden Triangle project and the overall reawakening of a new Pittsburgh." Rouse applauded the Allegheny Conference for, among other things, creating new corporate headquarters buildings "on a former 123-acre slum" as well as smoke controls, parking garages downtown, a new airport, and expressways and admired the "tightly organized, like-minded business leadership group forcing action."[24] Other cities also had groups of downtown interests pushing for radical transformations in the operations of the city: "Similarly, in St. Louis it is Civic Progress, Inc., in Cleveland the Cleveland Redevelopment Foundation . . . by which businessmen have responded to a new awareness of their responsibility for the way their city develops."[25]

Inspired by these efforts, Rouse nevertheless learned the most important lessons close to home. He already had some direct experience in urban redevelopment, and by 1951 he had "two redevelopment projects under way in Baltimore. One is a 29 block project in the blighted Waverly area, where razing has begun. Rouse said 291 apartment units for middle-income families and a drive-in shopping center will be built starting next spring."[26] Of questionable merit, these projects (discussed in the next chapter) nevertheless demonstrated to Rouse that comprehensive redevelopment of cities was possible if businessmen took the lead.

Rouse also became a leading figure in the redesign of Baltimore's downtown. The Greater Baltimore Committee, of which Rouse was a founding member in 1955, was modeled on Pittsburgh's activist Allegheny Conference and played a central role in both shaping downtown and the surrounding districts and highways. The redevelopment project Rouse helped lay the groundwork for, known as Charles Center, became a favorite subject in his many speeches on the rebirth of the American city and was one of the most famous postwar redevelopment projects. Here, according to Rouse, was a leading example of the potential of private sector planning operating on a massive scale to reinvent an entire central portion of a major city. Referring to Charles Center: "This was possible in the

city because a great plan was produced, because it was produced by the support and with the leadership of the business community, and the business
community is responsible for it and has honored it." Rouse understood well
that the scale of redevelopment proposed in the hands of government
interests alone would have been far more controversial.[27]

Charles Center began through a series of meetings of Baltimore businessmen concerned about the state of the city in 1952, including leading
retailer Louis Kohn, banker Guy Hollyday, Hunter Moss (Rouse's business
partner at this time), and Rouse. They decided to circumvent the more
conservative chamber of commerce, ascertain information about the
Allegheny Conference, and endeavored to identify other wealthy individuals they hoped to recruit.[28] In a memo Rouse articulated the idealistic flourishes that would distinguish his work for decades: "Small scale,
piecemeal approaches to this accumulation of neglect are futile, except to
the extent that they are useful as 'experiments' or 'pilots' to determine the
effectiveness of a particular line of effort." The aim of total transformation became a familiar Rouse theme during this period and helped gain
interest in the project among local elites.[29]

The Greater Baltimore Committee, officially established in 1955 by
these idealistic men, grew in influence during the mid-1950s and ultimately included a large number of leading Baltimoreans. By 1959 the
Greater Baltimore Committee (GBC) consisted of seventy-one members
and the upper limit was set at one hundred in order to maintain institutional focus.[30] A report on the Baltimore experience for potential imitators
pointed out that leadership in Baltimore redevelopment came not from the
chamber of commerce, but "from the financial and insurance firms that
have had few connections to the chamber." Not only were many of these
firms smaller and staffed by organization men with less attachment to place
(Rouse was a newcomer to Baltimore himself), but also "the crux of the
matter seems to be the orientation and philosophy of many C. of C.
groups. Traditionally they have been among the country's most active proponents of laissez-faire private enterprise and, in general, they have not
kept up with the enormous changes taking place nationally."[31] Postwar,
pure laissez-faire ideology was not closely tied to the businessman's utopia.
The GBC, then, represented the progressive voice of the business interests
of the city. An impressive number of Jewish business leaders, with whom
Rouse worked closely throughout his career, also became major players in
regional issues through the GBC, although before this period they had
been kept to the edges of local power politics. The emergence of a more
assimilated generation of Jewish business leadership played a role in redevelopment in many cities and merits further study.

Different subcommittees of the GBC worked hard, particularly the one associated with downtown redevelopment. Rouse was not a member of this committee but evidently played a leading role in bringing the group's work to fruition. Referring to redevelopment of business districts and explaining why private interests were involved in such a big study, "the sponsors of the study, particularly Hunter Moss and James W. Rouse, Jr., felt that there is a real role for a private planning organization. Their thinking was, and is, that such a private organization locally sponsored and financed can operate with relative freedom and confidential contracts of private enterprise."[32] In 1956 the Greater Baltimore Committee joined forces with the downtown Property Owner's Association's Downtown Committee to create a planning council. The designer in charge of the project was David Wallace, a professor of planning at the University of Pennsylvania.[33] Already the tone of the project was noticeably different from a municipally generated scheme. Wallace, not a mere government employee in a public office, was a leading professional from one of the top design schools in the country. According to Rouse, "Freed of budgetary controls and political pressures, the Council has been able to employ top-flight people at the salaries required to obtain their services."[34]

Through the Downtown Committee the businessmen collected $150,000 among themselves for the operating budget of the planning council, and the GBC gave $75,000. The leading lights of the administrative effort would become part of a familiar cast of Baltimore characters and included J. Jefferson Miller (a department store executive), Walter Sondheim (another department store executive), and J. Harold Grady (the mayor).[35] Miller led the charge on the Charles Center organization and later plans for the Inner Harbor. He in turn recruited Martin Millspaugh in 1960, a former journalist (who wrote extensively on urban renewal for the *Baltimore Sun*), who was then serving as assistant commissioner for Research and Development of the U.S. Urban Renewal Administration. The Charles Center–Inner Harbor Management Corporation, as it was known in time, featured Miller as chairman of the board and Millspaugh as president. The corporation worked on a contractual basis with the city and hired planners like Wallace to devise quite extraordinary plans.[36]

Although many leading individuals from the city were involved, David Wallace did not at first have a clear direction. According to Rouse, "[A]fter six months, Wallace came into my office and said, 'The whole thing is fruitless; there's no real interest in downtown Baltimore; nobody's planning to expand; there's no real prospect of any real vitality occurring.'" Rouse remembered, "We talked about it and agreed that what ought to happen was the largest do-able project that could be done in order to raise the image of the possible, to create a new attitude about

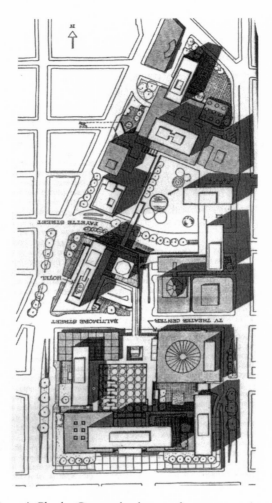

Figure 6. Baltimore's Charles Center plan became famous across America for its comprehensive yet sensitive approach to urban redevelopment. Although the project emerged from business support in the city, including Rouse, and rightly became a symbol of private sector talent, local and federal money made possible the completion of the project. *Architectural Forum*, 1958.

downtown."[37] Wallace explained many times that this brief conversation had a major impact upon his planning. Rouse consistently called for the most ambitious plan possible.

Emboldened by Rouse's enthusiasm, Wallace's Charles Center plan ultimately covered twenty-two acres of the downtown area and proposed to clear or rebuild almost the entire business heart of the community. City

Figure 7. Alternative view, Charles Center. Attractive plazas, modernist towers, plentiful parking, and selective historic preservation made the plan one that even Jane Jacobs could love. *Architectural Forum*, 1958.

voters approved a bond for Charles Center in 1958 to the tune of $25 million, and the Baltimore City Council approved Wallace's plan in 1959. The Charles Center plan was one of the most comprehensive reinvented downtown spaces of this period and included not only the obligatory modernist office towers, but separated automobiles and pedestrians, buried parking garages under plazas, made future provisions for mass transit, and offered relatively inviting and well-conceived public spaces. The reinvented urban landscape advocated by Victor Gruen at Fort Worth (1956), never built but much admired, was partly realized at Charles Center. A modern downtown, reflecting renewed capitalism, the demands of the auto age, and the capacity of competitive capitalists to cooperate partially reached its realization here.

Rouse boasted of the achievement: "The Charles Center project involves the demolition, through urban renewal, of all but five buildings in a 22-acre area at the very heart of the City. One of our main shopping blocks will be closed and all the stores on it demolished. Think of it—this project, including the ordinance to condemn, was approved by the City Council unanimously and without protest from property owners involved."[38] During discussion of the bond issue, members of the GBC went on the road "using slides and flip cards, before various local groups" and "insisted that there is no strong opposition, and that the public's attitude has been highly favorable."[39] The first parcels became ready by December of 1959 and brought significant interest from developers. Aside from the selective preservation of historic buildings, it looked at first as though a bomb had gone off in the heart of Baltimore's principal commercial district. By 1976, however, Charles Center–Inner Harbor, including the combined downtown and harbor commercial districts, represented a total of $375 million in private, public, and institutional investment. One thousand properties were acquired and 730 businesses were relocated during this massive reconstruction, but real estate revenues still increased by between three and four million dollars each year.

Nearly all of the critics at the national level found Charles Center to be a worthwhile addition to Baltimore's urban fabric. According to *Fortune,* "The Baltimore project is magnificently different. It looks as if it were designed by people who like the city . . . Charles Center is in downtown, and it is meant to bring its activities to a focus rather than distribute them."[40] Jane Jacobs, a tough critic of most redevelopment, praised the project plan, because it "blends the Center into the area that lies outside it. This means the Center will be less a 'project' than an integral, continuous part of downtown." The manner in which the "continuity" had been established included tall buildings on the edges of the project at similar heights to surrounding buildings and a series of new public spaces linked to existing streets and buildings. Jacobs celebrated that "pedestrians are to have a complete street system of their own" and that cars were tucked carefully into underground garages. She particularly liked that "a 68-foot drop in topography is exploited both for continuity with the rest of the city and for its drama." In sum, the planning "made possible, over the entire site, truly urban, concentrated, lively design." In accompanying diagrams she showed a line of model urban projects stretching from the Piazza San Marco through Piazza San Pietro, Penn Center, Rockefeller Center, and finally to Charles Center. This was good company for any urban renewal project from the period.[41]

In Rouse's mind an important aspect of the project was not merely the physical reconstruction and good design, but the means to this desirable end. Business interests should be proud of "the creation of Charles Center Management, Inc., a private, non-profit corporation set up outside of city government to contract with the city to get the plan executed. And it's still the best model in America for an enabling process to bring about a plan." Rouse also bragged that "there will be no Federal aid and no State aid in carrying the project forward . . . this project is a good, hard-headed investment for the city; [and] that the city's total cash contribution will be repaid within an acceptable term and that all the collateral benefits to the city will thus be free."[42]

This boasting turned out to be premature. Indeed, federal funding and buildings were eventually necessary to help complete the project. Rouse rarely mentioned government financial support in speeches that focused on private sector prowess. Charles Center, and the Inner Harbor areas added to the planning districts during the 1960s, in fact received $88 million in federal urban renewal grants and $20 million for federal buildings. In time the city itself provided $76 million in loans.[43] This was not a pure subsidy on the part of the government, as Rouse noted, because the project paid handsome dividends on public investment through enhanced tax revenues. It is ironic, however, to recognize that Charles Center, one of the leading examples of business redevelopment of the period, benefited mightily from government subsidy (some of which was originally intended to fund urban housing initiatives).

The federal government's important role in staking Charles Center and redevelopment projects across the United States always faded to the background, crowded out by the businessmen claiming credit for reanimated downtowns. These new business districts did not begin as, nor did they look like, government "projects," and businessmen did deserve most of the credit for generating and pursuing these projects; federal and local money served business interests well. At least in city center redevelopment, at Baltimore, Pittsburgh, New York, and other cities, capitalism had demonstrated both its resilience and its genius for urban form. The success of urban redevelopment gave businessmen the confidence to expand their field of action during the 1960s and 1970s.[44]

ACTION

During the late 1950s Rouse tried to reshape a national organization to suit his ambitious goals for the capitalist city. ACTION, the American Council to Improve Our Neighborhoods, primarily focused on neighborhood renewal, preservation, and housing (described in chapter 3). The organization played an equally important role in galvanizing movement on urban redevelopment on a national level. Rouse was a founding member and guiding force of the organization in 1954, along with Andrew Heiskell of Time-Life and other wealthy and well-connected Americans.

After becoming president in 1958, Rouse tried to imprint a far more utopian cast to the organization's efforts; his well-intentioned goal of using ACTION to promote unified urban redesign for cities as a whole exceeded his grasp.

ACTION had catalyzed business interest in urban renewal across the United States. New legislation and opportunities needed explanation and promotion, particularly outside America's largest cities. Through a series of Regional Urban Renewal Clinics held between 1956 and 1958, "some 200 civic leaders from 325 cities took part in the programs discussing vital questions concerning financing, legislation, citizen information, construction and other technical subject matters." A variety of Group Correspondents, local groups with an interest in new information, numbered about 150 by 1960.

Experts associated with ACTION created publications for the use of local groups. The "Urban Renewal Evaluator," for instance, was developed "as a self-survey instrument for local groups that wished to establish a factual basis for their efforts in renewal . . . The copyrighted 28-page Evaluator, especially attractive to businessmen, afforded an intensive means of determining the possibilities for economic development in their communities."[45] Note that this publication was "especially attractive to businessmen." It provided a series of formulas and categories to aid local business interests in determinations of whether urban renewal would be a solid business proposition. Businessmen were asked to calculate the number of blighted buildings, the extent of slums, the social problems related to slums (in everything from auto thefts to venereal diseases), the degree to which slums cost more in social and other services as opposed to non-slum areas, and the relative revenues and expenses derived from slums. The outcome of such math was nearly predetermined—there were few cities in America that did not face serious costs related to urban decline. The brochure did, however, force businesspeople to confront the cold facts they tried to deny, and was purchased by two hundred cities and clearly adopted by a number of urban centers, including Houston and El Paso.

If the amount of press devoted to ACTION in papers and national publications across America indicates influence, ACTION became a force in encouraging the extension of ambitious ideals about urban renewal across the country. The notion of designing perfect capitalist cities, however, became Rouse's personal goal for the organization. Rouse traveled around the country advocating thorough reshaping of cities and proposing demonstration projects that would create an example of a slum-less, perfectly planned American city in a certain number of years. In 1958 Rouse, recently elected president of ACTION, signaled the begin-

Figure 8. This ACTION illustration from the *ACTION Evaluator*, ca. 1954, reflects well the importance placed upon business leadership in civic affairs. Rouse was a founding member and leading force behind ACTION, the American Council to Improve Our Neighborhoods. Rouse Papers, Columbia Archive.

ning of a wider role: "The root of urban blight was the neighborhood and this is where ACTION had concentrated its efforts. But the decay of housing is only one problem of urban renewal, and now ACTION felt it must broaden its horizons and turn its attention to the problems of the whole metropolis." Rouse, "emphasizing that the decay of our cities had become one of our country's greatest domestic failures," cried out for "good housing in good neighborhoods . . . efficient highways and better transportation . . . vigorous commercial and cultural cores instead of obsolescence and scatteration . . . adequate financing for public and private improvements."[46] The utopian glow in Rouse's speeches flowed through numerous letters and interviews he gave during this period. He admitted to being "determined that ACTION shall take strong leadership in lifting the sights of the cities to the goal of total planning—total programming for slumless, blight free, livable, efficient cities in 'X' years." This was utopian thinking on a par with any in Europe or the Soviet Union—in this case, separated from socialist goals by the private sector means to the idealistic ends.[47]

This wider vision of the ideal city could be found in ACTION documents of the late 1950s. A 1959 definition of a good community created by ACTION for a major Newark conference reflects the businessman's utopia as conceived by Rouse and many of those in ACTION. This document, "Agenda for a Good City," gave a number of signs of healthy places, including high employment, peaceful social relationships, safe housing, low disease rates, good schools, and other facilities. This idealized vision of the capitalist city, although integrating an impressive number of civic and social improvements, would be created primarily with local government and business leadership and without altering the wider society.[48]

Rouse made serious efforts to create a living demonstration of the potential for urban renewal on a metropolitan scale in the early 1960s, but the project ultimately fell through. Nevertheless, many of his letters sent to leading individuals during this effort reflect his urban idealism. Rouse proposed that a series of cities across America create comprehensive redevelopment plans and that these plans be on display at the New York World's Fair of 1964–1965. According to Rouse, "It seems to us in ACTION that this lack of conviction [that the city can be made better] is at least partially the result of no one having seen (in our times at least) an efficient, slumless, American City equal to the full promise of our civilization, our political system and our productive capacity."[49] Rouse proposed that "Each participating city would study, plan and program the complete renewal and reorganization of that city into a slumless, blightless, livable community"; in other words, the planning would project a utopian vision onto existing cities. Such a major undertaking, he believed, would generate considerable excitement among professionals in a variety of fields: "The scope and challenge of the combined project would attract a variety and quality of talent never before applied in specific and detailed study of the problems of the city as an environment for living and working." Even more promising, "private corporations also would be attracted to apply to the undertaking their new-product development and research departments."[50]

The ultimate goal of this flurry of comprehensive planning was a display that would show what private interests could do, offer a new path for reform, and showcase America's commitment to urban improvement: "Upon completion of the studies and plans ACTION proposes that they be incorporated in an imaginative and dramatic presentation of a 'New Image for the American City.' This presentation would incorporate the most advanced and useful techniques for making real to the American people what American cities might be like." As in all of his projects, Rouse proposed that the project be multimedia, saying that "moving models, dioramas, pictures, charts, etc. would be put together in a mobile show of the 'new image' which would tour the town squares and public

places of America."[51] It also might show that America's urban management capabilities could match any in the world.

Rouse pitched the New Image to Ford Motor Company, asserting that
the popularity of automobiles could be paired with concern for the city as
a whole. Rouse noted that "This point is illustrated in the plan of Fort
Worth, Texas," developed by Victor Gruen (in 1956). While "the purpose
of the plan was to make downtown Fort Worth function efficiently and
well for people," such planning would result in an "almost ideal environment for the automobile."[52] Ford officials, although initially interested,
eventually backed out of supporting this idealistic scheme. General
Motors and Ford, however, both mounted glamorous futuristic urban
visions at the New York fair. Their displays substituted an emphasis on
auto consumption and futuristic designs for comprehensive planning of
actual cities. America was not quite ready for Rouse's utopian vision.

A Model Metropolis

ACTION may have faltered but Rouse sallied forth. Not only did he
launch the Columbia new town project during the 1960s, but he also led
one of the most sweeping urban renewal planning efforts ever undertak-
en. Rouse's utopian urban pitch reached its zenith in dowdy Hartford,
Connecticut, during the late 1960s and early 1970s. Jack Rosenthal, writing in the *New York Times* in 1972, called Rouse's massive effort there "the
largest, most visionary effort ever undertaken to renew and develop an
entire metropolitan area in America."[53] Rosenthal was not alone in discovering Rouse's ambitions at Hartford. Allan Talbot in *City* held up the
effort as one worthy of display for foreign visitors seeking the best in
American urban planning: "When the next planeload of foreign planners
arrives to see what's happening on America's urban front, the State
Department and HUD may well send them to Hartford."[54] Rouse proved
again that he had the ability to generate national interest in his private
sector solutions to America's urban malaise.

Even though Hartford was home to the headquarters of many wealthy
insurance corporations, the city suffered from a worsening divide between
central city and booming suburbs. In 1969 Daniel Moynihan, then
Presidential Urban Advisor, asked why after so much urban renewal
activity, as represented at Constitution Plaza (which he described as
"hideously separated from the life-giving river by a mindless submission to
the highway engineers") and other downtown redevelopment, Hartford
was still so distressed: "How could this city come to the point where riot
and disruption by minority youth should have become almost a constant

condition?"[55] Embarrassment about these kinds of comments spurred action by local business elites and would, at least for a few years, quickly shift Hartford from its position as one of America's worst-case scenarios to a leading planning model to the federal government. Arthur Lumsden, president of the Hartford Chamber of Commerce, acknowledged that times had changed from the days "when six or 12 men could decide on a major project for a city—like Pittsburgh's Gateway Center—and carry it through." Planning had to develop in partnership with the diverse constituents of the city due to "the revolt of minority people and the general agitation for involvement on the part of people little accustomed to being consulted."[56] Citizen participation, however, remained marginal in this mammoth undertaking by business interests.

Planners employed as part of a Rouse subsidiary, the American City Corporation, created the Greater Hartford Process, Inc. (initiated in 1969), an ambitious planning process and an eventual series of proposals for the entire region. Rouse and his planners did not decide randomly to focus their attention on Hartford, but were called in by "27 Hartford area businesses who have put up more than $3 million for the planning." This group of leading businessmen was known as the Greater Hartford Corporation and operated like the GBC in Baltimore.[57] As in Baltimore, success in downtown redevelopment emboldened progressive business leaders to look beyond business districts: "The completion of Constitution Plaza in the mid-1960s encouraged Hartford's business establishment to think more about how they could build upon the successful, albeit limited downtown project to do more for their home city and its surrounding suburbs."[58] According to the *Hartford Courant*, the businessmen viewed the problems of the region largely in management terms: "These businessmen were searching for some efficient way to pull together all the programs and money in the region to halt the disorderly sprawl of a growing metropolis."[59] Local press welcomed this growing public spiritedness in part because corporate wealth indicated a kind of talent that could benefit the region beyond the bottom line: "And since on all sides the prosperity of the business community here may be monumentally seen in quite a literal sense, the value of such acumen and energy is more than obvious."[60] The president of Connecticut General Life Insurance, Henry Roberts, endorsed the project, and his company had provided the primary funding source for Rouse's idealistic Columbia project. He and other leading businessmen chose Rouse because they knew he would not be afraid to propose what might seem to others like outlandish ideas.

Rouse, indeed, was not out merely to rebuild Hartford, but aimed to create a model of the utopian abilities of the private sector: "We have to believe that with the affluence and management capability that exist in this society, it is possible to produce a working urban environment."[61] Drawing on the abilities of on-site administrators and some of the same planners from the Columbia project, he provided less direct leadership in this particular project. His distance from the leadership makes it difficult at points to know which particular aspects of this comprehensive planning effort he endorsed. However, the planning documents produced fit so closely with almost all of Rouse's view of urban affairs that they can be considered part of his corpus. To begin with, this was no little plan. Large swaths of the central city were projected for redevelopment in tandem with a 20,000-person, multirace and mixed-income new town in a suburban region closely based on the Columbia model (see chapter 6). The center city redevelopment, an ambitious $780 million project, aimed to transform "40% of its population, and 75% of its commercial and office base." Planners sought to reshape existing neighborhoods through rehabilitation, planning, and clearance into new neighborhoods grouped around schools, community centers, and shopping (also on the neighborhood unit and Columbia model). The process of redevelopment, designed to last twenty years, included "rejuvenation of half the city of Hartford itself, including its downtown and some of its worst sections."[62] In terms of scale and ambition, Hartford Process matched Rouse's private sector ideals. A well-designed, socially just city would entirely replace the existing Hartford.

The Process reports, like Rouse's many projects, proposed massive changes in American society without fundamental shifts in social or political systems. Leading planner Leo Molinaro, in an early presentation, for instance, sounded like a socialist when he proposed some final goals of the project: "Social service will be available on the same basis as other public utilities and every family will have access to these services just as they now have to public utilities . . . every family will have the opportunity to earn enough income to meet their basic needs," and every adult "will be given the opportunity to perform in a community capacity appropriate to his talents and desires."[63] These goals would be achieved in Hartford, and any American city imitating the Hartford example, with a minimum of state and maximum of business direction. Nowhere in the documents is there a call for profound political or social reform to match these ambitious planning goals.

With the exception of creating a progressive state income tax to equalize funding across school districts, and limited federal money to create model programs, most of the money for these ambitious plans would come through a mixture of private investment, systematic organizational changes, and leveraging money from future local tax revenues that would accrue from effective center city redevelopment and new town construction—rather than state largess. One of the early planning documents indicates this faith in cost savings through management expertise: "That present resources are available in America, and in Hartford specifically, sufficient to allow the development of a much higher quality [of services] than presently exists . . . Resources range from knowledge of urban processes to financial capabilities, from management organizations to . . . communication techniques."[64] The planners had to steer clear of more extreme calls for funding, but their faith in future savings and earnings was hard to square with such mammoth changes.

Nevertheless, social change demanded ambitious programs for the city as a whole, including regional vocational training and job banks, education reform and an open university, integrated health systems and region-wide HMO, early childhood care, enhanced community development corporations, a recreation system organized on the community association model for the city as a whole, and unified systems for mostly nonprofit social welfare services administered through a system of neighborhood Community Life Associations. The planners took a "systems approach" to urban problems that they thought would integrate existing and new services in a more effective manner. Management skill would be able to create these new structures without significantly expanding a social welfare system.

The skeptical voices during the Hartford Process made their opinions known. Local citizens feared that the needs of the poor and minorities would not be taken into account, because much of the planning was developed in private. Although the planning team worked admirably with some local groups, transparent methods of citizen participation never crystallized. Christopher Feise and Peter Friedland, local activists, were unimpressed with participation by average citizens: "with a board stacked with establishment and corporate representatives, and the [public] forum not in existence, the clearest and most obvious power and constituency resides in the business community of Hartford." In addition, as a private organization, "Process and Devco [the new town development company] meetings are secret, the minutes are secret, the files of Process are not open to the general public," and local press sources took a less than critical approach to the project. These activists viewed Process as the leading edge of regressive national policy: "The commitment to citizen participation was and is being eroded by the Nixon administration in favor of strengthening the local unit of government. With the introduction of revenue sharing and fund cuts in the federal housing, poverty and model cities programs, Nixon places the responsibility for the poor and slum/ghetto back in the hands of local politicians and private corporations neither of which freed the slaves, gave blacks civil rights [etc.]." They documented numerous instances where Process planners kept activists and citizens (particularly minorities) at the margins of decisions, even bucking advice from The Rouse Company home office and former secretary of HUD, Robert Weaver, to expand citizen participation. Skepticism in the region, in part fueled by lack of access to the planning, grew and spawned conspiracy theories about Process's actual as opposed to stated goals.[65]

From a distance of many decades it does appear that the Process was, in large measure, predetermined to choose Rouse's preferred outcomes. Were neighborhood units and a new town really best suited to the needs of Hartford, or were they just the ways of looking at the world that the planners found most comfortable? Was clearing much of downtown and surrounding neighborhoods really the best way to rebuild Hartford? By creating high expectations for citizen participation, yet settling on familiar planning concepts, Process planners undermined rather than catalyzed public support.

Experts looking in from outside had doubts similar to those of the activists. A perceptive critic in *City* magazine noted the lack of a "new public mechanism" to carry out these ambitious plans, a shortsighted strategy designed to build local political support by not challenging existing politicians. He also was skeptical that the project without Rouse in situ could succeed in any measure. The project needed "a full time promoter . . . The problem with the Process report is that it has the Rouse touch, but it lacks his presence."[66] Another *City* article posed tougher questions: "Is the business consortium attempting tasks that belong in the public sector? Are the people of Hartford, particularly the poor and minorities, being offered elitist gifts and visions instead of fundamental change in public institutions and power arrangements?"[67] In 1972 the *Wall Street Journal* reported that although teams from other cities had come to see the Process in action, "What they have seen is so utopian in scope that, given the disappointing results of past urban-renewal attempts, the hoped-for results must be viewed with skepticism."[68]

All the attention notwithstanding, the visionary plans failed to garner sufficient community support. Among many reasons, aside from the utopian quality of the planning, both suburbanites and inner-city leaders remained skeptical about the goals and tactics of the planners (suburban whites feared black exodus to the planned new town, and black leaders feared massive urban clearance), and established politicians panicked over the potential loss in power to a new regional government that might grow out of Process. Rouse acknowledged the failure years later. In 1975 he wrote in a personal correspondence that Hartford Process "was acted upon favorably by the business community and set in operation. It has failed to receive the support in city government which it needs, and the economic recession knocked out the new town development after the land had been acquired. Thus, its hopes have not been fulfilled. However, I remain persuaded that the image is sound and that the strategy for achieving it is attainable."[69] Ever the optimist, Rouse always felt that execution rather than concept marred his failures.

Although achieving few of its goals, the Hartford Process, like the Baltimore Plan, complemented antistatist national policy. The *Hartford Courant* noted that in the late 1960s, when the concept was hatched, "Washington was pleading for the participation of private enterprise on the urban front."[70] Nixon wanted to shed even the small urban programs created during the Great Society. The president of the Greater Hartford Corporation, which sponsored Hartford Process, explained, "In one sense the program is a response to the new (Nixon) administration 'which has urged private enterprise to invest in regional development.'"[71] In 1970 attention from the Hartford Process reached the White House, and "In May Rouse and the top executives at ACC [American City Corporation] were invited to the White House to discuss their efforts with President Nixon's Urban Affairs Council. The President was originally scheduled to spend 15 minutes with the group; he lingered for an hour and in Rouse's description asked tough and penetrating questions."[72]

George Romney, Nixon's secretary of Housing and Urban Development, also announced in 1970 "that the comprehensive study financed by Hartford's business community may become the model for future metropolitan planning throughout the country."[73] In 1971 Romney still portrayed the Hartford Process as an ideal solution to stretching increasingly stingy federal dollars. An article in the *Wall Street Journal* summarized Romney's goals in its headline: "Romney Readies a Secret, Supposedly Cheap Plan to Attack Social Ills—and Help Nixon Win Votes." Through private sector regional planning, Romney aimed to show that "a better living environment can be provided on a less costly basis" in contrast to the Democratic "emphasis on pouring large amounts and varieties of federal aid into relatively small urban neighborhoods" ("large amounts" only in the American context, of course). A few cities with the best comprehensive regional plans would be selected by Romney for priority funds; metropolitan-scale planning as at Hartford promised savings through regional cooperation and private sector multiplier effects. This plan, highly controversial even when announced, never emerged full-blown from the administration. In the meantime, Rouse's utopian stances had proved valuable in lending legitimacy to antistatist political goals. As Romney made clear, his program responded to his sense that the federal government had so far "failed to tap fully the energies of private industry" in urban policy.[74]

A Contented Reformer

James Rouse may never have achieved his utopian goals for urban rede-velopment, but to the end of his days he believed that redevelopment on the whole had successfully reawakened the city center. This opinion stands in contrast to the successful critique mounted by Jane Jacobs, Lewis Mumford, 1960s radicals, civil rights activists, and many liberals: "In one city after another individuals less articulate than Jacobs but just as out-raged were expressing complaints and raising questions about the justice and economic feasibility of urban renewal."[75] Urbanist Roy Lubove, for instance, in 1969 called Pittsburgh's Golden Triangle a "keystone of the reverse welfare state" that "epitomized the managerial approach to the urban environment and culture." Under the leadership of the Allegheny Conference, "[t]he CBD has been transformed into an enormous filing cabinet. . . . The expressionless stainless-steel facades . . . tower over grass and walks; no shops, no entertainment, no restaurants of note, no nightlife."[76] Even today, in many circles urban renewal still conjures up nothing but bulldozers and ugly office towers.

Rouse could not have disagreed more with the negative assessments of urban renewal. In a speech from the 1970s he celebrated "a new life at the center of America's old cities" resulting from "the cumulative impact of what we have been about for 20 years." Rouse was quite right that the American city by the 1970s, particularly in central business districts, was a far more impressive reflection of the ability of capitalism to create attractive environments than the city he knew from the 1940s and 1950s. The American downtown welcomed automobiles: "[I]t's easier to get to the center of most American cities today than it was 20, 25 years ago . . . It's easier to park once you get there than it was 20 to 25 years ago." This was no small matter in downtown survival and had been a hard-fought battle that most thought cities would lose. Near the parking was an impressive amount of "construction of office buildings. We've seen them kind of one by one surprise . . . at the beginning of this, 20, 25 years ago, believing that the office market was going to be oversupplied, and it has been oversupplied. But that oversupply gets taken up and then we start again." This cycle had brought "a lot of new office buildings, a lot of new jobs, a strong work force at the heart of the city, many new institutions from art museums to stadiums, theaters." Rouse celebrated not only the postindustrial office complexes, but also the new "public squares, public places. Center cities on the whole are more rational, more beautiful, more livable than they were 20 years ago in America." As proof of the success,

Figure 9. The extra-governmental ambitions of business interests are captured well in this newspaper cartoon. Business interests, although working with city officials, led the line of attack in redeveloping most American downtowns. Rouse Papers, Columbia Archive.

he noted that by the 1970s the "most hopeful and long-awaited movement of all has been the clear pressure, and it is now a pressure, of middle–and upper-income people moving back in the center of the city."[77] Gentrification reflected the multiplying benefits of center city rebuilding.

Baltimore's Cinderella story featured prominently in many of Rouse's speeches. He bragged that "in the last 20 years in Baltimore, a city that nobody ever thought anything of, has had probably the most remarkable regeneration of economic vitality and spirit of any city in the country, with 18 new office buildings, with 15 million square feet of space, [and] nine new national corporations moving in." He rejoiced about the fact that "ten thousand dwelling units are built or rehabilitated or restored within ten minutes of the center city." The credit for this transformation went primarily to business leaders like himself: "The energy emerged from the significance of the plans and the cooperation between the business community and the city government and an organization set up to carry out those plans." Federal and local cash for land purchases, new highways and federal buildings may have made redevelopment possible in the long term, but that money faithfully served local business interests and their goals.[77] Baltimore's renaissance was not singular. Boston, New York, Chicago, and many other cities transformed their downtowns for a reenergized modern capitalism on a postindustrial model. New highways, middle-class housing, public plazas, fountains, and gleaming skyscrapers made a powerful statement about the transformative power of capital on the urban scene. Idealism and massive reconstruction along planned lines was not the sole property of socialists; in fact, businessmen had proven their abilities in urban artistry. Rouse and other businessmen were never content with reshaping the central business districts, however, and as indicated by Hartford Process, made a number of successful bids to direct wider urban policy in America.

CHAPTER 3

A Businessman's Search for Slumless Cities

If we desire to show our foreign visitors the results of our American civilization, chances are good that we would not be particularly interested in showing them the heart of our cities. This has brought an enormous demand for us to do something about our cities. To improve them, and their appearance. There is a gigantic task ahead in the next few years and we, the builders, will certainly be in it up to our necks.

James Rouse

The poor live in the worst fear in the United States. There's no equivalent condition to this in any other nation in Western civilization or in any nation that we would call a part of the free world . . . Think what a judgment this is on our civilization that this is true.

James Rouse

To Rouse and others financing and building them, new suburbs and glittering downtowns represented the ideal standard in American living, but they were not sufficient demonstrations of the ability of private enterprise to create an ideal society. Massive slums, sandwiched between up-to-the-minute central business districts and outward-spreading middle-class suburbs, inexplicably grew even as the United States became the richest nation in the world.

Rouse needed to look no further than his adopted hometown of Baltimore for displeasing slums. Many Baltimore neighborhoods were in a dire situation by the 1930s, a situation that grew far worse during and after the war. Cut off from much of the federally insured mortgage money of the 1940s and 1950s, housing for recent African American migrants from the South in the city's older neighborhoods reflected the worst nineteenth-century housing conditions. Families were squeezed into tiny rooms, many older houses lacked indoor plumbing, and outdoor privies and garbage filled back alleys. Other cities shared these shameful conditions; Baltimore was by no means alone. *Time* reported in February 1955 that "despite the biggest construction boom in U.S. history, the nation has notably failed to clear its slums, instead of growing smaller, slums are getting bigger and worse than ever."[1]

In a nation priding itself on a universally high standard of living, such squalor undermined the American consumerist model, because the "*Pax Americana,* though ultimately based on the most powerful military machine in human history, was really founded on the image of an American lifestyle endlessly adapted to national and regional particularities which all could obtain."[2] Any wrinkle in this vision inevitably raised doubts about the universal attainability of the consumer paradise. If the United States could not even uniformly achieve these standards, what were the chances that other, particularly less affluent, nations would? Domestically, business talent had to address slum conditions or likely faced draconian and expensive state solutions to the urban crisis.

Through a series of political and public relations efforts, housing of the urban poor in the United States was essentially left to private interests, landlords, and nonprofits. A mixture of approaches, combining political and social action with cultural creativity, convinced the American public that the private sector had the interest and ability to take on the challenge of righting slum conditions. Over a forty-year period, Rouse could be found intimately involved, and sometimes leading, these private sector initiatives.

The Baltimore situation shaped Rouse's sense of crisis and propelled him early into national housing policy debates. The notion of "blight" (a shorthand term for the spread of poverty and decline of housing conditions in urban neighborhoods) had been discussed in Baltimore since the 1930s in reference to changing older neighborhoods, but in the postwar period "blight" took on even more resonance as white flight was abetted by racist housing policies.[3] In 1950 the *Baltimore Sun* spoke openly of the manner in which Baltimore neighborhoods had changed: "The 303,000 persons that the United States Census Bureau's pilot survey showed live in Baltimore's blighted areas are almost evenly divided between Negroes and whites. But the most recent estimate indicates that Negroes make up a bit less than one third of the city's population. When these two facts are put together mathematically, the answer is that three fourths of Baltimore Negroes live in either a blighted or slum section of the city."[4] The city's black population was disproportionately represented in the poorest areas, and the situation was not improving as blacks streamed northward from the rural south. In this Baltimore shared a great deal with most American cities at the time. Rouse became active in fighting "blight" at a number of levels.

His first foray into neighborhood redevelopment was not auspicious and illustrated Rouse's early insensitivity to neighborhood needs and the issues of race. Early in his career he often boasted of these Baltimore projects he

financed (ca. 1951)—one in the neighborhood of Waverly and another near
Johns Hopkins Medical campus the same year—but as he became more sensitive to growing criticism of urban renewal, they dropped as models from
his speeches. In 1961, for instance, he boasted, "the first complete redevelopment project in the United States was represented by our Waverly
project. This was an old residential area, much deteriorated. The worst was
cleared to make room for 300 apartment units and a small, but successful,
shopping center. The results in Waverly prove that you can go into a slum
area, clean it out and do a decent job of redevelopment." Rouse also bragged
of another project near Johns Hopkins University that "included apartments
for Residents of the hospital, a shopping center and office buildings. This
project will do a great deal for Johns Hopkins and the city."[5]

Both projects, according to historian Arnold Hirsch, did little for poor,
minority inhabitants: "The Waverly plans called for the displacement of
nearly 200 families, more than half of them African American. All of the
291 new homes to be built in the area, however, were reserved for whites."
The same was true near Johns Hopkins: "In this instance, African
Americans represented about 90 percent of those displaced, while 85 percent of the new dwellings were set aside for whites." Rouse and others came
under fire from the Baltimore Urban League, which saw the plan as a successful attempt to confine blacks to the core and segregate formerly integrated areas. "Baltimore's experience early in the redevelopment
program," Hirsch laments, "both served as a model and set a precedent in
the adaptation of national legislation to a southern idiom."[6] Thus, one must
include Rouse in the creation of this unfortunate pattern; but his involvement in these projects was not Rouse's final or even most important role
in reshaping ideas about American urban neighborhoods. By the late 1950s
Rouse would move on to become a leading figure in the attempt to stop
blockbusting and racial change in Baltimore neighborhoods.[7]

Carving New Neighborhoods out of Old Cities:
The Philosophy

A native of the small town of Easton, Maryland, James Rouse preserved
throughout his life an abiding nostalgia for small-town living. This small-
town wistfulness became most evident at Columbia, Maryland, during the
1960s when he made such statements as "I hold some very unscientific conclusions to the effect that people grow best in small communities where
institutions . . . are within reach of their responsibility," or "a broader range
of friendships and relationships occurs in a village or small town than in
a city," and even that in small towns "self-reliance is promoted."[8] Small towns

and small communities also created the social structures that reduced the need for a larger government presence by creating forms of informal support and control. This preference for small communities, although most commonly associated with Columbia, manifested itself much earlier in Rouse's urban work.

During the 1950s Rouse merged existing planning concepts such as the "neighborhood unit" with admiration for small communities. In 1945 *The Nation* summarized the neighborhood unit concept (developed by planner Clarence Perry) for an elite general audience: "there is fairly general agreement on what the pattern of well-planned communities should be. Their nuclei should be neighborhoods comprising perhaps a thousand families. Arranged around a civic center, school, recreation area, and local shopping district, they should be self-contained units, separated from and connected with other areas by parks and parkways."[9] Rouse believed that the city should be reshaped into a series of such small neighborhoods within the metropolis; this vision of creating ordered and organized neighborhoods guided his activities in urban affairs throughout his career and is worth considering before embarking on a more detailed description of his actual activities in the 1950s.

In speeches during the 1950s around the country Rouse sketched positive portraits of a Baltimore neighborhood, Hampden, he knew from his own experience. A white, working-class neighborhood, and once a leading mill town of the Industrial Revolution, Hampden had been strategically sited along the rocky Jones Falls River. Rouse admired Hampden because, even after the departure of many of the mills in the 1920s and 1930s, its boundaries—including the river, railroad lines, parks, and exclusive Roland Park (and later a massive highway project along the river)—allowed it to develop small-town virtues: "Hampden is in fact a neighborhood. It requires no label on a map. It has its own churches, its own shopping street, its own community life . . . Hampden has a conscience, a spirit, a soul as a neighborhood." These boundaries also allowed the community to avoid the worst aspects of urban decline: "Had it not been protected by natural topographic boundaries, Hampden, as the oldest and lowest income area in its part of the City, would surely have been infected by the soullessness and hopelessness which spreads through the inner-City."[10] Rouse failed to mention in any speech that the boundaries of Hampden also allowed its white residents to defend the neighborhood against black incursion. Blacks who dared to move into Hampden were met with harassment. With clear boundaries, racial turf could also be tightly managed in a manner impossible in the average city neighborhood.

With the right design, neighborhoods that naturally lacked such natural boundaries could gain them through modern community planning, of which Rouse was an advocate. Using new master plans that included modern zoning and building codes, slum houses would be removed, "incompatible uses" such as stables or small workshops eliminated, liquor stores squelched, and new elementary schools and parks inserted to develop community cohesion. Rouse endorsed all of these activities in his urban activities. Speaking of renewal of slums in 1957 to the National Retail Dry Goods Association, Rouse painted an appealing picture of neighborhood planning: "This can be no limited paint-up, fix-up program, nor need it be a wholesale bulldozer operation. Through careful planning, healthy neighborhoods can be created out of these sprawling areas. Highways must be routed around, rather than through them. Worn-out buildings and obsolete uses must be removed through spot-surgery use of the condemnation power. Sound or salvageable buildings must be saved. Many streets must be closed; densities reduced, parks and playgrounds introduced." Neighborhood redesign at its best targeted higher income groups leaving for the suburbs: "These huge areas can be made attractive to middle-income families and to upper-income families, particularly to our aging population which will find the central city convenience especially appealing."[11] Rouse, in fact, while head of the Urban Renewal Subcommittee of the GBC during the mid-1950s, played an important role in the designation of the elegant but decaying Mt. Royal/Bolton Hill area north of downtown as an urban renewal area. Through a mixture of city demolition, citizen activism, and private sector redevelopment, the district was enhanced as an upscale, in-town residential neighborhood during the 1950s and 1960s. Public housing most notably did not find its way into Rouse's urban prescriptions, although it had been frequently associated with neighborhood planning up until this period.

Like many at the time, Rouse promoted massive highway programs as part of neighborhood planning. Not only did highways help renew downtown commercial districts and open new land for suburban development, but highways also could be adjuncts to neighborhood planning. Although his goals were different, he shared a similarly positive vision of highways with Robert Moses, the notorious mastermind of New York's reconstruction, who in a 1945 article in the *Atlantic Monthly* argued that highways offered many benefits to urban areas: "an arterial improvement, whether it be a parkway for restricted travel or an express route open to mixed traffic, is not simply a strip of pavement in a gasoline gully, but a genuine shoestring or ribbon improvement of the entire area through which it passes."[12]

Rouse took a slightly different approach to the potential benefits of highways as part of large-scale planning. Again borrowing liberally from the "neighborhood unit" ideas of Clarence Perry, he advocated the creation of new neighborhoods carved, partly using highway programs, out of old sprawling urban districts. In 1957, for instance, he argued, "We must make the city consist of communities which are in human scale . . . neighborhoods which are given shape and definition by natural boundaries, such as parks, playgrounds, schools, hospitals, public buildings of all kinds and, *most important of all, by our highways*"(italics mine). Not all highways, of course, accomplished proper community building: "A huge unplanned highway program will rip through and around the cities with little attention to neighborhood destruction or neighborhood creation." That bad highway programs existed, however, did not mean that all highways were bad: "But, a highway program that recognizes its enormous potential in partnership with urban renewal will relate every highway plan to its neighborhood impact." Highways could reduce internal traffic by rerouting traffic around areas, and "the highway is important in that its width and function automatically create[s] an effective boundary defining and protecting a neighborhood."[13] In an era when cross-town traffic remained a major problem, these concepts likely seemed less destructive than they do now.

That these concepts of neighborhood design have become passé should not lead us to think that Rouse and others did not genuinely believe these statements about the potential role of highways in urban areas. Rouse repeated his comments on highways numerous times at meetings around the country and continued to discuss them into the 1960s, when he finally was too embarrassed to talk about his advocacy of such destructive practices as creative tools. The Greater Baltimore Committee, of which he was a leading member, initiated and helped create a highway plan for Baltimore City during the 1950s that benefited downtown but played havoc on a number of surrounding neighborhoods (and was finally stalled by neighborhood activists). Rouse may have had nobler intentions for highways, but the distinction between positive and negative highway programs was most often lost in the neighborhoods facing demolition.[14]

The Baltimore Plan vs. Public Housing

Rouse focused on neighborhood renewal not only through promotion of his own redevelopment projects and advocacy of highway programs, but also through his leading role in a nationally known model of neighborhood conservation and enhancement: the Baltimore Plan. Rouse was only one of the individuals associated with the program, and not its originator, but by the 1950s he had become one of the most visible individuals associated with it. As a businessman he lent legitimacy to some rather idealistic and dreamy plans. His involvement with the project in time also propelled him to the leading edge of national government policy.

The 1930s were important years in Baltimore for discovering the failings of private enterprise. During these difficult times, Frances Morton, "a pretty young Smith College graduate spent a year prowling Wards 5 and 10 in Baltimore's worst slums." From a prominent Baltimore family, she listed privies, rats, and other slum problems and authored a master's thesis at the New York School of Social Work detailing these conditions and potential solutions. Clark Hobbs, the associate editor of the *Baltimore Sun*, took up the fight as his own in the leading city newspaper: "His humorous and sarcastic articles, framing shocking photographs of blighted areas, stung his readers."[15]

City officials felt pressured to respond in some manner, and "the Health Commissioner ordered demolition of a block of some of the worst housing." Although hardly a convincing start to slum improvement, on the heels of this demolition came legislation from the Baltimore City Council that created a "Hygiene of Housing" ordinance, "one of the nation's first attempts at a housing code." In addition, the Citizen's Housing and Planning Association (CPHA), a group of concerned citizens including Morton, Hans Froelicher, and later Rouse, formed as an adjunct to official efforts at city hall. During the 1940s the Baltimore City Department of Health, with the aid of the CPHA, undertook a number of small attention-getting "pilot" renovation programs in selected blocks around Baltimore, with "mixed results." More impressive was the creation of a separate Housing Court in 1947, led by a crusading judge who made a point of forcing landlords and others to comply with health and safety codes. The overall program gained momentum in the early 1950s with the creation of what became known as the Pilot Program—a larger-scale neighborhood-focused improvement project in East Baltimore. During this period Rouse took on a more prominent role.[16]

This Pilot Program grew out of a number of institutional changes both outside and inside city government. In 1950 a citizens' committee, with Rouse as a member, recommended "application of community education and other social service techniques" as part of the process of enforcement. In 1951 this citizens' committee became the Mayor's Advisory Council on Housing Law Enforcement, with Rouse at its head. A housing bureau, led by a crusading reformer, Yates Cook, was also created in 1951 within the health department to lead the cleanup charge and coordinate with the citizens' council and other redevelopment officials. Also in 1951, the housing bureau designated a twenty-seven-block "blighted section of East Baltimore" as the Pilot Program. "Within this Pilot area, the hygiene of housing, building, fire prevention, and zoning codes were systematically applied on a house-to-house basis by an inspection team from each of the various city agencies concerned. Neighborhood organizations and community

Figure 10. The Baltimore Plan as represented in Miles Colean's *Renewing Our Cities*. The plan, a series of code enforcement and neighborhood improvement projects, of which Rouse was a leading promoter, became famous across America and played a role in the battles over public housing. From Miles Colean, *Renewing Our Cities*.

education programs were employed to acquaint homeowners and tenants with the goals of the program and enlist voluntary support and compliance." Officials issued over 1,500 notices with over 16,000 violations to owners of housing—homeowners and slum landlords. At the end of two years, in 1953, approximately 90 percent of the violations had been addressed.[17] Fight Blight, a fund to help poor homeowners meet new standards, was established in 1951 by Guy Hollyday (a former president of the Mortgage Banker's Association and also a member of the Mayor's Advisory Council) and Rouse collected an initial ten thousand dollars from donors. The fund lent money but also steered poor people to reliable lenders and good contractors. By 1956 about four hundred cases a year were being addressed by the fund.[18]

The combined results seemed quite promising, and the photogenic aspects of the project catapulted it to national prominence beginning in the late 1940s. As early as 1949, Baltimore received flattering press in national magazines for its relatively modest results. Local *Baltimore Sun* reporters Edgar Jones and Burke Davis wrote a long article that appeared in the *Atlantic Monthly:* "Baltimore, alone among large American cities, has a plan already in operation to save itself from engulfment by slum blight . . . What is now known as Block Number One in the city's clean-up drive used to be a run-down collection of 63 small houses surrounding a courtyard cut up by rickety wooden fences, sagging outhouses, and piles of debris." With a wave of a wand, the writers described the same scene after its transformation: "Today that block of houses surrounds a paved and sunny courtyard in which children play on swings and seesaws. All the wooden fences and outside toilets have been removed. Every dwelling unit, now one room larger on the average, has an inside toilet, and there are no windowless rooms. Rat infestation has been entirely wiped out." What was perhaps more stunning was "the cost to the city was only the cost of an inspection staff and court action." Such rapid progress brought in visitors from out of town; "Block Number One is Baltimore's showpiece, and has impressed officials from scores of cities in need of a cheap approach to their slum problems. . . . Inquiries about its operation have come from almost every state and from points as far removed as Hawaii, Brazil, and Australia." These writers, however, saw some of the potential dangers inherent in this inexpensive type of program, particularly as the plan was adopted by more conservative forces: "Many of these inquiries, however, represent wishful thinking that can be traced directly to the widespread, misleading publicity given the Baltimore Plan by the National Association of Home Builders. Through magazine articles and a $20,000 film strip, the Home Builders have represented the plan as yielding 'immense dividends in health and property values,' 'gradually ridding this great metropolitan center of its slum areas,' 'providing much-needed minimum housing,' and 'markedly reducing the rate of juvenile delinquency.'" Why would the Home Builders be so fascinated with a cleanup program? They had their reasons: "The interest of the Home Builders in the Baltimore Plan is easy enough to explain. As part of the powerful real estate lobby, the Home Builders are exploiting before-and-after pictures of Block Number One as evidence that slum conditions can be eliminated through private enterprise without public housing and slum-clearance programs."[19] During congressional debates in 1949 concerning public housing, the Baltimore Plan was cited by Republican Congressman Joseph W. Martin (Massachusetts) as preferable to public housing: "Cities should be required through ordinances similar to those in Baltimore to take the initial step in slum clearance. It is remarkable how much can be done. Old, unsightly buildings can be repaired, renovated and remodeled."[20] Chicago and St. Louis also developed similar programs during the time, but Baltimore's remained the most famous.

As the program increased in scale, so did the press attention. The *Saturday Evening Post* in 1953 ran a long and laudatory article on Block One and the Pilot Program. An adventurous journalist went on a tour of some of the worst areas: "I went walking with Cook through some of his 'rock-bottom' slums for as long as I could stand it. He led me through so-called 'squeeze-gut' alleys—three feet wide—that were deep with excrement, muck and garbage. Hordes of persistent flies settled on us. I beat the air with a handkerchief in a not very successful effort to keep them off my face." According to this intrepid character, "Everywhere in the unimproved areas were ramshackle, rotting board fences behind which the slum dwellers piled their incredible debris; it was as if the people themselves were hiding behind these rotten screens . . . By the time Cook and I had picked our way through the litter to peer at a filthy, choked-up outdoor toilet that served two families of eight adults and ten children, I had had enough for one session." Cook informed his guest, "[T]hese are the neighborhoods where the maids, cooks and nurses for some of Baltimore's 'best families' live." The renovated areas, on the other hand, radiated a nearly utopian quality: "The Negro families around Block One are proudly tending little gardens, and thinking up home-made ways—such as whitewashing old tires as borders for flower beds—to beautify their neighborhood." James Rouse reported that "Five hundred people lived there, and 500 rats were killed as the clean-up progressed." The reporter detailed the transformations, many of which came from private sector efforts: "Today, a concrete-paved recreational area, equipped with playground equipment which was paid for by the Kiwanis Club, stands on the site of old rubble heaps in the former rat heaven. The property was donated by the landlords." Landlords seemed particularly chastened by the process, according to the author. A notorious slumlord admitted, "When the Baltimore Plan descended on me, it was a bitter pill to swallow, for it was going to cost me five hundred dollars apiece to fix up my places." After being shocked by conditions, however, he began renovating places and "It's been the best thing that ever happened to me." Rouse, ever the optimist, enthused that "we won't stop until Baltimore's slums are entirely cleaned up."[21] This was not to be the case, as we shall see.

The year 1953 represented a high point for Baltimore in the national media.[22] A nationally distributed film by *Encyclopedia Britannica*, "The Baltimore Plan," dramatized the effort on the silver screen. The film opens with a male narrator seriously intoning, "Like all large American cities, Baltimore, Maryland has extensive blighted areas—residential, commercial, and industrial 'slums' . . . And, like other cities, it has a program of urban redevelopment and housing, both public and private. But, integrated with these—is a program which has come to be known as . . .THE BALTIMORE PLAN." Although male narration sets the tone, the film uses the perspective of a white social worker to tell the story (standing in for Ms. Morton). Neatly dressed, wandering the back alleys of Baltimore's black neighborhoods, the social worker describes "gas-lighted streets, spotless front steps, colorful screen paintings—these, you say, are Baltimore. True. But Baltimore—like most American cities—is also block after block of incredibly bad housing." As she exposes this world to her viewers, she explains, "It *is* another world, I suppose, to most people—an urban jungle. But though it may seem a jungle in its ugliness and disorder, its real life is in the people who live here— *the only place they have to live*—people with the same kindliness and neighborliness as elsewhere." Viewers of the film are later treated to a panoramic view of Baltimore, and the narrator warned, "Here is the shame of our American cities . . . here is the face of our cities we hide . . . endless blocks of houses scarred beyond belief, overcrowded firetraps, tenements, shacks, human dwellings unfit for human beings to live in."[23] The notion that America had to be held to a certain standard drives the film's narration. A shocking slide show delivered by a well-dressed narrator (playing the role of a CPHA representative) exposes cigar-smoking businessmen to "rat-bite cases" and filthy backyards satirically termed "Baltimore Playgrounds." In another scene, preppy young white men see for themselves the sorry state of Baltimore slums.

The long and sometimes frustrating story of the development of the Baltimore Plan is recounted in a theatrical form by *Encyclopedia Britannica* filmmakers, with recalcitrant landlords, crusading judges, local community activists, and teams of city officials (black and white) attacking blight. A "Blitz Block" provides an opportunity for stirring music as the filth is removed: "The walls came a tumbling down." The most serious scenes take place in the Housing Court, where landlords are forced to confront their sins. One, a Mr. Gary, claims, "I stand on my rights as an American citizen" when confronted with demands to clean up his property. The judge replies, "I find nothing in the Constitution of the United States which says a landlord can keep his property in a disgraceful condition." Instead of simply fining the landlord, however, Mr. Gary is told that he may use his fine to clean up his property. Later scenes show the same landlord diligently cleaning up his property in a most impressive manner: directing workers, pulling off his sport coat, and ripping rotted wood from back alleys. According to the social worker, "Mr. Gary is a changed man." The film ends on a particularly ebullient note with before and after scenes set to dramatic music: "Blighted back yards [before] . . . had become flower gardens [after]." Children rush joyously forward into a new, clean play area and the narrator swings into the final, grandiose claims: "This, then, is the

Figure 11. Scenes from "The Baltimore Plan" film created by *Encyclopedia Britannica* in 1953. A) A social worker in search of neighborhood leaders; B) a "rat bite case"; C) more shocking scenes; D) Mr. Gary, the landlord, and citizen activist discuss the issues; E) the Housing Court cracking down on slum landlords; F) an attack on slum conditions by citizens; G) the renewed environment inside a cleaned up block. Photographs by the author.

Baltimore Plan. It cannot work miracles. There are slum areas beyond recovery, but for those worthy of rehabilitating, the Baltimore Plan can work, and together with a program of redevelopment and new housing, both private and public, it can remake a city."[24] It is interesting to note that this is only the second brief mention of public housing in the entire film; nor is public housing depicted at any point during the film. The hope that the Baltimore Plan, a comparatively low-cost program, had the power to "remake a city" without extensive state action or spending must have been very attractive.

The Baltimore Plan opened in 1953 and was broadcast on NBC-TV on a program entitled "Mrs. USA," devoted to the All-American Cities Awards, of which Baltimore was a recipient. The film was also distributed widely in schools, universities, and local film councils. The script made a number of overstatements that became common in the public perception of the plan. A CPHA document described one of these overstatements it hoped *Encyclopedia Britannica* would correct (although it did not): "It is premature to conclude, as the script does, that 'the plan *does* work' until a follow-up program has at least been set in motion." The following sentence, however, was removed after comments by the CPHA: 'Moreover, the Baltimore Plan—forcefully administered—can do this: it can attack the *causes* of slums and *prevent their spread into new areas.*' CPHA knows of no existing evidence in Baltimore to support this statement."[25] Small changes in the film to make it more accurate did not change the generally optimistic tone of the film. This was powerful propaganda for business-friendly solutions to urban problems.

The dark side of this publicity worried as many people as it excited. The Baltimore Plan again became part of a successful attack on public housing at the national level. Mayor Frank Zeidler of Milwaukee had nothing but negative comments concerning the Baltimore Plan on a visit to town in 1953. Zeidler, a "sewer socialist" who served as mayor from 1948 to 1960, was known for his aggressive construction of public housing (and would later head the social democratic Socialist Party-USA). He was not disposed to like the Baltimore Plan, as it had evidently become part of the standard artillery deployed by public housing's enemies. "He and other Milwaukee officials were in Washington earlier in the week to urge the Public Housing Administration to reconsider its decision to exclude Milwaukee from the cities allotted new public housing units under the reduced Federal program. He said that in both Milwaukee and in Washington he has frequently heard from spokesmen for the real-estate business the claim that the Baltimore Plan was the answer to elimination of slums." Although the mayor admitted that "the Baltimore Plan improved the appearance of slum areas by rehabilitation of buildings," he maintained that "the improvements might be regarded as a surface treatment . . . that the buildings for the most part were still slum buildings by reason of their obsolescence and age."[26]Mayor Zeidler's discomfort was easy to understand. The National Association of Homebuilders in a fierce battle to reduce public housing, had in fact again jumped on the Baltimore Plan as a likely substitute for grander public housing schemes. The *Baltimore American* reported to Baltimore readers, "efforts are about to be launched to spread the Baltimore Plan to every city in the nation. This was revealed by Alan Brockbank, president of the National Association of Home Builders following an all-day inspection of the actual working of the plan here." Brockbank heaped praise on Baltimore: "The work done in your city in fighting slums through the Baltimore Plan has convinced me of its effectiveness. I am going to work to spread this method of slum rehabilitation to every city in the nation."[27]

Trenchant criticism came from the labor press, which saw the adoption of the Baltimore Plan by housing interests as part of a strategy to kill funding for more generous housing schemes. The *Federationist* declared: "It is the realtors' story, garnished with deluding superlatives into a Utopian fairy tale of rainbows' gold, that is being told throughout the land to lull into oblivion the dreamers, plotters and planners who would tear down the fetid barricades and bring to even the lowliest of slum dwellers high standards of living, good health, clean minds and their inherent right to the pursuit of happiness." The plan's "chief value to real estate interests now is its use as a weapon of distorted propaganda to bludgeon public housing proposals pending approval in cities other than Baltimore throughout the United States." The skeptics at the *Federationist* had to look no further than those working on the plan for confirmation of failure: "The futility of The Plan is best illustrated by its own statistics, which show that from the inception of its all-out battle against blight in September, 1945, through five years to September 1950, The Plan 'rehabilitated' only 100 blocks totaling 403 dwellings in Baltimore's more than 2,000 blocks of sprawling slums." The Pilot area was particularly unimpressive: "Further evidence of The Plan's sluggishness is manifested in the Pilot Area, a neighborhood of 27 blocks which, since 1951, has been the new target of another all-out fight against blight. As late as June of this year housing inspectors were pressing for compliance with directives issued two years ago." Those areas that had succeeded at some improvement still fell "short of the standards for a minimum level of decency set by the American Public Health Association's housing code." Hans Froelicher Jr., president of CPHA, himself explained that the plan was never "seriously urged as a bar or alternative to the public housing program . . . To urge The Plan as anything approaching a full answer to the gruesome housing situation of large cities like Baltimore is treason to the truth."[28]

Following Ziedler's visit to Baltimore and his negative comments, the *Federationist* proposed that "Real estate businessmen, supported by some of the biggest magazines, have sold the nation on the proposition that the Baltimore Plan is a cure-all for slums and that new housing, particularly public housing, is not needed. Although no local official interviewed by unionists made such wild claims for the plan, neither have they countered the false propaganda circulated by the real estate men."[29] *Baltimore Sun* editorialists, too, disliked the fact that "The plan has been promoted as the answer nationally by those groups anxious to defeat public-housing pro-grams. To insiders, which includes the many private and public organiza-tions and agencies which have worked to push the plan along, the program for the most part has been more a matter of first aid."[30] A *Baltimore Sun* reporter, Martin Millspaugh, who became a leader at Charles Center and later worked for Rouse, described the mixed results of the effort: "The Pilot Area houses are freshly painted, with bricks pointed up and steps in neat and good repair. In the back yards, filthy privies and rotten, rat-infested sheds and piles of rubble have all but disappeared. Indoors, too, the houses have been transformed." Behind the glamour, however, the persistent problems remained: "Still, a tour of the area reveals gaping holes in the armor against blight. Individual houses have been rehabilitated, but the neighborhood as a whole is not yet a new place."[31] The plan began to disintegrate under the weight of both high expectations and internal fights. The *Federationist* reported the disintegration: "Frank Vidor, director of the enforcement program, proposed abandonment of the 'area projects' of the Baltimore Plan. . . . He is apparently dissatisfied with results achieved in the Pilot area. He is reported to have said that enforcement now should revert back to the old 'hit or miss' system in slum areas."[32]

Rouse himself grew increasingly disenchanted with the city government's slow pace of internal change. He acknowledged as well the mild effects of the program. In an editorial explaining why he had resigned as chairman of the Mayor's Advisory Council in 1954, he admitted, "The Baltimore Plan is not doing nearly the job that can be done; nor nearly the job that must be done if we really mean business about stopping the spread of slums and revitalizing worn-out neighborhoods. We corrected over 10,000 violations of the housing codes in the Pilot area in two years. That was good, but not nearly good enough. At that rate it will take us nearly 300 years to cover Baltimore's 2,100 blocks of blight." This pace would change only with a more businesslike approach to reform. In describing his and his associates' goal of unifying different efforts under one city department, Rouse explained, "It would cut out miles of red tape and months of delay. It would centralize responsibility for inspection follow-up and enforcement. It would tighten up the entire law enforcement program." A winning metaphor drove his point home: "If it took three traffic cops to arrest a motorist who had no lights, no brakes and no horn, we would have a lot more dan-gerous cars on the road. Well, it takes fives cops to arrest an unsafe house." Although he urged the mayor to support the legislation to create such a commission, the mayor refused to do so. After dramatically resigning the mayor's service, Rouse and other like-minded reformers successfully led the creation of state legislation for rationalization of housing improvement; but in a final blow to Rouse's efforts, the legislation failed to cover Baltimore, the largest city in the state. Apparently, according to Rouse, Baltimore, "at the request of the city administration, was excepted from its provisions."[33] Looking back on the experience, Rouse admitted the role the Baltimore Plan had played in undercutting public housing efforts: "As the public housing fight grew, real estate interests in a zeal to substitute alternatives grabbed at straws wherever they could find them. They grabbed at rehabilitation programs such as the Baltimore Plan which were hopeful, and they stated that they were panaceas."[34]

Although the slum dwellers saw only minor improvements, those involved with the plan caught professional fire and gained national prominence. Yates Cook left the Baltimore Housing Bureau and joined the National Association of Home Builders "to work with cities throughout the country in helping them set up effective neighborhood conservation commissions." Guy Hollyday, local businessman and the leader behind the Fight Blight Fund, also resigned from the Advisory Council and subsequently became commissioner of the Federal Housing Administration in 1953. Rouse also benefited handsomely. He wrote in 1953 that the press related to the Baltimore Plan had "attracted wide attention throughout the administration and among people everywhere who are interested in housing." Rouse would parlay his experience into direct service for President Dwight D. Eisenhower and a national stage for his ideas. Groups of businessmen, including Rouse, began to meet and discuss neighborhood renewal. Rouse explained that he had attended just such a meeting: "People from all over the country met for two days in New York and wound up with a very hard-hitting set of conclusions and recommendations which will be published in the October issue of *House and Home* and may well be highlighted in future issues of *Life* magazine. Roy Larsen and Andrew Heiskell (publisher of *Life*) were both tremendously impressed with the necessity for the kind of thing we are doing and the potential which it represents." Heiskell would prove a close ally with Rouse on many different projects and provided his considerable resources to Rouse's aid over the following decades.[35]

Rouse's experience with the Baltimore Plan likely played an important role in his later activities. The plan on the whole reflected his interest in carving the city into effective neighborhood units. It also confirmed his belief in the potential power of environmental changes to alter community and personal character. The challenges presented by implementation also illustrated the importance of streamlining urban government on a business model to better respond to urban needs (and Rouse, with the aid of the GBC, continued to press for reform at city hall until the early 1960s). Most of all, the Baltimore Plan promised ideal neighborhoods without an expansion of government social welfare. Although a notable practical failure, the ideas, according to Rouse, had been strong and possible; what they lacked was sufficient will and leadership. It was not the individual failure of private enterprise, slum landlords, or even government, but the failure of existing systems to manage neighborhood improvement.

Rouse on the National Stage

Defenders of public housing had been right to worry about the impact of the Baltimore Plan on public housing. The Baltimore Plan was not the only form of attack on public housing, but its reputation became part of lobbying and public relations that steered the Eisenhower administration, with Rouse's help, toward rehabilitation and away from public housing funding. What became known as the Housing Act of 1954 sounded a great deal like the Baltimore Plan reinvented for national application.

As a member of the Democrats for Eisenhower and an emerging leader in the growing fight for better urban neighborhoods, Rouse received a letter in 1953 from President Eisenhower: "Dear Mr. Rouse, I am establishing an Advisory Committee under the Chairmanship of the Housing and Home Finance Administrator to review the Federal Government's housing programs, activities and agency organization. I should be very pleased if you could participate. The aim of the review is to develop a series of recommendations which will clearly identify the proper role of the Federal Government in this field and outline more economical and effective means for improving the housing conditions of our people."[36] Note the emphasis on "economical" means. Rouse accepted the invitation and served on the Executive Commmittee of Eisenhower's Advisory Committee on Housing Programs and Policies and was a member and chairman of the Subcommittee on Conservation, Rehabilitation, and Redevelopment. In a letter from 1982, he recounted his role in the effort: "My sub-committee held hearings and invited people from all over the country to testify . . . There was a preponderant view that the individual sovereignties regarding housing solutions had to be overcome and that they needed to be combined in a single program which embraced the separate solutions as pieces of a total program."[37]

During this period Rouse created enthusiasm for the term *urban renewal*, which he borrowed from a well-known planner (who admired the Baltimore Plan): "I stole [urban renewal] from Miles Colean's book *Renewing Our Cities* in which he spoke of 'urban renewal' . . . The phrase and the report met with derision when it came before the whole committee, but because no one could produce a better phrase it stuck."[38] Rouse, and many people at the time, saw the concept of urban renewal as progressive. The Housing Act of 1954 in time demanded neighborhood conservation plans in addition to clearance: "I use the phrase 'Urban Renewal' only because it includes the physical rehabilitation of the neighborhood, an effective con-servation program and at the same time demolishing non-salvageable struc-tures and putting that land to its proper new use."[39] He did not use the term uniformly during his career, and urban renewal has not come to be associ-ated with progressive planning in neighborhoods; instead, it is most often associated with the large-scale programs in private sector commercial rede-velopment authorized in the Housing Acts of both 1949 and 1954.

The president's message that accompanied the proposed Housing Act of 1954 reflected the direction of the Advisory Committee and was thus controversial in much the same way that the Baltimore Plan had been. Eisenhower advocated "Prevention of the spread of blight into good areas of the community through strict enforcement of housing and neighborhood standards and strict occupancy controls. . . . Rehabilitation of salvable areas, turning them into sound, healthy neighborhoods by replanning, removing congestion, providing parks and playgrounds, reorganizing streets and traffic, and by facilitating physical rehabilitation of deteriorated structures."[40] New mortgage money and loans were to be made available to local agen-cies to facilitate this process, and comprehensive plans were required to address replanning of old neighborhoods and anti-blight/code enforcement efforts. As might be expected, labor interests were not impressed with what they considered to be pretty language and little real action.

The *Federationist* jumped on the administration's proposal: "The administration's housing program would rely primarily on rehabilitation and remodeling of old, rundown dwellings. These halfway measures are glori-fied and dressed up as an urban renewal program, but the fancy title can-not conceal the fact that the Eisenhower proposals amount to little more than a piecemeal patch-up and fix-up campaign." The hand of the Advisory Committee was rightly seen as the guiding force behind these pro-visions: "The administration's so-called urban renewal program stems largely from recommendations of the President's Advisory Committee on Housing" that had "pumped enthusiastically for the rehabilitation panacea."[41] Organized labor hoped for government support of 600,000 units of public housing over three years, far more than the 140,000 units pro-posed by the administration—numbers more in line with social democra-tic Europe. The Catholic Worker's magazine, *Work*, saw the dead hand of private enterprise behind the administration's tepid proposals: "The over-whelming majority of the President's committee was made up of bankers, builders, and real estate men."[42]

The good intentions of Rouse and other Advisory Committee members notwithstanding, application of the provisions of neighborhood conservation as part of what became known as urban renewal rarely had much effect. Gurney Breckenfeld, managing editor of *House and Home*, the leading magazine of

homebuilders, argued in 1964 that although the 1954 law meant well in trying to "broaden the concept from bulldozers only in the '49 Act to what we
have today, which is a triple-barreled program of clearance and redevelopment, rehabilitation and conservation" linked to comprehensive planning,
"Since 1954, almost every Housing administrator, who is charged by law with
annually reviewing and approving these city pledges, has admitted some cities
aren't doing what they say, especially in failing to enforce housing codes against
existing slums." More damning perhaps was the fact that "for a decade, critics have correctly complained that HHFA [Housing and Home Finance Agency]
has credited cities with workable programs and qualified them for renewal and
public housing subsidies when in fact their programs didn't work at all. New
York, of course, is the most flagrant example." He reminded his audience that
nationally "more than 148,000 urban families have been uprooted by bulldozers."[43] For a housing act, the 1954 legislation had a notably antihousing
effect and primarily expanded business district redevelopment, like Charles
Center, across America.

Urban renewal funds helped transform cities, but public housing, a small
part of the Housing Act, became the most controversial aspect of the legislation. Money for redevelopment was not questioned, nor were new regulations demanding local comprehensive planning, but even the small number
of public housing units called for by Eisenhower became explosive material
in a Cold War Congress. The lobbying of homebuilders, the private sector
bias of Eisenhower's own committee, and the emphasis on code enforcement
popularized by the Baltimore Plan (and similar but less famous efforts in a
few other cities) already watered the case for social housing.

The controversy that surrounded public housing proved particularly ironic
considering how little public housing was proposed or built in the United
States compared to Europe. Although the Housing Act of 1949 had set ambitious goals for public housing—135,000 units per year for six years—only
84,000 total units had been built by 1951 because of opposition from real
estate interests and restrictions created by the Korean War. Few public housing units were constructed in 1952 or 1953. Three positions emerged in
1954 on public housing during debate of the Housing Act—none of
which made a powerful case for social housing.

The Eisenhower administration and his Advisory Committee (including Rouse) supported a small public housing as a part of urban redevelopment, but not on the basis of a long-term social welfare program.
According to a document from 1958, "Rouse long ago gave up opposing
public housing. On this choler-laden topic, he commented last year:
'We're missing an enormous bet. Public housing could be an enormous catalyst' in wiping out slums and rebuilding cities. The nation,' he contended,
'should stop thinking of enormous projects,' and use public housing as a

'vehicle for moving people to the private market economy.'"[44] Public housing was no more than a necessary evil designed to compensate for business displacement.

Redevelopers like Rouse had been under attack for some time from liberal quarters as a result of displacement activities. The case of Metropolitan Life's Stuyvesant Town (1943) in New York was perhaps most notorious, when thousands of low-income residents were moved to make way for a for-profit, middle-class, all-white development (and Baltimore redevelopment projects, in which Rouse played a role, also generated controversy). Leading housing advocate Charles Abrams in *The Nation* condemned the fact that at Stuyvesant Town "present residents are to be crowded into other slums, making them more profitable for the owners." Like other liberals, he argued that "Alternative accommodations for the slum families to be displaced, at rents they can afford, must be made available by public housing agencies."[45] Although the residents of the future site of Stuyvesant Town were displaced, public housing programs indeed became a necessary part of redevelopment in cities such as New York and Chicago.

The proposed Housing Act of 1954 carefully limited public housing to meet the basic needs of redevelopment. The total of 140,000 units of public housing proposed over a four-year period were projected with the notion that "special preference among eligible families should be given to those who must be relocated because of slum clearance, neighborhood rehabilitation, or similar public actions."[46] In remarks to the Economic Club of Detroit, Albert Cole, administrator of the Housing and Home Finance Agency, explained, "I have always been a critic of socialized housing . . . Public housing cannot be considered an end in itself; it is a conduit through which people can move toward improved and permanent living conditions."[47] He admitted, too, that "it is fair to say that [the Advisory Committee] began their work with a predisposition, perhaps a hope, that the low-rent program could be ended. Again, I think it is fair to say that the Advisory Committee recommended its continuation, not because they were promoters of public housing, but because they were honestly convinced that for at least the next few years it is a necessary program." In order to clean out blight, "families must be moved out of slums and out of overcrowded and declining neighborhoods."[48] Charles Slusser, commissioner of the Public Housing Administration, defended the use of public housing as part of civic renewal by explaining, "citizens are neither creeping nor socialistic when they try to prevent their cities from running down at the heels—particularly when there is no infringement on local initiative and local authority."[49] Linking public housing to redevelopment saved the small number of units but should be seen for what it was, a calculation by business interests of necessary costs to their private sector rebuilding of city centers.

Liberals in Congress and elsewhere feebly attempted to use humanitarian antisocialist language to justify public housing in an era when public housing was closely linked to socialism. Anticommunist liberals argued that slums reflected a flaw in the American system that public housing could remedy: "Let us then strike a real blow against the dangers of any American acceptance of subtle Communist propaganda," Democratic Congressman Harold Donahue (Massachusetts) argued, "by giving our citizens who vitally need it, a fair chance to bring up their families in godly cleanliness, healthful happiness and patriotic loyalty by voting for the continuation of an adequate public housing program." Slum areas, according to Donahue, should rightly be seen as roots of social unrest: "Meanwhile the entire country is exposed to national welfare sabotage by creeping crime, corruption and social rebellion that find such devilish inspiration in slum areas. The history of public housing demonstrates these cancers can be successfully halted."[50] Joseph P. McMurray, the housing executive for the City of New York, in a speech to the Potomac Chapter of the National Association of Housing Officials, demanded that national leaders make good on their claims to superiority: "Our housing problem is not merely a question of clearing out slums. It is a matter of providing more adequate and comfortable dwellings for the people who are entitled to the standards we boast of so much in America."[51] "Slums are a blot on America. They are existing to the disgrace of our people," admitted moderate Republican Congressman William Widnall (New Jersey), and he cited a *New York Times* editorial calling for congressional leaders "to be aware of the importance of clean, decent housing in strengthening our democracy."[52] It can be said with some certainty that arguments linking public housing with antisocialism (without the labor or socialist justifications) had little effect in an era when social housing had become so closely linked to socialism and communism. New Deal liberalism had declined in the face of virulent leftism.

The Red baiting and antistatist position, which carried the day, proved far more compelling and persuasive in congressional debates, because conservatives could so strongly link public housing to both the New Deal and socialism abroad. Legislators whittled away at even the small number of public housing units called for by Eisenhower's already conservative committee. Anticommunist crusader Democratic Congressman Martin Dies (Texas) described what he considered to be the questionable social philosophy of public housing supporters: "They subscribe to the political philosophy that there is great virtue in big government. They believe that the ends justifies the means."[53] He admitted, "I respect a liberal if he is honest and sincere and if he believes in statism—but I just do not believe in it. I came up to understand that socialism is unworkable in any country."[54] A far stronger antisocialist position proved popular with many congressmen. Democratic

Congressman Don Wheeler (Georgia) worked himself up into a lather and imagined a vote for public housing as an act of treason to future generations: "But am I to excuse myself to my grandchildren for having cast a vote in favor of this socialistic program by telling them that I was blinded by the brass in the White House, that simply because the President of the United States asked for it I subverted my convictions and voted to impose this multi-billion dollar socialistic program on generations yet unborn?"[55] Public housing was also, apparently, a haven for subversives, according to Congressman Ralph Gwinn of New York: "Strangely enough, in every one of these big public housing projects where investigation has been made, right at the center or core of the tenancy is some very well acknowledged Communist or left winger tucked right into the setup." A survey allegedly found that communists had infiltrated all of New York's public housing projects, and that Detroit and Los Angeles faced similar dangers.[56]

The memory of the New Deal still smarted, and many of these representatives believed that a major public housing program would be no more than another step toward a socialistic state that the New Deal had initiated. Eisenhower himself undercut support for public housing by referring to the Tennessee Valley Authority as "an example of creeping socialism." Democratic Congressman Joe Evins (Tennessee) believed that "the President should not be surprised when members of his own party used his own words 'creeping socialism' to wreck and defeat the President's public housing program."[57] Democratic Congressman William Colmer (Mississippi), declared his opposition in the strongest terms: "But, out of all of this New and Fair Deal program, it is my considered judgment that this so-called public housing is the most inimical to the continuation of the Republic . . . It is socialistic in the truest sense of the word. It would destroy if permitted to continue to grow the principle of individual home ownership . . . [and] could end only in a socialistic state, or even worse, a dictatorship."[58] Not only did opponents fail to distinguish among New Deal, communist, and social democratic examples, asserting that all public housing led to "dictatorships," but also they were confused about causation—social democratic governments generally created public housing, and public housing certainly was part of their appeal to masses of people. Public housing, however, did not necessarily generate greater socialism or party loyalty in democratic nations (because of Soviet totalitarianism it is impossible to say what role public housing played in maintaining communist power). Labor and social democratic parties in most of Europe cycled in and out of office even with large numbers of public housing residents. Certainly there were better ways to gain party loyalty.

The opposition, using effective propaganda and colorful language, well supported by powerful groups of homebuilders and business interests, and

buttressed by the conservative mood of the white, middle-class public, ultimately triumphed.[59] The historian Roger Biles has written, "in 1954, a reluc-
tant Congress appropriated monies not for 135,000, but for barely 20,000
units of public housing." Similarly low amounts of public housing flowed
from Congress during the rest of the 1950s. The parsimony was "a tribute
to the successful assault on the program undertaken by foes such as the National
Association of Real Estate Boards, which branded the policy a 'communist plot' and the 'road to serfdom.'" The outcome was also a tribute to a
confluence of a variety of antistatist activities: the Baltimore Plan's
emphasis on code enforcement and private responsibility for slum conditions seemed to undercut the need for public housing; tepid support from
Eisenhower and his committee only justified public housing as part of business redevelopment; the genuine association of public housing with statism during the New Deal and abroad undermined humanitarian
justifications for social housing; and the use of anticommunist language in
Congress identified all public housing supporters as un-American. The Cold
War and the question of what constituted acceptable government action
thus played an important role in defeating social welfare initiatives.[60]

No Slums in Ten Years

Because of Rouse's leading role in the Advisory Committee and the
Baltimore Plan, in 1954 he was invited by commissioners of the District
of Columbia to propose a comprehensive plan of urban renewal for much
of the blighted sections of the city. In 1949 "several parties from Congress
went slumming right here in sight of the capitol building. The members
were shocked. They found a stinking, filthy, unhealthy mess . . . They found
hell constructed in the capital of the richest country, with the highest standards on earth."[61] *Newsweek* vividly illustrated the political dangers of these
conditions: "A favorite Communist propaganda picture shows some dirty
Negro kids playing in a yard of garbage against a backdrop of the sharply
focused Capitol dome."[62] Much more of the city suffered from horrendous
conditions; a more embarrassing situation for the United States government could scarcely have been imagined.

The 1955 report, optimistically entitled *No Slums in Ten Years*, was cowrit-
ten by Rouse and Nathaniel Keith, director of the Housing and Home Finance
Agency's Slum Clearance and Urban Redevelopment Division from
1949–1953. Rouse was described as the leader of "the highly successful Baltimore
Plan of slum rehabilitation, and his firm financed Baltimore's first two major
redevelopment projects."[63] Although the specific planning guidelines
likely came primarily from Nathaniel Keith, the document as a whole reflects

Rouse's utopian notions of the power of planning to create an ideal society, a transformation possible without extensive government spending. According to this optimistic report, "Slums can be eliminated from the District of Columbia within the next ten years. The city's sprawling blighted areas can be replanned and renewed into healthy neighborhoods. Machinery can be established for detecting and effectively combating future blight in its early stages." The plan itself called for a mix of "complete clearance of existing structures," "spot surgery," and "vigorous enforcement of strong housing and building codes and through large-scale rehabilitation." The neighborhood ideals of Rouse and others were also integrated into this ambitious document: "A comprehensive master plan will organize the city into logical neighborhoods centered, wherever possible, around an elementary school. These neighborhoods will be bounded by major traffic ways to take the city's traffic around the neighborhoods instead of through them, public buildings, parks or other natural barriers." Rouse and Keith called for general improvements in city services as well as this neighborhood planning.[64]

The potential of modern capitalist management is not overlooked in the report, either. Much of the plan is devoted to launching a smooth system of management that would prevent creation of slums, clean up existing ones, and replace the inconsistent and irregular process then in place. This new enforcement included both a crackdown on violations and a "preventive" program to stymie decline. Consistent standards and procedures would be created as well as a centralized office of enforcement. According to the authors: "A high standard of performance by property owners must be required. Stubborn non-compliance, irresponsible indifference, careless performance must be met by resolute and unrelenting enforcement." As in Baltimore, the authors also encouraged the creation of a housing court solely devoted to housing issues and proposed a streamlined process of bringing offenders, particularly slum landlords, into line. Rouse and Keith tied enforcement to a new and comprehensive code for the city. This code included expanded amounts of space per individual, kitchens, and private toilets, as one might expect in a modern society. Other notable and progressive aspects of the plan encouraged the creation of small public housing projects to be fit into existing neighborhoods and extensive rehabilitation of substandard housing.

From the perspective of Rouse's private sector ideals, one cannot overlook the report's call for a "A Private Renewal Corporation" that would carry out these idealistic plans: "To assure vigorous and financially competent leadership in rehabilitation at the outset of the program, it is recommended that a private corporation be formed in the business community to concentrate on rehabilitation work under the renewal program. It would be a pace-setting, trail-blazing profit venture with broad business support and a community gleam in its eye." It would also make use of new FHA (Federal Housing Authority) funding as part of the Housing Act of 1954 for capital and acquisition and might "set the pace in this challenging new field of private enterprise." The corporation was to focus on rental housing, but might expand to sell and build low-cost housing. Here one finds the first glimmer of what would become the philosophy of Rouse's Enterprise Foundation in the 1980s. In this early plan, as was projected for Enterprise, such an organization would take the place of public authorities. The larger context of the Cold War also crept into the language of the report: "public awareness of the problem" of blight "has been heightened by the anachronism of substantial slums existing in the national capital," and "Washington can become the country's first major slumless city— an appropriate and exhilarating role for the Nation's Capital."[65]

The local media, predictably, greeted the plan with great acclaim. According to the *Washington Post:* "The Rouse-Keith report is a sort of blueprint for the application of the 'urban renewal' concept to Washington. Before the city can take advantage of the Housing Act of 1954 it must have a comprehensive plan to mobilize all of its interested agencies in a concentrated drive against the slums. It must be prepared to bring together public housing, redevelopment, housing code enforcement, city planning, private enterprise, community and neighborhood efforts and tie them all in with the city's public works program already launched." The fact that most private land had already been developed within the district made redevelopment all the more important: "Failure to take this course would result in continued loss of population and business to the suburbs, with further deterioration of the city's inner core and consequent loss of municipal revenue. That would be a tragedy for the city as a whole and for the nation, which has much pride in its Capital." Tragedy was the result, however. From what I can determine the plan had little effect on most slums, and Washington, D.C., did not become a slumless city.[66]

The title of the report, however, turned out to be prophetic in one respect. The Southwest Urban Renewal District tore down 99 percent of the slum buildings and moved out most of the poor black residents for mostly upper-income whites beginning in 1952. According to *Fortune,* looking back from 1957, "The rat-infested hovels in the immediate shadow of the nation's Capitol, which were made famous by a generation of angry photographers, have been cleared in the past decade, largely, it appears, because of the worldwide attention those photographs got."[67] There were no slums in their place afterward, and William Zeckendorf was involved in middle-class, racially integrated housing projects, but the number of poor and increasingly angry people had not been altered. The initial process of relocating poor residents during the 1950s was considered progressive, but these high standards faltered.

According to Washington journalists Harry Jaffe and Tom Sherwood: "The city relocated twenty-five thousand people to public housing projects in the Northeast and Southeast parts of the city in the midst of stable, middle-class black neighborhoods . . . the housing projects were allowed to deteriorate, and the surrounding neighborhoods took a turn for the worse."[68] Although the Rouse report was more enlightened than many plans at the time, it was part of a "consensus" of opinion aimed at entirely reshaping the center city for highways, middle-class high-rises, and office buildings. Little more than a decade after the report was issued, the city was rocked by some of the worst riots in America.[69] Our national shame, a segregated and poverty-stricken capital, would not be so easily dispatched.

The Businessman's Ideal Neighborhood

> I believe an urban center, such as Pittsburgh, does not achieve true greatness until its people are well-housed—regardless of how many new office towers, expressways, and industrial plants are built.
>
> Richard K. Mellon

The President's Committee on Housing Programs and Policies recommended in 1954 that "a broadly representative private organization be formed outside of the Federal Government with congressional and/or Presidential sponsorship to mobilize public opinion in the support of vigorous and effective action by the cities in slum prevention, neighborhood conservation, and other urban renewal activities."[70] Such was the modest beginning of ACTION, the American Council to Improve Our Neighborhoods. Now forgotten, it was once a powerful national organization designed to research and promote neighborhood renewal.

The ACTION board of directors included corporate heavyweights such as the president of Owens-Corning; directors of housing authorities; representatives from the National Association of Home Builders; Phil Klutznick (developer of Park Forest, Illinois, and former head of the United States Housing Authority); the mayors of Philadelphia and New Orleans; Wallace Harrison (a leading Modernist architect); Andrew Heiskell; Richard Mellon; Stanley Marcus; Walter Reuther of the CIO; and Robert Weaver (then deputy commissioner of housing for the State of New York).[71] And, of course, James Rouse appeared among this powerful group. ACTION's first president was Major General Frederick Irving, former head of West Point. The Advertising Council lent its significant talent and resources to ACTION. Planner Martin Meyerson of the University of Pennsylvania played an important role in launching the organization and also led an ACTION research unit that published, in partnership with McGraw-Hill, a number of popular books on housing and rehabilitation.

Although liberals peppered the board, the businessmen, and Rouse in particular, set the tone for the organization. ACTION became a strong advocate for business leadership on urban issues: "Private enterprise will make the major contribution in the building and rebuilding of our urban areas. Private development can take place with assurance if there is knowledge of the goals to be achieved and that the particular project will contribute to those goals."[72] From the beginning, too, ACTION did not envision a major role for public housing in neighborhood improvement: "Public housing has played an important, although a minor, role in the housing programs of hundreds of communities. It is recognized in the Housing Act of 1954 as an adjunct to relocation of those slum dwellers who are displaced by clearance programs. We are an ingenious people, however. We in ACTION are sure that in times of such high national productivity we will develop many other tools in addition to public housing to broaden the opportunities for good housing for low-income people."[73] ACTION leadership believed that application of business talent to the issues of urban housing would obviate state solutions.

Cold War ideology provided much of the fire that fueled ACTION. Vice president of ACTION, Milton Veiser, a life insurance executive, proclaimed, "ACTION believes that businessmen are the greatest latent force for good in the cities of America" rather than elected officials. He noted, moreover, that the urban malaise imperiled America's leadership position: "For generations the image of American life has spelled hope and expectation to people all over the world, not just to Americans. Today, when the competition for men's minds is as vital to our country as the missile race, the image of how Americans live must not come under question. If we cannot appeal with more than words to the social needs and the hunger for fulfillment of the people of the world, if we cannot demonstrate with a gleaming sample case of our cities, we will lose those minds to other forces." American cities, where most Americans then lived, did not live up to claims of national grandeur, particularly in the race with the communists: "So long as our cities invite by their slums and disorder the down-grading of our cultural, our social morality, our values of living, we are vulnerable. Only when we make our American cities into an image to match our great aspirations, are we on the way to becoming invincible—a nation noble, free and beautiful."[74]

Fritz Close, a vice president at ALCOA, describing the ACTION-sponsored East Hills affordable housing project in Pittsburgh, remarked, "This is our Sputnik. This is the way we can do something with this housing business that will make us the envy of the world."[75] The ACTION chairman, Roy Johnson, former director of the Advanced Projects Agency, admitted,

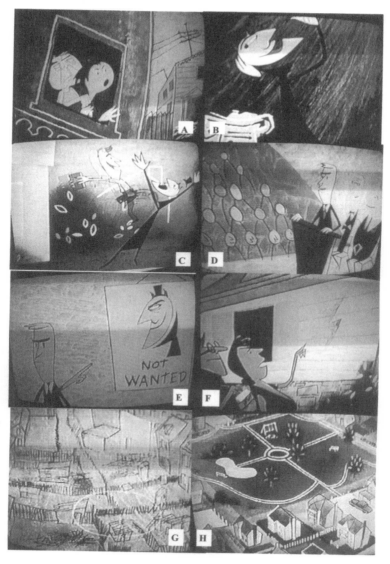

Figure 12. Scenes from the *Man of ACTION*, a mid-1950s propaganda film created by ACTION: A) A slum neighborhood where pathology breeds; B) the "Devil" mastermind behind the mayhem; C) the average citizen grabbing the "Devil's Book" (listing future urban disasters) in order to enlighten city officials; D) the citizen as civic sparkplug advocating neighborhood renewal (without extensive state action); E) the "Devil" threat revealed to citizens; F) the Devil's profile represented in elements of physical neglect in urban neighborhoods; G) transformation of slums like this into H) tidied neighborhoods from which the "Devil" has been driven by concerted citizen activism. Photographs by the author.

"[I]t is a national disgrace that so far we have been more successful in putting one monkey into space than we have been in putting all Americans into decent housing."[76] And the hero of our story, Rouse, could hardly be expected not to make similar pronouncements: "In no city have we been able to eliminate this [slum] situation, and the American city is the standard from which other nations see us. Is there no better standard?" As president of ACTION (he took charge in 1958), in a dramatic speech he "called upon the U.S. [Saving and Loan] League to provide powerful leadership in this fight to save our cities and to provide a vivid and vital answer to Mr. Khrushchev and all that he stands for."[77]

ACTION engaged in propaganda, network building, and research, but its primary goal was to build excitement about the possibilities of neighborhood preservation. With the help of the Ad Council (and funding from the Continental Can Company), ACTION created a short animated motion picture, *Man of ACTION*, released in 1955, to a national audience: "In its first seven months the 13 ½ minute epic of the citizen's role in urban renewal was witnessed by better than 22,000,000 people, largely via television. By 1959, some 700 television showings were reported to an audience in excess of 60,000,000. In addition, more than 600,000 viewers had seen the film at some 12,000 live showings sponsored by local business firms and civic organizations."[78] According to ACTION materials the film "effectively tells the story of the citizen's role in moving an urban renewal program forward . . . In a relatively short time it manages to tell the story of modernization and home improvement but also widens the story to include neighborhood improvement and slum elimination."[79]

Man of ACTION merits close examination. Set to melancholy jazz and a minimal but stylish animation, the film short is still entertaining. The story follows the attempt by a citizen both to save his own neighborhood and to organize the whole city for neighborhood renewal. The story begins as this average citizen awakens one day to find the devil at his door. This devil, who unconvincingly demands that he is actually one of the devil's project supervisors from Hell's "Division of Urban Destruction," is a humorous and likable fellow, but is clearly supervising the slow destruction of the citizen's own neighborhood. The devil claims, in fact, that he is not directly responsible for housing problems or neighborhood decline: "I don't destroy anything, I just keep track of the schedule . . . people do the destroying." Later, when showing the citizen a neighborhood more decrepit and dangerous than his own, the devil still demands, in a flip manner, "I can't really claim credit for it, people did it all."

The film then walks the viewer through the decline of a once idyllic neighborhood, Paradise Gardens. This is not the neighborhood of the main character; instead, it is considered to be the worst area in the city.

Although the neighborhood once featured trees and large homes, we are shown that automobile traffic, streetcars, and street widening undermined the suburban character of the district. The citizen admits that when the streetcar moved in "that's when grandfather moved out." According to the dramatic narration, that was also when "the neighborhood began to *change*" and factories and commercial uses piled in along with crowded housing. No mention of any racial politics is made in any of the film, an intentional and notable omission in this description of neighborhood change. Nor are comments made about bank disinvestment in urban neighborhoods. The devil admits that while he might not have created the conditions in Paradise Gardens, "this neighborhood is fine for our business—juvenile delinquency, alcoholism, crime—yep, this is a great little neighborhood!"

The citizen learns that his neighborhood is next on the devil's list and starts painting and repairing his house. Best of all, while being taunted for his spirit of improvement, he grabs the devil's book that predicts future slums and future disasters. He hurries off to city hall with this critical information. The devil isn't worried, however, because "Most of the facts are known to the officials." In fact, at city hall an idealistic planner is arguing in front of the council that "slum clearance is not enough, we've got to prevent slums from being developed in the first place." However, hikes in taxes and regulation to fund improvements are greeted by outrage from property owners and landlords listening in on the meeting, even when the citizen stands up to inform them that the streets on which they have their property are slated for decline by the devil.

A dramatic demonstration of the citizen's predictive power, granted by the devil's book, follows as he correctly predicts the collapse of a landlord's chimney to disbelieving citizens and officials. The demonstration that the predictions in the devil's book are true gives him enormous power and leads to the formation of a "city-wide group to study the whole problem." The citizen becomes an outspoken advocate, an idealistic firebrand (modeled on Rouse), and the music swells as the civic organizing begins. One of the most striking scenes depicts the citizen illustrating how the devil's profile can be found in cracks in the sidewalk and other physical signs of distress. The profile is dramatically laid over broken windows, busted fences, cracked sidewalks, and other signs of urban blight.

The devil is on the retreat as the citizens of the city fix up their homes and neighborhoods; the familiar before and after scenes similar to the Baltimore Plan demonstrate the effectiveness of these efforts. The devil flees on a train from the town but laughs, knowing that "This isn't the only town in America." The narrator warns that the devil "may be on his way to your community right now . . . He may be there already." At the end of the film, however, the narrator reminds the audience, "you know how to handle him . . . He

Figure 13. More ACTION publicity distributed nationally during the 1950s. The focus on external signs of decay and "blight" avoided the more complex reasons for the creation of slums in American cities. Rouse Papers, Columbia Archive.

can't stand organized groups where people work together. If enough of us work together we can run him right out of the country." It is hard to overlook the obvious Cold War, anticommunist paranoia in the film, but the more important aspects of the Cold War story here are reflected in omissions. Nowhere in the film is public housing or social welfare discussed as a solution to the housing problem. Home repair, code enforcement, citizen committees, and cleanup projects are offered as the remedies to slum problems; these were the solutions businessmen supported for solving urban social issues.[80]

A flashy road show developed by *Life* magazine for ACTION built further excitement for urban renewal at the highest levels of finance and politics: "Our Living Future: A giant panoramic screen presentation combining motion pictures and photographs, both in color and black-and-white, making use of three-dimensional animation technique and in-person lecture, the show spotlights the menace of decay faced by America's cities." A writer and actor, David Keith Hardy, narrated "the story behind the pictures, speaking before a gigantic screen (30 feet by 15 feet) and directing the showing by means of an intricate keyboard controlling projectors, lights and sound." Mayors, city managers, legislators, and executives raved about the show, and audiences were particularly impressed with local examples woven into the narrative. "This live show was taken to more than 100 cities from coast to coast. It played to more than 100,000 persons, including about one-third of the members of Congress at a special showing at the Hotel Statler in Washington."[81] By no means was this minor propaganda with only local reach.

ACTION experts created publications to complement the film and traveling show. A brochure, reprinted in newspapers and magazines, asked the ominous question: "Is Your Neighborhood Going to Seed?" and offered a checklist of danger signs, including the following:

> 1. "For Rent" and "For Sale" signs are a familiar sight; people are leaving to live elsewhere. 2. Houses need repairs or paint; lawns are weedy, fences broken. 3. Commercial buildings and stores are beginning to appear on residential streets . . . 5. Residences are being converted into rooming houses on your block . . . 8. Abandoned cars stand on the street for months . . . 9. Juvenile delinquency and crime are on the increase . . . 10. School buildings are dingy, outmoded, perhaps unsafe . . . 11. Children play in the streets . . . 12. Trucks and fast-moving traffic pass through your neighborhood . . . 14. There are accumulations of rubbish in back yards and vacant lots . . . 15. People aren't investing in home improvements or new construction . . . 17. Shopping facilities are poor or remote, with inadequate parking facilities . . . 19. Your neighborhood has no identity, no focal point or center of interest.

The list was as notable for what it excluded as what it included. For instance, it did not list "banks are redlining your neighborhood" or a "highway project is scheduled for your district." Using familiar language of blight as disease rather than the result of policy choices or inequality, the brochure cautioned, "Blight is like an infection, spreading from house to house, apartment to apartment, neighborhood to neighborhood with alarming speed. No house or community is immune from its attack."[82] Blight imagined as akin to a medical condition was not invented at ACTION, but in the context of the Cold War minimized the political ramifications of slum conditions.

These materials seem almost silly today, but they were taken seriously at the time. According to ACTION documents, "In the first nine months of the campaign, more than a thousand newspapers requested ACTION material. More than fifty national magazines embraced the campaign and allocated space to it. Radio and television spots received the widest acceptance and use of any of the campaign materials. . . . The Advertising Council estimated that more than 100 million readers were exposed to ACTION articles in consumer magazines alone." All of this public relations effort had an effect; at the end of three years "ACTION was widely known throughout the country as a symbol of home and neighborhood improvements, thousands of inquiries had been answered, and local urban renewal officials testified that the campaign had increased public support for their local programs."[83]

ACTION also promoted networking by creating "little ACTIONS" at the local level, including "neighborhood groups, public service community organizations, and special private interest groups." Through scheduled meetings and regular publications ACTION spread word of successful programs and inspired a great deal of interest. Conferences seemed especially effective: "The ACTION Regional Urban Renewal Clinics provided training opportunities for all levels of leaders. [Seven] clinics reached 2,000 leaders from 300 cities in almost every state in the Union. More than 100 urban specialists provided content."[84] These activities integrated ACTION's support for both business district and neighborhood redevelopment activities.

In its final years of activity during the early 1960s, ACTION likely played a role in setting national policy under the Kennedy administration. On March 9, 1961, President John F. Kennedy gave a speech that, according to ACTION administrator James Lash, reflected ACTION's message almost perfectly: "The message went on to vigorously set forth many of the principles ACTION has been emphasizing to the nation in its six-year history." Robert Weaver, a cofounder of ACTION, was also appointed head of the Housing and Home Finance Agency under Kennedy.[85] A proposal by Rouse for a conference on urban problems in 1961 at the White House, directed at leading executives of companies, suggested that the secretary of state could "Point up [the] 'show window' aspect of American cities. What does central city squalor say to the world about the effectiveness of a democratic society, a free enterprise economy, a God-inspired nation?"[86] It is unclear if this meeting ever transpired, Rouse's Cold War language notwithstanding.

ACTION faded by the mid-1960s, but it had played an important role in legitimating the notion of the businessman's utopia. Rouse acknowledged that many of ACTION's ideas had become a normal part of urban renewal activities by 1961: "When ACTION was formed, it had a clear-cut objective. Our ads, billboards, radio, TV, and Advertising Council program were enormous and effective. ACTION then had to respond to the excitement it stimulated. We held dozens of meetings, bringing in the best official and professional talent. This worked and people became organized. Before we knew it, we were participating in a tide that was running across the country. We've had trouble keeping up and, therefore, trouble defining what we are."[87]

ACTION may have been fading, but it had served its purpose. At the leading edge of private sector efforts, ACTION was perfectly positioned to promote the notion that American cities should be improved as part of international competition, and that this improvement could come without a massive commitment of federal funds or enhanced government direction (and definitely not public housing). By focusing on the potential for renovation, local neighborhood action, city government reform, and the leading role of private efforts in urban affairs, ACTION had more than carried out its mandate; it helped keep the nation focused on market or managerial solutions to the growing problems of urban neighborhoods.

Inventing the End of the American Welfare State and Creating a Private Sector Alternative

> At our last Board Meeting, Bob [Robert] McNamara banged the table and said, "Jim, we are building a new national system in America through the work of the Foundation and the Development Company. It is very important, and you must tell it that way."
>
> James Rouse

> When Patty [Rouse] and I go to other countries, we always ask, "Show us your worst areas." And we go to the worst areas in London or Sydney or Tokyo or wherever. And we'd love to have them in an American city.
>
> James Rouse

During the 1960s and 1970s, the growing malaise in America's urban neighborhoods dimmed the image of the United States abroad. The riots and the persistence of massive slum districts, barely addressed by Eisenhower, ACTION, or the Great Society programs, further distinguished the United States from both its industrialized allies and the Soviet Union. In this period the social welfare state abroad reached its apogee, and countries like the Soviet Union, Britain, France, and Sweden were still constructing massive new housing estates for poor people while generously expanding social benefits. This optimistic expansion hit the wall in the 1970s, but by then these countries had already rebuilt significant sections of their existing cities and even created new districts that reflected socialist values.

During the era of the Civil Rights movement and Great Society initiatives, and the golden age of European social welfare, Rouse primarily devoted himself to malls and new towns that sought reform of the urban order but not through direct rebuilding of declining neighborhoods. Most notably, Rouse's Columbia project, which began in 1963, included subsidized housing without the direct aid of county officials. A Rouse subsidiary and local faith-oriented nonprofits used federal mortgage subsidies to build hundreds of subsidized units in Columbia. The town became a leading example of suburban class mixture, although not without occasional tensions.

Rouse's retirement in 1979 from The Rouse Company (at age sixty-five), however, opened a grand new chapter in his approach to *urban* neighborhood renewal as well as a return to the fundamental principles articulated in the 1950s. The much publicized faltering of the European welfare state and Soviet Union in the late 1970s and 1980s, as well as extensive coverage of problems in American public housing and social welfare, gave Rouse a receptive audience for his reengineered private sector ideas and projects. Even though Rouse did not see any role for public housing in rebuilding poor neighborhoods, he did believe that renovation and new home construction by nonprofits, paired primarily to private sector social welfare, could turn whole neighborhoods and cities around.

The creation of the Enterprise Foundation in 1982, a private sector project designed to create slum-free American cities with only minor government interference, made Rouse a darling of politicians, both Democrats and Republicans, throughout the country. The vacuum created by the Reagan, Bush, and Clinton administrations' destruction of national housing programs and social welfare was partly filled with Rouse's vision of private sector solutions. Although it is true that the Enterprise Foundation remains one of the most important national organizations sponsoring affordable housing and community development corporations, and has thus helped to partly rebuild some distressed urban neighborhoods, the emergence of the Foundation during the 1980s also helped legitimize destruction of federal housing and social welfare programs. In the meantime, the promised national private sector social welfare network Rouse envisioned, which would create not only housing but also "slumless cities," failed to materialize. In much the same way that the Baltimore Plan had played a role in undermining a federal commitment to public housing, so Enterprise helped ease the destruction of subsidized housing programs and welfare.

Rouse's vision of poor neighborhoods had significantly sharpened by the 1980s. For the first time, his religious ideals merged with his faith in private enterprise. Rouse remembered in a 1979 speech entitled "Utopia: Limited or Unlimited" that during the late 1960s in a course in Christian doctrine at the Church of the Savior in Washington, D.C., taught by Gordon Cosby, "we studied a book that had a very profound impact on my life and work . . . Paul Jones' *Recovery of Life's Meaning.*" Jones's most important message, according to Rouse, was that "creation is not—was not—a single act but a continuing process, and that man—each of us—is God's instrument for carrying that process forward." Humans should not, then, take a fatalistic approach to life on earth, but should become "co-creators with God in this continuing process: co-creators in what happens to the natural environment, what happens to the institutions we create." These inspiring religious ideals demanded that true Christians "raise up the vision of the beauty,

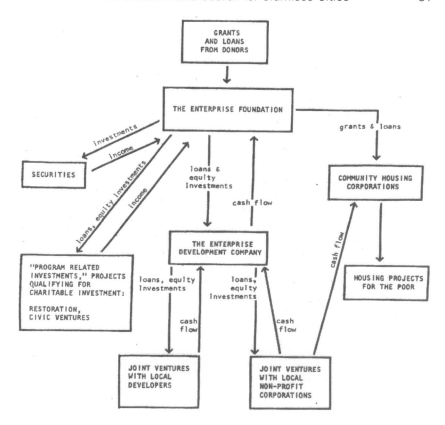

Figure 14. The idealistic template for Rouse's national private sector social welfare system only partially realized at the Enterprise Foundation. Rouse Papers, Columbia Archive.

the well-being, the community of people, the creative support of one another, the brotherhood, the functioning of love that might be God's city." Idealism aside, Rouse acknowledged that these ideals were still distant: "Nor is it difficult to discern our performance as co-creators when we observe the ugliness and the poverty and the crime and the violence and the suffocation of the human spirit, the hopelessness that pervades much of the inner city."[88]

Through his involvement with Church of the Savior he was introduced to community leaders in Washington in the early 1970s. Although at first skeptical of the community development process, he quickly joined in the effort, particularly after leaders gained control of two older apartment buildings, in such bad shape that Rouse admitted on his first visit, "the stench was so bad I couldn't have gone beyond the lobby." The women, however, "had a vision that they could make these buildings fit and livable," and

Rouse "helped them to buy the buildings, which they bought very cheap." Using nearly fifty thousand hours of volunteer labor, the buildings became "decent places to live." This became the start of Jubilee Housing that expanded into social service projects, including job placement, health clinics, and a homeless shelter. This experience inspired Rouse to create "a whole new system in America of working from the bottom up, through neighborhood people, into restoring life into the very poor neighborhoods of the country, and we set a goal to make all housing for the very poor in this country fit and livable within a generation."[89]

The Enterprise Foundation became the umbrella organization for Rouse's private sector social welfare system. Rouse originally intended to create a for-profit development corporation that would plow its profits back into a nonprofit wing that would build affordable, low-cost housing in partnerships with community development corporations and local foundations. Dartington Hall Trust in Britain, where subcontracting businesses run by local farmers generated income for cultural institutions, provided the initial model.[90] The Enterprise Development Company, run by Rouse and Martin Millspaugh, became "a for-profit commercial real estate development company based in Columbia, Maryland, specializing in the development and management of quality urban centers."[91]

Although more active during the 1980s, and still offering consulting services on development and property management around the world, the development company never yielded the massive profits for reinvestment because of a rare financial miscalculation on Rouse's part. Applying the festival marketplace concept (described in chapter 5) to smaller and poorer market areas led to now famous flops in Toledo, Flint, Battle Creek, and Richmond. Two projects still prosper in Norfolk, Virginia (Waterside), and Baltimore (Brown's Arcade, a small redeveloped shopping area near Charles Center). The high-profile failures have come in for criticism, particularly Flint, because of the market's near comic role in the ham-handed city management portrayed in Michael Moore's humorous documentary, *Roger and Me* (1989). City officials made the mistake of opening the marketplace at the very moment General Motors was laying off tens of thousands of workers. Subsidy of the marketplace by city government looked heartless in light of the many hardships so many faced during that time. Rouse admitted in 1990 that the development company "has not yet paid dividends into the foundation."[92]

The majority of funding for the Enterprise Foundation actually came from major national corporations and individuals, including AT&T, Atlantic Richfield, the Mott Foundation, ALCOA Foundation, the Rockefeller Foundation, Ford, and Richard Mellon (both David Rockefeller and Mellon had been participants in the ACTION activities). Money raised from these sources—and

Rouse was a tireless and winning fund-raiser—was used to leverage further investment capital to be distributed to community development corporations. During the early years the board of the Foundation lent a great deal of prestige to the effort and included Gordon Cosby (spiritual mentor to Rouse), Andrew Heiskell (longtime supporter of ACTION), Patricia Harris (Secretary of HUD under Jimmy Carter), Robert McNamara (then a former president of the World Bank), Senator Charles "Mac" Mathias of Maryland, and retired liberal Congressman Henry Reuss.

The social investment dimension of the business suited Rouse best. The Enterprise Social Investment Corporation developed "new sources of capital for low-income housing and administers The Enterprise Loan Fund, Inc."[93] By 1989 Rouse reported, "The Enterprise Foundation has raised $45 million from the private sector, is working with 100 nonprofit neighborhood groups in 27 cities and the State of Maine. Through its network of local nonprofit, grassroots groups, 8,500 units of decent housing for very poor people are being provided and 13,000 hard-to-employ people have been placed in jobs through 18 job placement centers."[94] Rouse created relationships among different groups concerned about housing and had great success in New York: "We have had much help from the state, the city, private investors, and over 20 nonprofit neighborhood development corporations in rehabilitating 2,000 dilapidated apartments into fine dwellings" in the South Bronx, the Lower East Side, Harlem, and the Williamsburg area of Brooklyn.[95] Mayor Koch's commitment of five billion dollars in city funds during the 1980s made New York's program the most successful in the nation.

Enterprise was also devoted to discovering ways to make renovation cheaper so that more housing could be renovated: "To cut housing rehabilitation costs, Enterprise formed the Rehabilitation Work Group, a panel of experts in every aspect of housing rehabilitation, which works with the neighborhood groups to systematically review rehabilitation budgets for our network organizations. A reduction of rehabilitation costs of 20–40 percent has been achieved in most cities."[96] Enterprise programs are now larger; over 120,000 houses have been built in partnership with Enterprise, and 3.9 billion dollars of financing (as of 2002) have been arranged over these two decades of efforts.

Enterprise has played a central role in the community development corporation (CDC) movement of the 1980s and 1990s (with organization such as LISC, the Local Initiative Support Corporation). The timing could not have been better for launching Enterprise not only because of new attention to the problems with social welfare abroad and at home, and the growing interest and organization level of Community Development Corporations (CDCs), but also because the Reagan administration successfully destroyed housing programs still in existence during the early 1980s; the general groundswell of antistatism paralleled closely Rouse's own ideas about the virtues of small government and private action. By 1988 the pattern of cuts had become clear: "Since The Enterprise Foundation was launched in 1982, federal housing assistance has decreased by over 75 percent, from $33 billion [primarily Section 8] to less than $8 billion today."[97]

In private, Rouse was critical of the Reagan administration. Numerous letters and even some speeches to select audiences reflect his distaste for the Reagan, and later Bush, administrations. As Reagan was such an outspoken Cold Warrior, this criticism may appear to be contradictory, but Rouse remained an old school conservative with a genuine concern for fiscal restraint. He also was an antimilitarist who had opposed the Vietnam War openly during the early 1970s and did not believe in military adventures to advance American interests abroad; he believed that the Cold War had to be won on the fields of social policy. Rouse, for instance, attacked the Nixon administration in 1970 by arguing that resources devoted to the Vietnam War would be better spent on "improvement of the environment and the advancement of health and education throughout the world." Although Rouse might have been expected to support the tax cuts and budget trimming pursued by Ronald Reagan during the 1980s, he grew increasingly upset with the swelling defense budget that kept federal spending high and thus created mammoth budget deficits.[98] Referring to Reagan budget deficits, he remarked, "If this had been a Democratic president he would be run out of the country by now . . . This actor in the White House has been able to make the country believe the unbelievable and to look like a conservative president while engaging in the most radical budget/financial methods the country has ever seen."[99] In a fund-raising letter for Allen Cranston he blasted "The fruitlessness and danger of the bellicose, provocative posture of this Administration."[100] In 1988 he accused the Republicans of being conservatives in name alone: "There seems to be a protective blindness by which a pumped-up, debt-driven economy allows those who have [money], to avoid facing where we are headed and to enjoy the reckless indulgence of an undisciplined Administration that operates under the ridiculous banner of being 'conservative.' In fact, they have been the most reckless spenders in our history."[101]

This titanic shift of the 1980s was not all bad. In 1985 he admitted, "I have not been sympathetic to this administration's elimination of support for housing at the local level, and it has virtually been eliminated. Almost nothing anymore." Rouse, however, saw opportunity in Reagan's policies, and in speech after speech he argued that cuts in federal money presented opportunities for more creative action:

But the fact is that the vacuum that has [been] created has energized initiative and creativity and resourcefulness that wasn't happening before.
We had become dependent, so dependent on federal grants, federal programs, that it was the government's job. And we've all said it was the government's job. And then all of a sudden we turned around and said, "Get
the government off our backs." And now the government's off our backs.
And now whose back is it on, except those of us who have wealth and
power in the country. . . . The private sector needed to step up to the
plate. It just takes the resourcefulness of a businessman and business
money to be out there working on this to change this country right from
its base on up.[102]

Budget slashing by conservatives, then, allowed the end of dependency and
a renewed sense of social justice among businessmen. This was Rouse at
his most Panglossian.

As in his earlier projects, Rouse did not reject federal largess, just federal direction of programs. Money that potentially supported his locally based
projects—tax credits and grants most notably—remained acceptable:
"This should not mislead anybody to thinking that this whole housing problem can be solved without money from the federal government and lots of
money. It's got to come, it should come . . . but it shouldn't come in big
programs defined by the federal government and laid down as projects on
a city. It ought to come as cash, and it ought to come as cash that will stimulate and encourage and support these kinds of initiatives at the local level."[103]
In particular, Rouse wanted federal funds to "reduce the cost of money, and
develop new ways of producing, financing and owning housing."[104] In 1985
Rouse successfully defended tax breaks before Congress that allowed him
and others in the nonprofit field to arrange money: "The Enterprise
Foundation has stimulated corporate and other private sector participation
in nonprofit housing rehabilitation in distressed neighborhoods at the heart
of our cities through the use of existing tax incentives for low-income housing." "Without the availability or use of the tax incentives," he warned,
"providing approximately 20–25 percent of the financing costs, these reha-
bilitations could not be done to meet the needs of the poor . . . The use of
tax incentives provides the 'equity money' . . . that leverages the other private sector resources."[105] Rouse understandably sought low-cost versions of
the FHA system of middle-class mortgage insurance.

Rouse's support for tax incentives notwithstanding, in letter after letter
and speech after speech he became one of the leading proponents of an
enhanced role for business executives in finding new ways of improving
society, particularly poor neighborhoods. In a letter to an insurance executive he lamented the chronic addiction some had formed to government

money: "we have become too dependent on government—not just the poor and the cities, but our whole society including, particularly, the American business corporation. . . . If the American business corporation will begin to feel responsibility for the cities in which we all live, work and do business, we can contribute more than money and individual civic leadership. We can create with local government and voluntary agencies new processes, new systems, new structures for dealing with human needs and public issues."[106] The Reagan administration, demanded Rouse, had to promote this sense of social responsibility. "But I wish that somehow the White House would make clear to business the need for a new state of mind regarding our cities and human needs which will not be supported in the future, as in the past, with Federal funds."[107] Rouse overestimated the numbers of businessmen interested in "human needs" in cities.

Like many people at the time, Rouse developed a story to explain the end of social welfare in America. Because any direct social spending from the federal level was suspect, he tended to see any federally designed social welfare activity as essentially too much. The comparatively small American welfare state of the postwar period inflated in Rouse's story to a scale comparable to its European counterparts. Referring to the poor and homeless: "'It is their own fault' is a valid charge in far too many cases. There is too much idleness, too much welfare, too much violence. It costs us, literally, billions of dollars each year to pay for these conditions. At a recent meeting I attended with President Bush at the table, a member of the White House staff estimated that cost at 750 billion a year. Think of that burden on our country."[108] How this official arrived at these numbers, and exactly what he counted as costs, is unclear, but what is crystal clear is that Rouse was ready to inflate the cost of the welfare state to his audiences.

Rouse's treatment of an article by Robert Kuttner in his files, entitled "The Erosion of the Welfare State," affirmed his view of big government history while avoiding the writer's largely positive assessment of the welfare state in Western Europe. Rouse underlined phrases such as "the welfare state is a kind of sand castle. As the benefits are piled higher, it continuously erodes" and "a basic family allowance which gives everybody a thousand dollars per child is expensive for society, but fails to eliminate poverty." This criticism of social welfare directed at Europe he applied in speeches when referring to the problems of so-called big government programs in America. In fact, Kuttner argued just as forcefully in the same article that universal health and social welfare systems had many benefits, but Rouse did not underline a statement such as: "To fiscal engineers, the word entitlement has become a term of opprobrium. Yet a tour of Europe's welfare state cannot fail to leave an American visitor impressed with the simple humanity of common programs that provide health care, retirement benefits, homemaker assistance, family allowances and other basic needs as rights of citizenship."[109]

Rouse's criticism of an American social welfare system, paired to that of Reagan and Bush, has come to be the standard version of the cycles of government in America, but was always as much imaginative as real. American social spending did increase during the 1960s and 1970s, according to the Ford Foundation, jumping from 12 percent of the Gross National Product in 1965 to 20 percent in 1980, and changing from 30 to 54 percent of all government spending.[110] These figures are misleading when discussing social welfare, however. The majority of social spending was devoted to paying benefits collected through contributory retirement insurance (46 percent in 1980 as opposed to 21 percent in 1965) and senior medical benefits (health and medical spending increased from 13 percent to 21 percent primarily for Medicare in this same period), whereas "the increase for public assistance was from 10.6 percent to 14.7 percent." The largest forms of social welfare spending in America, then, benefited "citizens with incomes well above those of the 'deserving poor.'"[111]

Rouse had decided that America had developed a large welfare state during the New Deal and the Great Society even though conservative forces had spent the recent decades making sure that America retained comparatively low social spending targeted at the poor. Repeating his critique over and over again in front of the leading audiences of the United States and in major publications nevertheless made his version authoritative: "The people of the country have said whether we like it or not and whether we believe we should have it or not, the people of the United States have said they are tired of big, expensive, inefficient bureaucratic government and we think there has got to be some better way."[112] Repeated enough times, it started to seem true.

The problems of public housing contributed ammunition to the private sector approach. Rouse had softened his position on public housing over the years, but he still saw public housing in America as part of dangerous big government programs. In testimony to Congress in 1968, he explained his rather complex position on public housing: "I guess the first time I ever appeared before this Committee was 20 years ago opposing the Wagner-Ellender-Taft Bill, and I think the main reason for my then opposition to it was in opposition to public housing. And my opposition to public housing then was based not on the fact that there was no need for public housing, but that the need for it was being incorrectly stated, that it was incorrectly stated as the solution to the problem of the slums." Rouse preferred the alternative Baltimore approach to urban reform that depended upon civic action and municipal power rather than massive state spending. He disliked particularly that "there was a practice in America for a long time of parading before a Committee such as this the statistical horror of the slums and then presenting public housing as the only solution."[113] To what long period of time Rouse was referring in 1968 is unclear. Public housing appeared only in small amounts in the 1930s and was equally devoted to making "work" as social justice. The Housing Acts of 1949 and 1954 also generated modest programs.

The general scale of public housing programs, Section 8, the Model Cities program, and other forms of subsidy to cities had clearly been inflated in Rouse's mind by the 1980s, as reflected in the following statement from 1983: "Compassionate concern for troubled cities and troubled people in those cities has led to a succession of big Federal programs which, although well intended, have had the cumulative effect of increasing dependence." Although he offered legitimate criticisms, including high building costs for public housing and questionable income limits, he overlooked the ways in which public housing in most cities had become part of what historian Arnold Hirsch has called "second ghettos" for warehousing and sealing off poor minority residents of the city displaced by the redevelopment that Rouse supported. Rouse argued, questionably, that the housing projects themselves almost entirely generated the primary problems of the urban poor: "Public housing, too often, has produced huge ghettos which separated the poor from the mainstream of life; generated drugs, violence, vandalism, fear—highlighted by the necessity of demolishing two huge projects." Ironically, and in contrast to Rouse's environmental determinism, most of the projects of the Enterprise Foundation would focus on equally rundown neighborhoods of which public housing was not a major part.[114]

As one might imagine, Cold War ideology paralleled this critique of the social welfare state. Cutting government programs would test the free enterprise system's capacity to create forms of social welfare, as in this 1982 statement to urban leaders: "We really have the test, to demonstrate that a free enterprise business system in a democratic society can invent the processes, the structures, the systems, the solutions, for all of the people in this country and if we don't do it, who does?"[115] One might ask if the private sector really has to create, or has the desire to generate, all the solutions for the people in this country. The *Wall Street Journal* in 1983 explained, "Mr. Rouse says the foundation stems, in part, from his belief that the United States has fallen behind the Soviet Union in meeting the 'human needs' of its poorest citizens. 'The free enterprise system—our system—just doesn't do it at all . . . But it can."[116] Against mounting evidence of social breakdown in the Soviet Union, Rouse still seemed to be convinced that the communists, for all their failings, had devoted a great deal more national effort to solving the problems of its poorest urban citizens. And he was not wrong, even then; the communists probably bankrupted themselves on these efforts. His optimism that businessmen could outfox the communists on social policy nevertheless proved overly idealistic.

The conviction that American corporate leaders like himself could create more successful social policy than communists became a recurrent theme in his speeches and interviews from this period: "We are the wealthiest country in the world with the greatest problem-solving capacity in the history of man with tremendous management capacity and unequalled leadership. It is our opportunity—our responsibility—to put that capacity, creativity and energy to work—to invent new answers, create new systems, new structures—to deal with deep human needs."[117] These statements reflected a remarkable extension of the notion of business expertise. The hubris that led communists to create factories similarly fired Rouse's hopes for business-inspired urban social welfare. The same year, 1985, he warned businesspeople of the dangers of ignoring their social responsibilities in antisocialist terms: "We are cultivating a growing Third World subculture of disaffected, untrained, jobless people—fertile soil for radical leaders who neither understand nor support American values."[118] In an era when many had stopped treating the socialist threat seriously from a social perspective, Rouse still remained fearful of the attractiveness of left-wing ideals.

The final link in this ideological edifice, including both a critique of the social welfare state and Cold War rhetoric, was utopian rhetoric he matched to his efforts. Through the Foundation, Rouse did not propose to improve *some* housing or clean up *a few* neighborhoods; instead, he was intent on creating a parallel system of social welfare run on a business model that would remove *all* the slums in America. At a time of massive cutbacks in federal social spending, the thought that the private sector as a whole had a concern for social welfare, and would actually transform whole cities, was attractive. In numerous speeches and letters during the 1980s, Rouse promised that this was no ordinary endeavor. In Chattanooga the Foundation aimed to "make all housing for the poor in Chattanooga fit and livable within ten years. It's absolutely doable, and it's doable in every city in America."[119]

During the 1980s Enterprise was "developing new systems for helping poor people help themselves move up out of poverty and dependence into fit and affordable housing and self-sufficiency. Our purpose is not to work at the problem, but to solve it—to see that all poor people in this country have decent, affordable housing within a generation."[120] To billionaire Warren Buffet he bragged, "perhaps of greater importance is the increasing demonstration that we are, in fact, building a new national housing system for dealing with the problems of housing the very poor and helping them lift themselves out of poverty into the mainstream."[121] In 1989 Rouse planned "to go into 230 cities in the next three to five years. We will use success in one city as a demonstration to others. We will build a true national campaign to house the poor and homeless."[122] Also in 1989, he promised that this "is truly a new system for working with the poor—to make their housing livable and to help lift them from dependence to the capacity to cope in our society. It is not a big, top-down Federal program but works from the bottom-up with neighborhood groups using their ingenuity, energy, and diversity to create a new kind of national program with hopes of housing 200,000 families a year and moving tens of thousands of families out of poverty to self-sufficiency and independence."[123] These are just a few examples from numerous speeches and letters. Although he slowly distanced himself from some of the more grandiose claims, by the 1990s he had already made quite a stir with his splashy utopian rhetoric.

In practical terms, Rouse proved quite useful to both Presidents Reagan and Bush. His many speeches helped legitimate conservative policy changes. During the Reagan and Bush administrations Rouse served on a number of task forces designed to reassess government policy. It is fair to say that these task forces aimed in part to legitimize cuts in social welfare. Rouse likely would not have argued with this assessment. In 1982 he announced to Congress that the "The President's Task Force can be extremely useful in saying to business that if you want to get the Government off your backs you'd better put your backs out to some of these problems."[124] That social welfare had become business's new responsibility likewise signaled the government to take a backseat in social programs.

The most important leadership role Rouse played in national policy came in 1987–88, when he led the National Housing Task Force, a nonpartisan, privately funded effort to reexamine housing policy. Participants included representatives from business, banking, state government, and education. In testimony to Congress Rouse made a familiar pitch, stressing the localism that guided much of his career: "The Task Force also believes that government closest to the people is best situated to identify and respond to the varying conditions and needs of local housing markets." The task force laid the groundwork for Hope VI, the national program to replace the most distressed public housing with mixed-income developments: "The Task Force was deeply concerned about the nation's most valuable low-income housing resource—public housing—and made a series of substantive recommendations regarding the need for modernization, resident involvement, and special help in remedying the most seriously troubled projects. . . . The call for a National Commission on Severely Distressed Public Housing to develop a national action plan to eliminate unfit living conditions in severely distressed projects is a good step." The National Affordable Housing Act (1990) followed from the recommendations of the task force, including modest provisions for affordable homeownership, rentals, low-income public housing, rural housing, and special needs.[125]

Democratic Senator Donald Riegle of Michigan described Rouse's impact on the legislation that emerged: "as Chairman of the National Housing Task Force, Mr. Rouse established the foundation for the National Affordable Housing Act. This Act marked a bold new direction in Federal housing policy and will enable states, local government and nonprofit organizations to provide affordable housing in a manner that is best tailored to the needs of low income people for many years to come."[126] The Act, although well-meaning and admirably designed to make the most of very little funds, provided only three billion dollars over twelve years and encouraged matching funds from private and state sources, federal/state partnerships, and aid to community development corporations—in other words, it was a very conservative bill. A 1988 *Journal of Commerce* editorial by Professor David Schwartz of Rutgers University made the case for the bill: "Overall, the new housing policy that seems to be emerging is pro-business, efficient and cost effective. It deserves consideration and support from the U.S. business community and from the public."[127]

Rouse became friendly with conservative Secretary of Housing and Urban Development, Jack Kemp, during this period. In a letter to Kemp in 1989, Rouse praised him, saying, "You have diverted the river and the Augean stables are being cleaned." Rouse further wrote, "Your leadership, energy and compassion are turning HUD into the kind of agency it ought to be. It is rightfully time to turn to energizing the private sector in combination with new HUD initiatives."[128] At an Enterprise meeting in Washington, "Kemp invoked the memory of Martin Luther King and declared 'I believe we are forging a common and bipartisan agenda for waging a new and successful war on poverty.'" Kemp must never have spent much time looking at King's radical speeches on poverty. Rouse nevertheless singled out Kemp for commendation: "Almost alone among 'movement' conservatives, Kemp has shown genuine concern for the deteriorating condition of the nation's inner cities and for families caught in the housing squeeze."[129] Referring to changes at HUD, *Business Week* illustrated the synergy of Rouse and Kemp: "The great new hope is public-private partnerships, an incantation that HUD Secretary Jack F. Kemp and legislators increasingly hope will cause shiny new housing to materialize in their swamp of slums and red ink. Washington provides a dollop of seed money, and the private sector and local governments leverage it to finance housing for the poor."[130]

Rouse's close work with the Kemp administration could occasionally frustrate his liberal allies. Michael Seipp, a local developer and housing advocate working with Enterprise, wrote to Rouse after talking to Senator Barbara Mikulski: "She raised some concerns she had about our national role." Mikulski "is becoming increasingly irritated at Mr. Kemp's position on housing and the information he or his staff is providing her

committee. . . . Although she understands the needs of the Enterprise Foundation
to raise money and maintain a working relationship with HUD, she has
a feeling that the Foundation is becoming too closely aligned with the Kemp
administration."[131] Rouse was far too pragmatic to limit himself to one party,
and he was certainly sympathetic to the direction of Bush housing policy.

Rouse, equally appealing to both political parties, remained powerful during the moderate Clinton administration. According to Henry Cisneros, conversations he had with Rouse on "front stoops of homes in cities such as
Chattanooga and Baltimore" led to Rouse speaking with President-elect Clinton
at the Little Rock Economic Summit in December of 1992. Cisneros
remembered that Rouse "told the President-elect that I should be Secretary
of HUD. From his lips to the President's ears." Cisneros admitted that at
HUD, "I saw Jim's street-level, people-centered view of the nation's inner-
city problems."[132] Hope VI goals—the enduring monument of Clinton-era
housing policy—of replacing distressed public housing with a mix of market and subsidized units, in smaller-scale contextual communities, illustrates
in part the influence of Enterprise on national practices. Community
development corporations, many partnered with Enterprise, grew in scale,
but no significant new housing programs flowed from the federal government during the 1990s (and welfare reform at the national and state levels
further cut social spending). Anna Borgman in the *Washington Post* in 1996
nicely summarized the Clinton-era approach to urban neighborhoods:
"Gradually, a new urban thinking is beginning to emerge that argues
against employing altruism as the primary tool to fix our slums. Better, these
innovators say, to focus on pure self-interest, on economics."[133] Rouse could
not have said it better himself.

Pilot Program Redux/Sandtown

It is our purpose, in at least three neighborhoods, in three different cities,
to make all housing fit and affordable; to uplift the neighborhood environment with attention to sidewalks, curbs, alleys, street trees, street lights,
little parks, and other conditions which would make the neighborhood
an attractive place to live.

James Rouse

The most impressive demonstration of Enterprise's ability to transform
urban neighborhoods represented a bittersweet homecoming for Rouse. Returning
to Baltimore's impoverished urban neighborhoods, where once he had quit
in frustration yet gained so much national attention, he set out to create a
version of the Pilot Program that could dramatically transform urban neighborhoods. Rouse had made efforts in Chattanooga to make it the "the Columbia

Figure 15. James Rouse in the Sandtown neighborhood of Baltimore. Rouse, during the 1980s and 1990s, was one of the few businessmen in Ameica who invested not only his money but also his time and energy into urban revitalization. The Sandtown project has demonstrated that massive spending by both foundations and the state has the ability to improve conditions in the most distressed urban neighborhoods, but the project has more commonly been celebrated as a leading demonstration of private-sector prowess in urban social welfare. Patrick Sandor, *The Baltimore Sun.*

of housing the poor," but had failed to generate much attention for his efforts. And although Enterprise played an important role in the much watched community development corporation movement in the Bronx, that effort was overshadowed by Mayor Ed Koch's massive investment in the borough during the 1980s.

It was in a neighborhood on Baltimore's west side, known as Sandtown-Winchester, that Rouse focused the resources of the foundation and government. Sandtown's close proximity to Enterprise headquarters in Columbia, and Rouse's local power base, helped generate local attention and resources. Here, at long last, would be demonstrated the ability of the private sector, in partnership with the city and other nonprofits, to revolutionize life in the American city. Rouse, who devoted enormous personal time to the project, came closest to achieving a vision of private sector social democracy at Sandtown, but he died before the effort would bear significant fruit.[134]

Rouse chose a particularly down-at-the-heels area. He reported in a letter in 1990: "Planning is underway in our first Demonstration Neighborhood, Sandtown-Winchester, Baltimore—population 12,000; average annual family income $6,900; 44% of men jobless; over 90% of families are single parent households; neighborhood ranks among top 5, among 34 in the city, in violent crime."[135] Here was one of the most chilling examples of the failure of American urban welfare and housing policy. Rouse needed to show that this type of neighborhood was not beyond the capacities of the private sector.

Although hatched at Enterprise, Rouse aimed to generate maximum neighborhood involvement. In a series of meetings residents and local activists created ambitious plans, "laying out what they wanted in Sandtown in the areas of housing, education, public safety, employment, health care and more." Over a five-year period they hoped "to cut the unemployment rate in half, to 11 percent, to make sure 95 percent of Sandtown youth meet state education standards; to build or improve 3,000 units of housing, to reduce crime to the level of a middle-class neighborhood." Rouse stood strongly behind these idealistic plans, "but post-planning letdown set in when residents realized how little funding was available to implement their lofty vision." Ralph Smith, of the Annie E. Casey Foundation, explained that "Jim's vision was bold and compelling but its one flaw was that he wanted to privatize everything, get programs out of the hands of the bureaucracy, but he couldn't. . . . Gradually he grew to see he needed to be more supportive of meaningful public participation and working through bureaucracy."[136]

Rouse did adjust and Enterprise worked closely with neighborhood and city officials. Mayor Kurt Schmoke devoted considerable city resources to aiding the effort, in time earning criticism for putting too much effort into the Sandtown project. Mayoral support came as a surprise to Rouse, who recounted a meeting with the mayor: "He has been reserved, cautious, interested but very uncommitted. This time I let him speak first. He came out firing. 'I am absolutely committed to this.' 'This will be the most important project in Baltimore.' . . . All special grants will be focused on Sandtown . . . He has enlarged the neighborhood, estimates 30,000 people +."[137] Physical rehabilitation of housing would be closely paired with social service improvements, many of them faith-based, to transform "the lives of the people along with the housing in the neighborhood."[138]

Over time some notable successes have been registered at Sandtown. Approximately one thousand homes have been renovated or constructed. Programs in job training, health care, mental health, public safety, playgrounds, and education have attained measurable improvements. The area is cleaner and better managed. HUD, Habitat for Humanity, the Annenberg Foundation, Baltimore City, B.U.I.L.D. (a faith-based multidenominational ecumenical organization), and Enterprise have funded and led this diverse mix of activities and raised $100 million for over a decade of activities.[139] Serious problems nevertheless persist in the neighborhood: "While hundreds of these homes have been fixed up and sold over the past few years, many other homes in the community have become vacant, with the pace of degradation exceeding that of rehabilitation." Many residents have simply moved from an older house in the area to a renovated or new one, leaving the older house to decline and creating no significant increase in local population (approximately eight hundred homes are vacant). Other neighborhoods have become "resentful over the amount of city funds that were earmarked for Sandtown-Winchester."[140]

Against great odds, Enterprise and its partners are trying to create an island of private sector social democracy in an impoverished city, without similar governmental and private resources for surrounding areas. As laudable as their efforts are, it is difficult to imagine how a neighborhood demonstration project can become a successful piece of utopia with transient and impoverished populations, lack of access to good jobs, and surrounding neighborhoods lacking equivalent social investment. One hundred million dollars for every distressed neighborhood in America would make an enormous difference, but such spending dwarfs the resources of private foundations, local governments, and existing federal programs. Leading housing analyst Peter Dreier explains, for instance, that CDCs "cannot produce even close to an adequate supply of housing for the poor primarily because of the lack of subsidies to fill the gap between what it costs to develop housing and what the poor can afford to pay." In spite of all the publicity generated by CDC activities during the 1990s "the nation's CDC sector has produced only 30,000 to 40,000 housing units a year. . . . Too few public resources are available to CDCs."[141] Rouse, always optimistic, believed that these resources would somehow materialize, but in an era of tightening public budgets and great competition for foundation dollars, such hopes have not been achieved.

The appeal of Sandtown to the right wing is nevertheless obvious. In a 1996 column George Will wrote that Sandtown at first glance gives "the impression that all commercial and social energies have congealed like oil in the crankcase of a jalopy: Ignition will be impossible." Will surprised his readers by arguing that such an "impression is wrong. There is a quickening of community life because Jim Rouse willed it. He knows a thing or two about urban resuscitations." While acknowledging the serious problems in the neighborhood, Will was impressed with what he considered to be a renewed Jeffersonian sense of participation: "Here scarcities of material resources and deficits of social skills are so severe that federal, state and city governments toil to empower people to participate in their own improvement. However, the high rate of participation may be what Jefferson had in mind as democracy. Residents are a majority of the board of Community Building in Partnership; 100 block captains, some with walkie-talkies, supplement police patrols." Will ended on a particularly sanguine note: "If freedom is more than freedom from restraints imposed by others, if freedom is a consequence of self-government, if freedom is active engagement in the affairs of a community controlling its fate, then the energized residents are free in a way that most Americans, who in most ways are more fortunately situated, are not. . . . Call them citizens of the Republic of Sandtown-Winchester."[142] Marginalization and abject poverty, in this rosy view, lack only a catalyst to reorganization. With more tact, Rouse would certainly second these sentiments.

⁕

At key moments in postwar urban policy Rouse could be found making a powerful case for private sector social welfare policy. Not only was Rouse often directly involved in national policy, but he also used the power of mass culture to maximize his impact. In contrast to the expediency of center city redevelopment, business-led social welfare was far more weighted toward propaganda than concrete action. Urban housing conditions have not changed much after fifty years of business-friendly policies, notwithstanding the few bright spots created by Enterprise and CDCs, and in many cities conditions have likely declined. Many problems of traditional urban neighborhoods are being identified in older "inner ring" suburbs as they undergo social change. Rouse's hoped-for imitators in cities across the country have not materialized.

Even in the face of these wretched and dangerous conditions, with no equal in the industrialized world, and certainly more embarrassing in light of national wealth, the antistatist outlook steered the nation around the dangerous shoals of social welfare expansion. The deficiencies of socialist urban policy have been well documented, especially after the dramatic implosion of the USSR in 1989, but urban policy of the businessman's utopia still awaits a fuller critique. Excessive idealism, after all, affected urban policy on both sides of the Atlantic.

CHAPTER 4

Public Life as Consumerism: Businessmen Monopolize Main Street

It's clear that we have built in America a business, a major new American business that's equipped with [the] knowledge, experience, organization, and techniques to build the new Main Streets of America and that's just what we're doing.

James Rouse

The regional mall is a very good place to shop. And we built a lot of them. We own a lot of them—55, as a matter of fact. But that is a very special purpose. It doesn't create community among people, in the sense that the center of the city can.

James Rouse, "Planning the City"

He was one of the chief architects of post–World War II America, helping GIs and other new residents of the suburbs transform the look of neighborhoods, and redefine Main Street as the enclosed shopping mall, with its fountains and food courts.

"A Model Builder," *Philadelphia Inquirer*

Like many American businessmen, Rouse frequently confused consumer choice and fundamental democratic processes. In 1976 he made one of the business community's most powerful statements of the importance of consumer democracy: "The merchants of America man the polling places where people cast their votes every minute of every day and where the fantastic communication system that operates over the counter stimulates response to the votes of the people." This constant contact with consumer choice, said Rouse, made merchants "more open, more liberal, more concerned, more responsive to the arts and to the private institutions for human services. It is the merchants who are the leaders of democracy in this country."[1]

This was quite a statement, and difficult to square with the reactionary politics of chambers of commerce across America, but in its general sentiment

107

such an idea was hardly unique to Rouse. His belief in consumerism as the bulwark of democracy, shared by leading businessmen, shaped Cold War–era public opinion. "*Life* [magazine] often equated democracy with consumption," says Wendy Kozol, "arguing that the right to choose which good to buy signified American freedom."[2] This daring philosophy found its most succinct expression at the famous 1959 Nixon-Khrushchev Kitchen Debate at the American Exhibition in Moscow. While the Soviets featured their industrial and scientific might, cultural achievements, and new towns in their displays, Americans displayed their smooth consumer democracy. Karal Ann Marling believes that "the American kitchens in Moscow . . . provided a working demonstration of a culture that defined freedom as the capacity to change and to choose and dramatized its choices in the pink-with-pushbuttons aesthetic of everyday living."[3] Consumer choice has been an important aspect of American society, but the concept of consumerism as a democratic practice swelled uncomfortably during the Cold War.

Shopping malls, of which Rouse was a leading pioneer, could not be shipped to Moscow, but they were the domestic arenas in which "free enterprise" ideology found its purist realization. Consumerism and business interests now crafted public life and public space for massive new suburban regions. Privatization of public life in America had rarely been envisaged, much less carried out, on such a scale. In America's central cities (and most older suburbs), dramatic swings in land use patterns and economic cycles had mixed with changing fashions in retail, religion, and public patronage to create complex urban places of which commerce was only one part. This process of incremental growth created layers of public and private uses that made for urban places with great strengths and equally complex problems: "The traditional central business district was an unpredictable and unexpected amalgam of old and new buildings, parks, strange characters, public spectacles, high- and low-end shopping, and locally owned stores."[4]

This layering came under attack during the great postwar suburban boom. Not only were new suburban places strictly zoned into distinct areas of housing, office parks, and shopping strips, but also downtowns and many small towns were quite ruthlessly simplified to fit new expectations of the urban environment. Complexity, bringing with it urban fear and parking headaches, came under fire during the postwar period. The public demanded new standards of security, design, and management; Rouse, among others, was there to provide this new model.

Central gathering spaces were sorely needed in the new suburbs, but their genesis was unclear. Would old main streets and towns in the vicinity of new subdivisions grow to meet the needs of new suburbanites? Would developers create new public spaces as part of every residential development as had occurred at famous planned suburbs like Forest Hills (New

York) and Country Club District (Kansas City)? Would suburban town centers, combining civic and commercial functions in an intimate blend, as pioneered in Britain and other European new towns, be adopted for the United States?

The regional shopping mall that emerged as the leading force in new suburban districts was an unexpected answer to the problems of new suburbs, but it was in step with changing ideals of public life from the period. Antistatist ideology dominated 1950s suburban politics and was coupled to an increasing focus on professionalism in government (as contrasted with urban patronage). In 1959 Robert Wood found that "function by function, more and more public activities in suburbia are called administrative and professional." Mall developers, professional themselves, delivered a new main street overnight, centralized management made malls shine in ways old main streets never could, and booming towns found themselves with impressive main streets without government spending. Already taxed by new developments and rising expectations in services from newcomers, local governments willingly turned main street development over to businessmen.[5]

As in other areas of his career, Rouse first experimented with what would become a national phenomenon close to home. At first the Moss-Rouse Company financed a number of conventional strip shopping centers, taking advantage of the booming automobile suburbs. Mondawmin, an old and grand estate within the Baltimore city limits, owned by the wealthy Alexander Brown family, became available in 1949. A large mall was not an immediate answer to the property's development, as none existed in the area at the time. The lack of a local example did not intimidate Moss and Rouse, who, "using market research, traffic analysis and eye-catching graphic displays, proposed the then untried concept of a large mall with a department store anchor. They got a ten percent share for putting the deal together and handling tenants." The mall was slow to launch and not enclosed: "After six years of planning, construction began in 1955. In the last stages, the developers lost their nerve and dropped the idea of enclosing the mall. But for its day, Mondawmin broke new ground, a two story mall with acres of parking—the biggest commercial project in Baltimore's history." In 1958 Rouse opened Harundale Mall in Anne Arundel County, "the nation's second enclosed mall by two months."[6]

Rouse boasted that "Harundale Mall is more important than Southdale (the only other enclosed mall center) because it was done by a developer not by a department store as an institutional venture."[7] The Cherry Hill Mall, located in New Jersey in 1961 not far from Philadelphia, was Rouse's first regional-scale enclosed mall and brought him national attention for the first time as a mall developer (and saw his first upscale department store, Strawbridge and Clothier). Rouse would lead the development of approximately thirty-six malls across the country (through Community Research and Development [CRD], the mall development and management subsidiary of The Rouse Company) by the time he retired in 1979. Rouse was not the largest mall developer and manager in the United States, but he had become a developer with truly national scope and powerful ideas.[8]

Although now taken for granted as the answer to suburban main streets, the regional shopping center was not the natural and inevitable answer to development on the suburban fringe. Idealistic designers had created innovative retail mall designs during the 1930s and 1940s, advocating the separation of pedestrians and automobiles, but these concepts were not integrated into existing centers until the late 1940s, and then not on a wide scale. Nor were central pedestrian malls essential to making money just after the war. As Rouse admitted many times, the development of strip malls in the new auto suburbia in the early years was akin to shooting fish in a barrel: "There was no experience behind what was being done; there was very little planning that could grow out of experience which hadn't yet occurred. We proliferated this country with strips of stores we called shopping centers."[9]

Rouse remembered that during the 1950s a few developers began to grow more sophisticated, paying more attention to overall design, sites, leases, and promotion. This attention to comprehensive planning set the new regional centers apart. A 1960s letter to a Connecticut General Life Insurance Company executive (insurance companies financed many of Rouse's projects) set the stage: "Haddonfield (two miles away from Cherry Hill), without any department store, has developed one of the finest, highest quality shopping streets in the Philadelphia area. It developed largely since the war, but it is ill planned, inconvenient, and without sufficient parking." He noted, optimistically, "Eight Haddonfield merchants are currently negotiating for space in Cherry Hill."[10] Indeed, merchants moved in step with their customers, but when given the choice between an older main street, an unregulated strip commercial thoroughfare, and a comprehensively developed mall with ample parking and organized promotion, many more chose the mall. Rouse knew that the shopping center was more than shops; it was the next and most important urban form in America: "it has been widely recognized that in the development of major regional shopping centers, we are really building new, well planned central business districts."[11]

It is worth considering what made malls new as retail operations, beyond the accommodation of the automobile. Had the mall been no more than a shopping area with adequate parking and attractive interior spaces, the story of malls in America would be quite different. Rouse led the way in recognizing that money could come as easily from managing malls extraordinarily well as it could from selling goods. His memos over the decades are filled with careful notes to subordinates calling for closer attention to management of these spaces so that they would perform better. The mall, as Rouse realized, was a marketplace that could be controlled to great advantage, much better controlled than the traditional downtown. As he reminded planners in the 1970s, the "steady bleeding out of retailing at the heart of the city" was due not only to the flight to the suburbs, but also to a whole new conception of retail management. "When the regional shopping centers were built that means that a single owner developed, operated, managed, promoted a center with two or more department stores and a hundred and fifty small stores," Rouse explained, "and therefore there could be the kind of resourceful management and administration that single ownership could provide when a store got weak and couldn't make it[,] that owner saw that it was replaced, expanded some other store, contracted one when it had too much space . . . there was an administration of that space, a merchandising of that space."[12]

In a different speech Rouse contrasted this centralized form of management with that in existence in most American cities: "a retail center in the conventional structure of the American city . . . is this tremendous diffusion of ownership, 150, 200 owners along the main street, 150, 200 different tenants paying rents to different owners. Nobody's in charge." Rouse pointed out what he saw as the dangers of this weak, multilayered system: "A tenant gets weak, a man gets old and dies, somebody just doesn't tend to his business, and it gradually goes till it collapses and then up goes the sign, see Bob Jones or consult your own broker. And another, and another, and nobody looking over that whole retail situation for the city as a whole, for the people as a whole." Laissez-faire management could not create ideal urban environments. Rouse explained that at his malls "we're working intensively all the time in the merchandising and management of those stores in that space. Not unusual at all in a center for us, in the first three years, to have to replace or change, reduce as many as 30, 40 stores out of 150."[13]

Malls were more than buildings, atria, or shops to Rouse; malls were complex systems demanding careful control. Although seemingly trivial, the management differences between his malls and those malls created by department stores meant a great deal to Rouse, because "to the best of my knowledge CRD is the only fully integrated operation in the shopping center field. By this I mean we do our own market analysis, our own planning, leading, construction, financing, management. All this work is with our own staff of exceptionally bright, eager, able young guys (average age 34)."[14] Control and profit flowed from expertise and organization.

In his suburban malls Rouse had thus seized on a powerful idea; he was not promoting a single store but space as a product to be crafted and engineered over time. From Rouse's perspective, malls should be seen less as places and more as products, "merchandized" space. As exciting as these management concepts were, Rouse also set in motion a hyper-Darwinian process that would much more rapidly filter out the strong from the weak than ever happened in old main streets or downtowns. Marginal spaces in cities and old main streets often became professional offices, or marginal retail ideal for businesses with a narrow niche such as printing, professional offices, storefront churches, galleries, antiques, or even food stores with lower returns and specialized clients. Decentralization in ownership did in many cases permit decline and blight, but it also allowed diversification of uses as each property had its own complex web of ownership. At malls, centralization, with an emphasis on yearly increases in revenue of the mall as a whole, and demands for a proportion of sales included in most leases, would in time filter out many essential but marginal businesses, most services, and even groceries that would have added to the convenience of centers. There were many small stores, but increasingly they became the same small stores and types of stores (first-quality retail) in all the malls.

This system in time created cookie-cutter repetition, because chain businesses, connected to national retail marketing efforts, competed best in this superheated selling environment.[15] "The regional shopping center," explains urbanists Bernard Frieden and Lynn Sagalyn, "was for the most efficient merchants, not the start-up businesses or unprofitable, failing, or marginal enterprises."[16] Although much blame has been heaped on chains themselves for creating a uniform environment in malls, much of that blame (if one believes anyone deserves blame) should actually be placed on mall managers like Rouse who created an environment where only the well-financed chains could compete.

The marginal businesses, services, and even food stores that dominated traditional retailing generally withered in a Rouse mall. In the early years Rouse management determined rents and policies on an analog basis. By 1976 he explained to department store owners how his system hummed: "A computer print-out reports monthly to us the sales of all space in our centers by tenant, type of merchandise, size of store and other relevant factors. It spots trends; predicts and supplies the basic intelligence data that allows our leasing people to focus attention on changing performance among merchants and changing attitudes among shoppers," leading to "prodding, counseling and changing merchants" to better respond to market demands.[17] Those companies with deep pockets would in most cases be able to survive the tough times and adapt their stores to suit these directives. The Rouse malls and others became a gated community for retailers as well as consumers, where in time only the richest players could afford the high level of amenities that malls offered their tenants. Private control in the free enterprise context proved surprisingly restrictive.

Although the malls engaged in a fierce struggle for survival, and included tight control of the plazas by a private authority, the image of the mall, quite understandably, could in no way reflect this antidemocratic reality. In speeches and articles that appeared as his malls grew, Rouse was careful to explain that the mall deserved to be the new home of American community life and was in fact just the latest version of the American small town. The mall as Main Street became an essential part of Rouse's Cold War utopia. In truth, and in contrast to many arguments made by academics over the years, Rouse and his associates proved successful in creating the illusion of Main Street life that in all likelihood was sufficient for (or even exceeded that demanded by) most suburbanites. This is not to say that suburbanites were simpletons, because they were not, but Rouse and those he worked with were illusionists of the highest degree. The following sections will look briefly at the physical design of the malls and the methods of cultural sponsorship that heightened the illusion of mall as Main Street.

Rouse did not invent the design of the shopping mall at his Harundale, Mondawmin, or Cherry Hill malls nor did his postwar contemporaries. The first shopping malls in America were the many shopping arcades, designed on British and French precedents, that could be found in American cities in the nineteenth century, including The Arcade in Providence, Rhode Island (1829), and the Cleveland Arcade (1888–1890). Early suburban shopping strips like that at Roland Park, Maryland (1896), first brought convenient shopping to wealthy suburbs at the turn of the century. It is nearly universally agreed that J. C. Nichols first realized the possibility of the auto-oriented shopping plaza at Kansas City's Country Club District. Rouse, and many mall developers of the period, owed and acknowledged a great debt to Nichols. Nichols set in motion some of the management techniques Rouse would adopt by encouraging unified promotions and tight management at Country Club Plaza (1922). He had many imitators during the 1920s, and the period is notable for the revival-style shopping areas—exuberant Spanish and Tudor revival style in many cases—created in exclusive suburban areas. As in most areas of development, the 1930s saw few great innovations in commercial design, with the exception of Greenbelt, Maryland's town center design separating pedestrians and autos. During the 1930s and the immediate postwar boom, the strip model of suburban development proved most popular. Strip malls, composed of bland, modern commercial buildings fronting large parking fields, reflected almost no aesthetic vision and in time clogged arterial roads leading out from cities.[18]

Leading designers of the postwar period adopted older traditions for the enormous regional shopping centers as part of a response to the worst aspects of strip shopping centers. Rouse worked with many of the famous designers of the postwar era, including landscape architect Dan Kiley and architects Victor Gruen and Pietro Belluschi. These designers believed that they were creating a special urban environment in suburbia, with attractive landscaped plazas and light-filled atria, but they carefully ignored the limited commercial vision that created a numbing and controlled experience. All the elements that gave traditional urban places great character—a sense of history and additions to an existing urban fabric, diverse stores and uses, religious and civic buildings, fine materials—designers jettisoned as these great warehouses metastasized in enormous parking fields. Cherry Hill, designed by Victor Gruen, for instance, originally devoted eighteen acres to buildings and public spaces and sixty-two acres to parking. One might profitably ask if the attractive interior spaces really mitigated the sprawling parking fields and blank walls encircling the mall. In public, at least, designers kept a straight face as they described their new projects as satisfying pedestrian places on a European model. And as long as one talked of the pedestrian courts alone, it almost seemed believable.

Victor Gruen's focus, and upon which he staked his reputation, was the notion that the mall was an innovative pedestrian environment for the suburbs. Gruen, an Austrian refugee based in Los Angeles, made a number of visionary designs for shopping centers and over time translated them into action. He first perfected his style at the enclosed Southdale Mall in Minneapolis, adapted, he said from the nineteenth-century "*gallerias* in Milan and Naples." He argued that the regional shopping center "is able to play the role not merely of a commercial center but of a social, cultural and recreational crystallization point of the up-to-then amorphous, sprawling suburban region." The centers formed "a cluster of great compactness, with spaces between them reserved for pedestrian use only and equipped with such amenities and improvements as landscaping, rest benches, fountains and, even in some cases, works of creative art."[19] Gruen showed that, with sufficient parking, American shoppers and developers could be coaxed to support pedestrian plazas and attractive modernist design.

Other high-profile designers who worked for Rouse made similar connections between their work and European antecedents. Pietro Belluschi, a noted architect from Italy, who had made a career for himself in the Pacific Northwest by mixing Modernism with close attention to local building traditions and landscapes, designed Rouse's Mondawmin Mall in the 1950s. He made the following comparison of Mondawmin to European models: "We were also after the scale you find in the old shopping streets of France and Italy—perfectly logical in a pedestrian center. With the short distances, the variety and no dead areas, it should be a lively place—lots of things happening wherever a person walks."[20] To compare Mondawmin with a European city tests credulity. Mondawmin—a shed of metal, glass, and tile of a notable uniformity and cheapness—has little in common with European spaces even though it might have been an improvement over ordinary strip malls.

These designers had their notions, but Rouse was not quite as romantic. His vision of design acknowledged that the regional mall's appearance "will have much to do with standards of taste and maintenance and concern on the part of people throughout this country,"[21] but he argued, "it is not dramatic architecture; elegant materials; formality, spectacle . . . Within the center, the structure should be almost unimportant. It should be so good that it unselfconsciously contributes to the environment without standing out."[22] Few great European spaces idolized by designers faded to the background in the way malls did. In malls, attention to overall appearance and consumer experiences yielded benefits, particularly in the face of regional competition, but it was not through dazzling architecture that one built consumer loyalty.

The mall democratized luxury and became a mass consumer paradise. Rouse explained to a group of designers his brand of design patronage—a fantasy interior world where amenities abounded: "This has led to great improvement in landscaping; it has led to the enclosed mall; to the pools and fountains; to improvements in the design of benches, trash receptacles, signs, and the little details of a center."[23] Malls were not much to look at, particularly from the exterior, but they felt comfortable and luxurious. In 1966 Rouse even cautioned his employees from minimizing greenery in their malls: "We have seen a lot of our own Centers and we may, therefore, be getting a little tired of the large quantities of planting. However, it continues to distinguish them from all other centers I see. Most developers have neither the imagination, taste nor patience to handle large planting areas."[24]

Rouse and those with him set out to create a simulacrum of the street that would be one better than reality. "Landscaping should be natural; growing out of the paving, seldom boxed in planters. Sitting, eating, watching should all be a part of the 'street,' not separated from it. Malls and courts must be free of trash and clutter, spotlessly clean like Disneyland is clean, but not cold, sterilized like a museum."[25] Describing the Columbia Mall in the 1970s, Rouse even claimed that this mall and others he had built met the high standards set by William Whyte in his famous study of street life and plazas in New York City, *The Social Life of Small Urban Spaces*. Rouse recalled that Whyte "has examined where people stop, sit, talk and why. He has interesting slides and movies and some of his conclusions are potentially important to us. He reports, in his words, 'the staggering discovery— that people like to be with people' and 'that people like to sit where there are seats.'" According to Rouse, "Every one of his observations checked out to affirm why the fountain court in Columbia Mall is such a busy, comfortable place for people to be—plenty of seats, in the main traffic way, with water, and trees, and eating places nearby."[26] The street, minus certain key elements, had been reinvented by Rouse and his designers.

Nor was Rouse static in his approach to design over the decades. In the 1970s he realized the growing power of the youth culture and increasing numbers of women in the workforce. "'Shopping is Fun' is a banner held high by our leasing teams and our center management—lots of small stores— independent merchants—attention to youth—wide variety of eating places—lively courts—signing and graphics and playful good taste." He pioneered the food court to meet the needs of working women in the 1970s: "In two of the most productive centers we have grouped fifteen to twenty over-the-counter eating places around a clean, colorful, carnival-like court where men, women and children can find a wide variety of food; eat quickly, inexpensively, in an attractive environment."[27] The food fairs were the first food courts, and Rouse is generally credited with creating this now ubiquitous mall institution. These innovations emerged out of Rouse's careful study of demographic trends and consumer habits.

On the heels of his early success, Rouse had announced with fanfare his vision of the new role of the private developer in 1960 when he proclaimed proudly that "in Shopping Center development a single man or a single company builds the Main Street, the town square, the 'home town,' and is largely responsible for the atmosphere it creates, for its chain reaction effect on the local community."[28] He made this remarkable statement with great pride to a gathering of fellow mall developers in 1960 and would do so many times afterward. It is unsettling that Rouse, devoted to local government and democracy, should celebrate paternalism without any sense of the dangers that went with such a restricting ideal for a democratic society. For if Rouse was right—and there is really no reason to believe he was not—the mall developer of the postwar period, although lacking control of residential areas, had a kind of de facto community control last seen in the nineteenth-century mill town.

The notion of the mall as Main Street was maintained through a regulated and highly censored system of inoffensive mall culture. Not only would space be better managed, but cultural and community life would also be directed. Rouse insisted to certain audiences beginning in the 1960s that the cultural and civic life of his malls was not merely symbolic, but functional. The better a mall was designed and managed for public life, the better it could compete with other malls and retail areas. The mall developer had "to discover all sorts of ways in which that environment can be used to serve the community so that it becomes central to the community, that the community adopts it as its center and develops deep feelings of pride and enthusiasm and concern about it."[29]

Rouse's point man on mall culture was Ned Daniels, known informally as his "Czar of Taste" at The Rouse Company. Daniels began his promotion of Rouse projects at Mondawmin and recalled: "I had a pile of money that the merchants had contributed and that I was supposed to use to promote the center. So we had sidewalk sales and the typical things. But then, there was this big open courtyard . . . and in Baltimore, there was no summer music . . . I got the idea of having symphony concerts in the mall. We hired 21 members of the Symphony and got some potted palms and some folding chairs and 1,000 people showed up!" As the firm expanded in the mall business, so did the scale of the cultural promotions. "So we did things design-wise in commissioning local sculptors[,] in marketing concerts, building branches of museums in shopping centers, having ballet companies in residence in centers, art shows, high school proms" as "an effort to make these centers the new downtowns of the suburbs, where people felt comfortable, where things happened."[30] Rouse, in fact, paid his managers to develop a fairly broad, albeit paternalistic, approach to community life.[31]

Rouse boasted of movie theaters and symphony concerts that have "drawn audiences double those of the regular downtown concerts." He spoke proudly of community halls in the malls, where "there will be about three meetings a day; ten thousand people . . . every month coming in and out of each of these community halls [to] attend all kinds of meetings, many with names you never dreamed of. We have started three churches in our centers, and the last one decided it didn't want to leave."[32] Company publications celebrated "art shows, little theaters, ballet, automobile and boat shows, charity benefits" as well as community-created events such as "Charlotte's Symphony Ball—an important annual social event held in Charlottetown Mall; The Cherry Hill High School Junior Prom in the Mall at Cherry Hill." The community hall received a great deal of attention as an incubator of suburban social life: "In each center CRD builds a Community Hall and meeting room for the use of civic, service and recreational organizations. In one CRD Center alone, 400 different groups totaling over 46,000 people used these facilities during a 10-month period."[33] Rouse even offered free office space to local legislators at its Paramus Mall in 1973, and Rouse "Throughout the 1960s and 1970s . . . let various groups leaflet and solicit signatures" inside his mall.[34] Rouse also noted in 1967 that "Cherry Hill Mall is where politicians speak."[35] By 1979 Rouse could count eight museum galleries in his malls.[36] To top it off, CRD explained "there is no natural conflict between profits and people and that the soundest base for a new 'main street' is to make it an indispensable servant of its community."[37] Another speech found Rouse boasting, "The promotion becomes a part of what's happening in that 'home town': it takes the place of the band concert in the town square."[38]

What happened to these community rooms, galleries, churches, politicians, and public performances? Quite simply, they have been largely eliminated or restricted for reasons of cost and lack of interest on the company's part in both Rouse malls and those managed by other companies. In addition, as suburban communities grew they developed their own community meeting halls, churches, and performance spaces less tightly controlled by the developers. The inhospitable climate of the malls meant that the most important community plazas of American suburbs, where the public most frequently gathered in large numbers, would be forever locked into a purely commercial role.

Most journalists, unlike academics, have uncritically accepted the new role of malls as Main Streets. At Cherry Hill, residents reported that old and young now had a place to gather, and one resident even enthused "that until Cherry Hill was built, there was no sense of community in the area."[39] In a 1962 issue of *Reader's Digest,* Don Wharton expressed his admiration for Cherry Hill: "It was a raw, windy January day in New Jersey, with the mercury down to 14 degrees. Yet in the central mall of the Cherry Hill shopping center I saw tiny children playing around a fountain, sticking their hands into the splashing spray. Nearby their mothers watched from benches, unconcerned at the cold." Wharton concurred with the "mall as Main Street" ideal: "Many shopping centers are actually becoming community centers with art exhibits, flower shows, charity balls, symphony concerts."[40] In functions, too, the early malls were mixed, much more than they would be in later years. At Cherry Hill, Food Fair and two drug stores were part of the initial mix.

On a visit to Cherry Hill in 1964, a journalist from Howard County, Maryland, found much to like: "We saw children taking ballet lessons, attending a movie, playing in a recreation center, looking at exhibits of live birds or boat models. We saw their parents shopping leisurely in the year round 70 degree temperature in stores ranging from exclusive specialty shops to the practicalities of two department stores. In the court, with its well-kept trees, plants and fountains, we saw older people, sitting happily watching the crowds go by, a part of life but free of its push." The journalist believed that Cherry Hill "is far more than a marketplace, it has become the heart of the community."[41] There is every reason to doubt the extent to which malls had become the heart of American communities, but it might be far more radical to accept these observations at face value. When first created, Cherry Hill and malls like it were nearly utopian in their appearance and functions. The attractions existed and the general satisfaction of suburbanites kept them coming back. The success of these malls as places, not just as selling tools, encouraged other communities to entice developers, which in turn often undermined the popularity of first-generation enclosed malls

Figure 16. Cherry Hill. The enclosed mall interiors felt like Main Street, only better. No inclement weather and a type of luxury the middle class could scarcely have imagined. Mall promoters, at first, even offered special events to make their malls the new civic centers of growing communities. *Howard County Times* (1961).

such as Cherry Hill. The private sector model of Main Street planning seemed to have satisfactorily replaced older and broader notions of public life.

Rouse built only a few of America's malls, but he had plenty of company in the business. By 1971 the International Council of Shopping Centers reported the existence of "nearly 13,000 large scale shopping centers in the country, many of them built within the last decade. In 21 of the nation's largest metropolitan areas, shopping centers now get more than 50 per cent of all the retail trade. In some communities . . . the proportion is even higher."[42] Most American cities found themselves hemmed in by malls, and Rouse's company even began to build malls in downtown locations in the 1970s. The Gallery at Market East in Philadelphia (1977), The Gallery in Baltimore (1987), and Pioneer Place in Portland, Oregon (1990) offer nearly the identical management styles and retailers as their suburban counterparts. During the 1990s, even with the growth of "big box" retail, malls still accounted for 75 percent of all retail space in the United States.

Even small cities proved to be fair game. Although Rouse himself demanded, "there's no excuse for a metropolitan area, 300,000 people or less, ever having a regional shopping center," he admitted, "We're building centers in . . . Augusta and Tallahassee that I really think shouldn't be built." Mall dominance was not his fault, but that of incompetent city leaders. "If the city was doing the things to make it unnecessary," he would not need to build these malls.[43] Such reserve on his part sounded convincing but overlooked the calculus his company knew all too well. Accepting Rouse's figures of minimum-size cities for regional malls (300,000 or fewer), what would happen to a city, such as Baltimore, with one million people and four or five (or even more) malls on its edges? No doubt it would mean near complete destruction of downtown shopping. Rouse was not blind to the impact of his malls but remained something of a fatalist on this point: "What is the effect of these big high-powered centers on the existing community? There is a variety of effects. The effect on the little towns close by is devastating. The effect on the old, worn-out, obsolete sub-centers is devastating. They have nothing with which to compete."[44] "Obsolete sub-centers" is a euphemism for the downtowns of medium-size cities.

Although the shopping mall did become the dominant Main Street of the postwar era, Rouse began to express doubts about its utopian claims. His actions as a mall developer dominated public life, but his thoughts and sentiments reveal discomfort with what and he other developers had accomplished. He most often expressed his reservations to designers and other businesspeople—these were not comments for mass consumption. A conference at Harvard in 1963 dubbed "The Future of the American Out-of-Town Shopping Center" found Rouse discussing the future of the mall with some of the world's leading designers (Rouse maintained a relationship with Harvard throughout his career). According to a summary printed in *Ekistics*, "After two days of panel meetings and discussions . . . the conference concluded that a good deal more governmental control should be exercised over the selection of sites for regional centers." The architects and planners, in general, condemned the new malls for undercutting traditional downtowns, and Edmund Bacon, a famous planner and theorist from the University of Pennsylvania, asked "that we decisively reject whatever vitiates the life of the central core" and, with other panelists, "cautioned that cub scout dens, fashion shows and barber shop quartets should not be mistaken for urban culture." The designers generally disliked the new malls for failing to integrate a wider civic vision and for focusing solely on merchandise. Rouse, perhaps unexpectedly, agreed.

Although Rouse's general address at the conference celebrated the possibilities for malls as civic centers, with new theaters, churches, and meeting halls within the new regional shopping centers, in later discussions at the same conference he distanced himself from the claim that business could create a genuine civic realm. Rouse argued that "if this elaborate commercial development is the product of public investment—of the public roads system (for expressways and highways produce these opportunities) and the sewer system that brings the houses—why should the fruits of this public investment be turned over at random to an individual land owner and developer? Why shouldn't there be a process by which local government or state government or a metropolitan authority acquires the land in advance of development, plans it and sells it to department stores and developers, locates the spots for public libraries or court houses or fire stations or police stations or whatever else it wants in the public interest, and then turns it over to the market for development?" Just in case anyone thought that Rouse was actually arguing for left-wing controls, he reminded his listeners that such a view "isn't a radical view. It's a conservative view of the role of local government. It's simply applying an easier way and in a much more obvious area the process that has been forced upon us in the urban renewal programs in the inner city." Rouse proposed that local government, instead of developers and department stores, should take on the role of developer. Maybe Rouse did not think this style of development was radical, but likely most of his audience did.[45]

Rouse gave a speech to a tougher audience in 1964 and expanded upon these ideas. In his address to the Real Estate Board of Baltimore he admitted, "I'd love to see a local government insist upon the power to condemn the key land at the clover-leafs and take over the spots where the town centers are inevitably going to unfold, and to engage in excess condemnation . . . and recapture to the local political subdivision the enhanced land values that are brought about only as a result of public means."[46]

In a speech over a decade later to department store merchants in 1976 Rouse still encouraged his listeners to think more ambitiously about their public responsibilities. "We have glimpses of the possibilities in the use of malls for all sorts of public events—educational, entertaining and cultural—that are important to the community and help build traffic in the centers," but he argued that "the focus is largely promotional, and the substance is thin." Here he sounded like Edmund Bacon and mall critics from the 1960s. He then offered the more radical vision: "But suppose merchants and developers worked with government and private institutions to plan the centers and their public spaces so as to provide the most resourceful and productive possible relationships between the center and public agencies, educational and cultural institutions." He wondered, for instance, "How might a library, schools of art, ballet, theatre, churches, centers for crafts, older people, youth, and day care be physically connected to the center so that each benefited from the other in the convenience of their relationship to their users; in their combined traffic; in communication to the public; in the use of public spaces for exhibition and performance. . . ." Obviously, public life of any merit had not actually developed naturally at his malls. He ended on a particularly critical note: "The marketplaces that are called malls have come a long way from the strip center with department store attached and

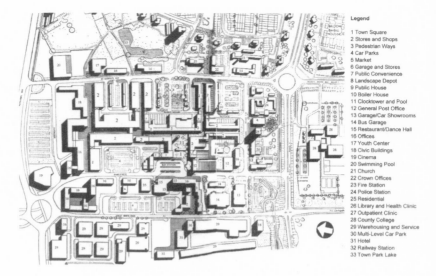

Legend

1 Town Square
2 Stores and Shops
3 Pedestrian Ways
4 Car Parks
5 Market
6 Garage and Stores
7 Public Convenience
8 Landscape Depot
9 Public House
10 Boiler House
11 Clocktower and Pool
12 General Post Office
13 Garage/Car Showrooms
14 Bus Garage
15 Restaurant/Dance Hall
16 Offices
17 Youth Center
18 Civic Buildings
19 Cinema
20 Swimming Pool
21 Church
22 Crown Offices
23 Fire Station
24 Police Station
25 Residential
26 Library and Health Clinic
27 Outpatient Clinic
28 County College
29 Warehousing and Service
30 Multi-Level Car Park
31 Hotel
32 Railway Station
33 Town Park Lake

Figure 17. Stevenage (United Kingdom) town center combined a great number of private and public functions, as did town centers in most social democratic new town projects. Rouse set out to duplicate this type of town center at Columbia, but depended almost entirely upon private sector efforts. Adapted from Osborn and Whittick, *The New Towns* (1963).

from the old downtown street. But they have become routine; are limited in their community service; monotonous in their repetitive alikeness." These comments came not from a jaded urban academic, but from one of America's leading mall developers. And of course they fell on deaf ears, even within his company. Without a formal mechanism requiring public use, long-term survival of these functions could not be expected. [47]

This criticism must in part be connected to Rouse's trips to European new towns for his Columbia project. With his planners he visited new towns across Europe in the early 1960s and encountered alternative visions of new Main Street, or "Town Center," development. In Europe, and through published accounts, Rouse thus encountered public entities organizing the commercial needs of new suburban districts around the demands of public life. Like American shopping malls, they separated pedestrians from automobiles and provided sculptures, plantings, fountains, plazas, and abundant seating (although usually only partially enclosed). The similarities stopped there.

A plan like that developed at Stevenage indicates that although the attractive pedestrian zones with stores were similar to those at American malls, the post office, youth center, civic buildings, swimming pool, fire and police stations, public plazas, a county college, housing, railway stations, and churches

Figure 18. Columbia, Maryland, Town Center blended civic and commercial functions like its social democratic counterparts, but the massive mall and private sector management undermined Rouse's idealistic goal of creating a vibrant, urbane center of his new town. Courtesy of Columbia Archives.

intimately grouped with the commercial areas made for a very different and more expansive type of town center. The comparatively small areas for parking are also notable and allowed for the tight grouping of different uses.

Directly reflecting the European new town influence, and Rouse's interest in the social democratic model, Columbia had a "town center" like its European counterparts, with blended commercial and civic functions. Again, Rouse was determined to show that business leadership could equal or even outdo its social democratic rivals. The planned town center at Columbia would be better than the traditional downtown as promoted to potential residents in 1966: "The heart of the city will be the home of art and music schools, theaters, museums and galleries. . . . By day, one edge of the lake will be a park . . . with restaurants, coffee shops, carousels and entertainment for children; by night, it will be transformed into a gay and playful wonderland for people of every age. There will be restaurants, bars and clubs, music, theaters and gaiety, life, laughter and nostalgia."[48] Here was a true suburban downtown with a wide range of activities and no grimy edge. Surrounding a galleria shopping mall, built and managed separately by the mall division at The Rouse Company, was a lakefront, offices, a community college, park space, and town government (a private homeowner's association). An old-fashioned clock in the Columbia Mall and folksy signs completed the civic symbolism. Mathias Devito, Rouse Company president in 1973, when asked by the leading Soviet urban planner, then on a tour of Columbia, if "he felt The Rouse Company had done a great service for the people" by building such an attractive mall, admitted "that [such a claim] would be an exaggeration, but we've made life better. The mall is more than a shopping place; it's the heart of the community."[49]

Such a claim overlooked salient defects of the Columbia town center design as a whole. Unlike European town centers, the Columbia Mall was surrounded by massive parking fields, was not well integrated with the rest of the town center activities, and company planners did little to encourage potential connections. Early years of fairly extensive nonconsuming activities in the mall and assorted cultural events and displays also gave way to rigid control by mall managers at The Rouse Company. The company turned against many of the remaining small businesses in the mall and replaced them with larger chain stores. The mall has become truly massive in scale in the recent renovation completed in 2001. Columbia still has quasi-public lakefront for other activities, but it is not nearly as heavily trafficked as the mall and is tightly regulated by a private homeowners' association. The town center is a failure as a casual, uncensored, everyday central public space. The shopping mall even ruined Rouse's most idealistic civic scheme.

The regional shopping center was a convincing transformation of the prewar commercial order and seemed to demonstrate yet again the ability of business interests to create a utopian environment. The outdated downtown department stores and main streets were replaced by far more luxurious and organized environments for consumption and even civic life. Everything was clean, attractive, modern, and easy on the eyes. At the time, plantings, fountains, and numerous public events must have made malls appear as satisfactory substitutes for older forms of urban space. Eventually, however, the disadvantages appeared. Regional suburban malls became a thin form of civic life that better reflected the Cold War notion of consumerist democracy rather than actual democratic life as it had developed over two hundred years. A narrowing of the freedom of thought took place by strategically removing anything but commercial allusions at the heart of new American suburbs and small towns. Whereas the modern city and even the small town had become fractured places of multiple voices, uses, and functions, the sole function and exclusive idea and iconography of the mall, effectively the most important common space in most suburban communities, remained the retail of comparatively expensive goods.

Much has been written about the lack of true freedom of speech in malls without considering what free speech in a mall environment would mean. In reality the lack of visual and functional linkages of the mall to public life has proved just as dangerous. Even states where freedom of speech and assembly has been legally extended into malls have gained noticeably few actual improvements in access.[50] Not only have malls continued to closely regulate speech by creating complex rules for access, but also religion and government—the other poles of civil society—have no real and symbolic presence in malls. The carefully designed and programmed mall environment easily overwhelms civic and other rituals. Even grocery stores and professional services have been eliminated in malls as too distracting and unprofitable. No local characters, town lawyers, or alternative authority figures could prosper or linger. Politics as a community process and daily custom has withered. In the words of historian Lizabeth Cohen, "the commercializing, privatizing, and segmenting of physical gathering places that has accompanied mass consumption has made precarious the shared public space upon which our democracy depends."[51] Declining political participation in America may be partly related to the substitution of informal networks with consumer practices. Music, light, architecture, and even art and plants helped keep the citizen's eyes too closely fixed on the new goods for sale. Even though malls have been surrounded by strip retail and a variety of community functions, and a new generation of massive regional malls has littered a number of suburbs with dead malls, these changes have in no way diminished mall centrality on the suburban national scene.

America had again taken a distinct path from European nations along a business-dominated/consumerist model with its own disadvantages. Businessmen had always formed the nucleus of Main Street, and they were *necessary* to urban health, but by insisting that consumption and private management was *sufficient* to civic life they had gone too far. This model, so appealing and seductive, has even started to undercut the more expansive notions of European planned town centers and suburban towns; the enclosed luxury mall has become one of America's leading exports. Europeans have every reason to be concerned.

CHAPTER 5

The For-Profit New Town Mirage

In Columbia, (Rouse's] ideas about what private capital and private
enterprise can do about the problem—and at the same time make a profit
for investors—appears to be proving correct at a rate that surprises Mr.
Rouse himself.

"James W. Rouse, The City Builder"

You've seen and heard them. Bleeding heart do-gooders tiptoeing around
the countryside. Trilling over poverty. Wailing over slums. Sobbing over
environmental rape. Professional hands outstretched to the Federal
Government for the unlimited funds they feel must surely cure the
nation's ills . . . The whole New Town concept (by contrast) is pure capitalistic entrepreneurship. At its best, the New Town answers real social
needs in a realistic manner. . . . On maturity, the successful New Town
can be expected to return upwards from 25% per year in return on initial
investment.

American Industrial Properties Report

In 1824 Robert Owen, the eccentric British philanthropist and utopian, addressed
the United States House of Representatives and asked America's nascent
political leadership to adopt his plan for a nation of parallelograms, comprehensively planned communities arranged around grassy quadrangles and
cooperative ideals. At New Lanark, his company town in Scotland run on progressive principles, Owen had demonstrated to great acclaim new possibilities
in social experimentation and reform, and in America he had just founded an
ambitious utopian project, a future parallelogram known as New Harmony. He
promised his audience in Washington that "the system which I am about to
introduce into your states is fully competent to form them into countries of
palaces, gardens and pleasure grounds, and, in one generation, to make the inhabitants a race of superior beings." Although politely received by then President
James Monroe and President-elect John Quincy Adams, as well as many members of the House of Representatives, his model of a new cooperative society,
including a quite expensive and impressive model that he later displayed, did
not lead to ambitious federal investment in his scheme.[1]

126

Nearly 150 years later, a similarly wealthy and idealistic businessman, James Rouse, would on many occasions address the American Congress in support of governmental underwriting for an ambitious program of privately planned and constructed new towns. Like Owen, Rouse had just embarked on an ambitious utopian venture, the new town of Columbia, Maryland, and thought that his success augured well for a nation of new towns. The similarities between Owen and Rouse end here, however. Columbia was less communitarian than Owen's parallelogram, and although it included careful social and racial integration and modern architecture, the utopian aspects of the new town tradition merged equally with the profit motive. The American new town was not to be the darling of starry-eyed idealists, communists, or social democrats as it was in Europe. Environmental preservation, social experimentation, transit innovation, educational reform, and neighborhood planning would be shown to be a good investment for even the most calculating developers. The reform potential for private sector new towns in Cold War America, however, proved as illusory as Owen's parallelogram.

⌒

The postwar suburban housing boom began as America's convincing answer to state-constructed housing in socialist and social democratic nations. The scale and satisfaction of the new subdivisions, built with the aid of federal highways and mortgage insurance, seemed from many perspectives convincing proof that the private sector had the ability to solve complex, mammoth social needs. Working-class and middle-class white Americans became consumers of quality housing on a scale never before witnessed, and the postwar housing shortage ended by the 1950s as over a million new, comfortable houses were constructed every year. The new suburbs at first indicated most of all the bounty and extent of America's consumer society compared to the rest of the world.

The criticism of this new suburban abundance mostly from urban loyalists grew in step with these burgeoning communities. As early as 1945, journalist Frank Fisher lamented that new suburban "communities are built with as little forethought as the central areas, and soon pleasant residential suburbs show the same signs of blight as the cities themselves. Invaded by factories and mushrooming slums, the suburbanites move again."[2] During the 1950s and early 1960s, growing unease traveled upward in waves from the commuter stuck in traffic to government officials concerned about air pollution and bulldozed farms and forests. Even many suburban Americans could not help but notice that certain trade-offs had been made in the great suburban bonanza. Casualties included increasingly isolated and forlorn older cities, ever more urbanized suburbs, and the loss of rural and wild ambiance around cities.

Criticism could be found in both highbrow newspapers and popular magazines, indicating an interest far beyond an elite circle (if not the suburban mainstream itself). Ada Louise Huxtable, the award-winning architectural critic at the *New York Times,* summarized a variety of suburban failings for her cosmopolitan readers: "The sociologists tell us of the disasters of the one-class community where mass-produced developers' housing herds one age group, one economic level and one color into homes as alike as their owners. The psychologists tell us that bliss of togetherness has turned into neurosis of development-sponsored ennui. The statisticians tell us of the disenchantment that has started a trend back to the cities. The critics point to the devastated countryside and the minimal dwelling of a sameness that promotes stultifying monotony." An article in *McCall's* denounced the "vast proliferation of housing developments which are neither city nor country, which stretch with dulling monotony across our land, devouring and obliterating it . . . Same supermarkets, same parking lots, same shopping centers, same lawns, same bushes—same kind of life."[3] *Reader's Digest* illustrated the problem of suburban sprawl in graphic terms for its readers. While one house might be lovely, "multiply the house by 1000 and the green country turns into a desert of pavements, roofs, electric poles, TV antennas. Trees come down. The side yards are useless. The houses stare at each other."[4] By the 1960s, finding fault with suburbia was not a radical stand; nor was offering solutions to the crisis.

There existed no single path to addressing the issue of suburban sprawl. Federal, state, and local governments might have embarked on a more aggressive policy of planning (as did their European counterparts), federal agencies like the FHA might have come under closer scrutiny or exercised greater control over participating developers, highway planners might have taken issues of suburban growth into account, and the federal government might have embarked on a massive project of carefully planned mass transit construction. The option actually selected for controlling sprawl in the 1960s and 1970s, private new town development, was not the only option for addressing suburban sprawl—it only appeared as such. Out of the competing voices the new town emerged as the most cost-effective and politically viable way to guide suburban growth.

The American new town became a practicable American option only after Rouse's success in launching an idealistic new town close to the nation's capital during the 1960s. Columbia, Rouse's fifteen-thousand-acre project in rural Maryland, ultimately set the terms of the debate about sprawl in the 1960s. Although the new town of Reston, Virginia, started earlier and was bolder in architectural concept, it quickly accumulated a great deal of damaging publicity related to its financial problems. By 1967, the same time that the government was ramping up its new town programs, Reston was widely known less for architectural innovation and more for its perilous financial situation. Columbia was different from Reston not only in its modest architectural goals, but also in its aims of combining social experimentation with excellent financing. Unfortunately, those who would imitate Columbia failed to understand that Columbia only seemed to be in sync with the American mainstream. Columbia occupied a special place in national consciousness, attracted a national group of idealistic suburban residents, and was guided by a gifted developer with remarkable financial backing for a land development project.

When Rouse had secretly accumulated his thousands of acres in rural Howard County by 1963, he promised nothing short of a reinvented American community. He would create a suburban-style city that would not only yield a stunning profit, but would also provide a projected one hundred thousand residents urban-level services without a city government. A small planned community experiment by The Rouse Company in Baltimore's elegant Roland Park neighborhood, Cross Keys, had already proved popular. After the opening of his Cherry Hill Mall in New Jersey in 1961, Rouse had also noticed that "rental projects (in surrounding areas) with twenty percent vacancy filled up," and he therefore hoped, by planning areas surrounding his malls, to reap those improvements in land value for himself,[5] but Rouse's ambitions went far beyond profit alone. The suburban-style city that Rouse proposed to create, although integrating split-levels and a shopping mall, was not familiar to the average American. With his planners, Rouse created a unique version of the new town tradition for modern American suburbia.

The new town concept was unfamiliar to most Americans, but it held an irresistible attraction to reformers and planners of the 1960s caught up in an exciting, international new town movement. In Europe, in particular, the new town was enjoying its greatest popularity and was closely tied to aggressive land and transportation planning by leftist governments. The new town or garden city originated with the ideas of turn-of-the-century visionary Ebenezer Howard, and had led to picturesque planned towns like Letchworth and Welwyn with community-owned property (and were inspired in part by Henry George's Single Tax ideas).

By the 1950s and 1960s the new town form had become intimately tied to comprehensive reshaping of European society. Hitched to social democratic and communist policies, new towns had become an experimental new world for workers and middle-class citizens alike. Enormous public and private investment in new towns, directed by public authorities at both the national and local levels, was designed to create new cities that would avoid the problems of older cities and reflect the social idealism of the postwar era. Tapiola, Farsta, Runcorn, Stevenage, Cumbernauld, Harlow, among others, were model new towns that transported their residents to a world with fewer social distinctions and abundant recreational and social resources. They truly were "slumless" cities for a post–laissez-faire urban order. Blended commercial/civic town centers, residential villages (with neighborhood shopping centers and the separation of pedestrians and motor vehicles), mass transportation and highway links, industrial parks, acres of open spaces, and abundant recreational facilities characterized most European new town environments.

These towns had tremendous influence far beyond their borders. Planners from America, including Rouse, who visited the towns, admired the bold designs from afar as well as their government funding but did not necessarily rush to imitate them.[6] American new towns of the early 1960s were entirely privately funded, unlike their European counterparts. As Reader's Digest explained in 1967, "American New Towns differ from those of Great Britain—the British have built 20 in 20 years—in that they are private-enterprise, done in the hope of profit, and the profits are potentially huge."[7]

As government money receded into the background in America, so too did modernist designs that dominated at European new towns. Only Robert Simon closely adopted an overall modernist style, for his Lake Anne Village Center, featuring concrete structures in rural Virginia (although some more traditional housing styles were included). More successful American new town proponents like James Rouse did not imitate European modernist styles as closely.[8] According to Robert Tennenbaum, an early planner, Rouse did not much care for the design of postwar British new towns, because there were "a lot of apartment houses—multifamily. . . . They were very hard. Most of it was hard, not warm. The landscaping hadn't matured yet."[9] Modern styles would be available at Columbia but would not set the community's tone or palette. Social planning, ecological preservation, and abundant community resources dominated at Columbia. The planners at Columbia admitted being influenced by the ecological visions of Scandinavian new towns, like Farsta, that "seemed to relate their buildings to trees rather than other buildings." Architectural innovation took a backseat as the planners carefully fit development (and builder's conventional housing types) to river valleys, existing trees, and older farm buildings.[10]

Rouse hired what he called a "work group" to help him with the planning of the new city and spent nearly $250,000 on their services. This work group met over a series of months in 1963 and was composed of academics from a variety of disciplines from planning to the social sciences and education. The work group encouraged Rouse and his planners to experiment on interfaith projects, health care, new theories of education, subsidized housing, cultural patronage, new governmental forms, and mass transit. This work group also lent academic prestige to the Columbia project and helped to attract a number of idealistic residents over time. Rouse, in fact, adopted many of the suggestions of the work group, and his planning team integrated many of their suggestions. The scale of the nine villages, guidelines for socioeconomic mixing, cooperative health and religious plans, educational reform, a minibus system, an activist homeowner's association, a community magazine, and even an amphitheater all emerged from the work group meetings.

As the planners developed the concept for the community, the high-quality level of development attracted attention at both local and national levels. Rouse Company planners trumpeted the future amenities of the new city in sensational publicity materials. What Burnham's 1909 Plan of Chicago was to the City Beautiful movement, the Columbia vision became for the American new town movement. In the same manner that Burnham and his associates—through lantern slides, calculated announcements, lectures, and publications—had galvanized support for their vision of Chicago rebuilt as a "Paris" on the shores of Lake Michigan, Rouse and his planners developed attractive visions of a redesigned suburbia.

In a variety of instances, publicists for The Rouse Company patched together stock photography from diverse sources with idealistic and upbeat accompanying text. Shots from Rouse Company malls illustrated the excitement and dazzle of mall interiors; scenes from Copenhagen and Rome gave a sense for the promising nightlife of the downtown district. Numerous photographs captured preppy suburbanites in the natural world, fishing, and relaxing. Columbia, a more perfect blend of town and country, was directly offered as a solution to the problems of suburban sprawl and urban decline. The Rouse Company even criticized the land development that had made it rich: "Our development process must find solutions that are long overdue: better answers to the cruel scarring of the countryside, to shameful and tasteless clutter along our highways, to monotonous rows of sterile subdivisions stretching across the land."[11]

The physical model The Rouse Company presented to the public offered a grand vision that was no less remarkable. Great effort had been devoted to covering the miniature wooden landscape with trees in green and gold, and in the town center white office towers with tan vertical lines poked politely and neatly above the trees. Miniature wooden sailboats winked from the lake. The model "was a wondrous thing, a great white vision of Utopia stretching across rolling countryside. . . . The model was almost too magnificent, and James Rouse had some acute last-minute qualms about showing it all as part of the presentation. 'Here we are talking about low density, villages, and open space,' he said, 'And then you look at that big white beautiful thing, and you know it's a city we're building.'"[12] This white

Figure 19. Columbia, Maryland as portrayed in the Columbia model (ca. 1963).
Rouse's appealing vision of social democratic ends with private sector means captured
America's attention. Courtesy of Columbia Archives.

city in nature was to be a place of small-scale residential villages center-
ing on grassy greens where residents could linger over an ice cream cone,
talk to the neighborhood doctor, or take in a show at the community center. The children would walk in underpasses to neighborhood schools, frolic
in convenient pools, and play harmlessly at teen centers and nature
reserves. Rouse believed that elements of small-town life could be restored
through careful planning.

From the beginning, Rouse even promised that his city would be open
to racial minorities and the poor—a major risk for Rouse but one that matched
perfectly the idealistic spirit of the 1960s (and particularly the
Baltimore/Washington region). This new town environment, ideally,
would transform stormy relations in American society: "We must believe,
because it is true, that people are affected by their environment—by space
and scale, by color and texture, by nature and beauty; that they can be uplifted,
made comfortable, important; become more productive workers, more agree-
able clients, more expansive customers."[13] Here was a version of utopia, built
not by socialists or the government but by a large corporation and its institutional backers (Rouse received his main financing from Connecticut General).

What had eluded society for thousands of years—an ideal city—would be achieved in a matter of decades.

A welcome center at Columbia raised the utopian pitch even higher. The exhibit, housed in a low-slung Frank Gehry building on the lakeshore, offered "an impressive presentation of the cacophony of unplanned cities then contrast(ed) it with the calmness, orderliness, yet the excitement of a planned community."[14] Publicists used cutting-edge technologies to stimulate the imagination of visitors and convince them that The Rouse Company would create a meaningful alternative to suburban sprawl: "In the slide theater, the first section of the exhibit, four 35 mm projectors present a coordinated show at continuously changing locations on a wide 3-panel screen. . . . From the slide show theater, the visitor walks through a combination of display structures which include floor-to-ceiling photo panels, dimensional maps, and illuminated transparency boxes, some of them with an automatic sound track." Rouse and his publicists were borrowing methods from cutting-edge exposition exhibits and museums to sell their vision of a reformed suburban community that would rise on the former farm fields and forests: "The central display of the Next America Exhibit begins with a summary of land use in Columbia, then views of downtown Columbia—now and in the future, the villages and their neighborhoods, the extensive use of open space, and employment opportunities."[15]

By 1971 one million people had visited the exhibition center, including tourists from around the world. A million more would visit during the next decade. Columbia had thus escaped its local orbit and became a national model of the potential of private new town development. A journalist described the experience of visiting the new town in 1970: "Columbia is set up as a showplace. Out on Route 29, touristy blue and white signs beacon you in with all the graciousness of Colonial Williamsburg. By the lakeshore an attractive, holiday-gay exhibit center offers a lively tour of the city in motion pictures, slides, models and graphics. Visitors stream through the Exhibit Center every day of the week, including cold, rainy Monday mornings in dreary February. They come from Arizona and Australia, Vancouver and Vietnam." "Columbia is a booming tourist attraction," explained another journalist, who found that "Families swarm in on weekends to see the 'Next America' exhibit, visit the model homes, tramp the woods, and skip stones across man-made Lake Kittamaqundi."[16]

Rouse committed his company to building roads and community facilities, while builders would construct houses and apartment complexes on land purchased from the company. The Rouse Company built the shopping centers in village centers as well as a mall in the town center. A community association in Columbia, dominated by the developer in early years but eventually elected by homeowners, managed recreation and open lands,

Figure 20. Columbia Association promotional materials, 2002. Columbia, unlike a number of new towns from the period, remains a socially innovative community. The idealistic public relations have in part been realized; the imitators, unfortunately, have been few. Reprinted with permission of the Columbia Association, courtesy of Columbia Archives.

a minibus service, and regulated housing maintenance. The county would see to the educational needs of the town and provide fire, police, and overall planning (which the county effectively yielded to The Rouse Company). Banished was a city government. Gone, too, was a city planning department responsible to citizens, and forgotten were a wide range of social services provided by many city governments. A solution to sprawl had been found that would preserve direction by the development corporations and the private enterprise system. Democracy at Columbia would be best reflected in terms of market forces, according to Rouse: "The profit purpose was alive and creative throughout the planning process. It was using the marketplace to cast votes for what people really want and care enough to pay for. It recognizes the dynamics of the market system as being fundamental to the democratic process, for it is through the marketplace that a free people can best make the complex judgments of how, where and when they wish to spend their earnings."[17] As at his malls, consumer choice took center stage in community life.

What is striking about Columbia is that Rouse and his planners proved remarkably successful in carrying out their market-based utopian planning. Unlike most other developers who embarked on these projects, Rouse was able to achieve a rather close facsimile of the original plan, and Rouse's adherence to these idealistic plans was evident by the late 1960s (and first residents moved into the town in 1967). The Rouse Company indeed built village centers that combined community facilities, public spaces, and shopping areas, a grand shopping mall modeled on main streets and shopping arcades of the past, and an attractive lakefront recreational area with bold architect-designed structures. The company preserved one-third of the property as open space; achieved an impressive level of subsidized and affordable housing (built by both a Rouse subsidiary and local nonprofits using a mix of private capital and federal subsidies) and attracted black residents in large numbers; and even encouraged fairly ambitious cultural activities. By the late 1960s and early 1970s Columbia had symphony concerts, dance recitals, a funky alternative college, integrated social events, new lakes and lovely forests, and lively village centers. This was no ordinary suburban place. Even the recession of the 1970s did little to dim the vision of The Rouse Company. Temporary cutbacks in services were soon restored as the project regained its financial footing due to the deep pockets of Rouse's main investor, Connecticut General Life Insurance.

This is not to say that all was a success. As discussed above, the town center failed by all accounts to become the vibrant center of the community projected in early publicity materials. Residents did not necessarily linger in the carefully planned public spaces in village centers or show much interest in mass transit. Nor did Columbia achieve the degree of social integration originally sought; the nonprofits and Rouse subsidiary lost funding for their efforts during the Nixon administration, and even when they tried to build more affordable housing they began to face stiff resistance from local residents who felt that Columbia had more than its fair share of subsidized housing in Howard County. The goal of 10-percent-subsidized housing has not been reached, although aging housing has recently taken on the role of affordable housing in some of Columbia's older villages. Aesthetically, too, Columbia won few awards. Although young Frank Gehry designed a number of Columbia's signature town center buildings, architectural critic Wolf Von Eckardt found Columbia unimpressive in 1979: "Columbia . . . looks like an ordinary suburb. Although well planned, the village centers, playgrounds, schools and even lakes seem to disappear in wide ribbons of macadam and well-groomed architectural mediocrity. Most buildings were designed by builders rather than architects. That was deliberate."[18] Design of new villages and districts further declined with the thinning of the staff of Howard Research and Development (HRD), The Rouse Company subsidiary that developed Columbia, during the 1970s.

Private government presented its own challenges. Some residents during the past decades chafed under the leadership of the Columbia Association. As in his other projects, Rouse had massively expanded the role of private entities in managing public life. Built into every home and apartment complex is the code enforcement system that he had hoped to achieve in existing slum neighborhoods. Homeowners in Columbia, as at many other planned communities, must maintain their properties to certain standards and are forbidden to make major external changes without permission from local committees. Even though enforcement has been uneven, regular controversies have emerged over the years as residents have tried to alter their properties in direct violation of the community codes. Recently the Columbia Association, facing declining values in certain older neighborhoods and growing numbers of absentee landlords, has increased its vigilance and enforcement of the codes. Rouse may have been frustrated in urban neighborhoods, but his concern for code enforcement may prove prescient in the suburb he created.

Private governance, as the enforcement situation illustrates, remains controversial. The association is still managed by professionals under the direction of an elected board, but many residents believe the professionals have been heavy-handed and insensitive to citizen concerns. As the board is only part-time, the professional staff has traditionally taken the lead in policy direction. The board elections have never attracted many voters, because the association is not taken seriously as an independent body and because voting is based upon a confusing one vote per household system. Rouse helped fight incorporation of Columbia in the 1990s; he and many other Columbians felt that the Columbia Association provided excellent services at reasonable cost, but still admitted that the system of household voting "ought to be changed. I think the voting ought to be one person, one vote."[19] These much discussed problems—auto dependence, elitism, architectural mediocrity, and private governance—were mere details, however, that did not become perceived as problems (and then only by some) until the later 1970s and 1980s.

Columbia, moreover, attracted many idealistic residents from across the region and nation. Not only was Columbia close to Washington, D.C., thus attracting a politically savvy group of leading residents, but also Columbia's growing reputation for racial integration attracted black and white residents who had been involved in civil rights struggles and were looking for ways to institutionalize the racial progress for which they had worked so hard. These idealistic residents, although never a majority, quickly set about developing local institutions to augment the work of the planners. A newspaper with left-leaning politics was launched, local cultural organizations began, a variety of cafés and galleries opened, numerous parties and festivals were organized, and civil rights activities remained important. Residents of Columbia also moved rapidly into county politics, circumventing their relatively weak position in the local community association (in essence controlled by the developer until 1980). The Columbia Association, although imperfect in the eyes of many residents, showed a tendency toward idealism, running not only recreational facilities, but also market-rate and subsidized after-school programs and summer camps, a serious-minded community magazine, concert series, an archive, art centers and festivals, and mass transit. The association also transferred much of its budget to locally controlled village associations that developed unique programming at village community centers. From the beginning, a foundation created by Rouse has augmented citizen efforts in the arts and social services. Rouse himself became a beloved community figure who lived in a modest home in Columbia's first village. He could be seen at local stores and events, and involved himself, even after he retired, in community affairs.

Columbia was remarkable and likely inimitable. Reston limped along financially, and the residents showed an impressive level of organization against a series of developers, and Irvine pioneered many new town concepts for California, but Columbia was truly the flagship new town project of the period. Columbia became a great platform for Rouse. It became his new ticket to national magazines, banquets of businessmen and government officials, and the circles of academe. Hundreds of articles in magazines and newspapers both in the region and the nation helped keep attention focused on Columbia's success and Reston's problems. As one of Rouse's staff members explained, "No paid advertising of any note was done (during the first two years), but thousands of stories and articles appeared in publications around the world, pointing up the deep dissatisfaction with the course taken by so much suburban development in America and the hope for something better."[20] In 1967 the *Washington Post* celebrated the first settlers of Columbia and claimed, "No community of this scale has ever before been begun in this country with such careful and conscious regard for the quality of lives that its inhabitants will lead." The editorial praised the developer for "providing the widest possible diversity of people, occupation and pastimes," and explained that the community was holding fast to its "original promise to offer housing to anyone who works there, from corporation president to janitor . . . Columbia is now setting a national standard for the art of building cities." This was just as Rouse had hoped, and similar sentiments multiplied across the nation.[21] That Columbia was close to Washington made it even more powerful when discussions of reforming sprawl became active in the 1960s. Coverage, as indicated above, was extensive in regional publications.

Columbia played a role in discussions at the national level not only because of press attention, but also because of Rouse's direct testimony to government officials. Federal sponsorship of private new towns had appeared for the first time in President Lyndon B. Johnson's 1964 housing proposals as a part of Great Society legislation. Johnson, responding to both suburban criticism and a growing wave of national studies, believed that new towns could be part of urban reconstruction along more sane lines. In 1964 he even criticized urban growth occurring in a "sprawling, space-consuming, unplanned and uneconomical way" and argued forcefully that "future growth must take place in an orderly fashion."[22] New towns like Columbia and Reston seemed to point the way to orderly suburban growth without great cost to the government.

A series of congressional acts, tied partially to Great Society idealism, progressively increased government underwriting of privately developed new towns. No action emerged in 1964, but in 1965 Congress, responding to executive pressure, allowed the Department of Housing and Urban Development to insure mortgages, up to $25 million, for large-scale planned projects. Known as Title X, it attracted little attention. New town legislation still remained a blip on the urban landscape.

While the legislation was growing, new town proponents faced significant opposition from big city mayors, small builders, and antistatist politicians who feared "complex forms of Federal control." Opponents also feared that the new town proponents were "contemplating Federally designed and constructed new towns where families of differing income classes and races will be mixed by Federal fiat. . . . This fear has been fed by confusion between our proposal and the way in which the English built a certain number of new towns."[23] However, the administration, and a growing number of congressional supporters were not contemplating close imitation of the social democratic example.

Rouse and other supporters of new towns carved out their unique position on government sponsorship of new towns that created a space between their proposals, European direct action, and even the statist approach of some other Great Society initiatives. In 1966 Rouse testified in Congress in favor of new town legislation that was then only in its infancy: "Let me remind you that I am a private developer and a private mortgage banker. I believe in the private enterprise system. The home building industry in America is the most productive in the world. But there are some things it cannot do without assistance—the very assistance it now resists. There is absolutely no means whatsoever by which the home building industry, as it is now constituted in America, can develop the sensibly organized new communities that America needs to accommodate its future growth." Rouse explained that without government funds "the enormous number of individual operators . . . will continue to build our cities in little bits and pieces."[24]

Appearing again in front of Congress in 1968, Rouse dangled the vision of Columbia, a "14,000-acre 'color-blind,' environmentally aesthetic new community." He then proceeded to deliver "a plea for enactment of experimental and innovative federal programs, such as financial assistance to new town developers who in turn would be required to provide low–and moderate-income housing." Such action, Rouse hoped, would "aid in the forging of a comprehensive national strategy to counteract the forces of division and disorder which plagued the nation in the 1960s."[25] This testimony in favor of federal action seems to run contrary to Rouse's notion of private sector leadership but in fact is consistent with his ideology.

Rouse had a sophisticated, although predictable, view of the proper role of government in reforming sprawl. He was not opposed to government involvement in ambitious planning schemes; he was only opposed to government involvement in the actual design, construction, and management of new towns themselves—qualities associated with the New Deal and European new towns. He acknowledged his special situation, the generous and patient support he had received from insurance companies, but he nevertheless came out strongly in favor of federal help in other private projects in an interview in 1970, because most developers needed "new resources made available to them, and I think some form of public support is required to bring it about."[26] As in other areas of his work, Rouse saw the government as the force that would leverage private action and private profit in doing the right thing.

His numerous testimonies during the 1960s and early 1970s proved crucial, at least according to Gurney Breckenfeld, who in a call to Rouse in 1971 "said that [Rouse's] testimony was quite critical to getting [new town legislation] into law."[27] Miles Colean wrote to Rouse after one of his testifying stints, scolding him for his upbeat promotion of federal aid to new towns: "I have read your 'new town' testimony with great interest and, as you suspect, with no little distress." Colean argued that the new towns would not prevent sprawl, "would impose another measure of federal control over local matters," would slow innovation, and would impose new regulations on private developers.[28]

The unique aspects of Columbia were forgotten as the apparent success of Columbia as a model launched the federal government on a disastrous program of underwriting more private new towns. The creation of a federal new town planning program would not have been possible without Columbia, but it also benefited from a variety of national commissions during the late

1960s, staffed with many planners and urban specialists, that issued studies calling for national action on metropolitan sprawl of which new towns
might play a part.[29] Reformers in Congress and the president understood
that they stood little chance of convincing housing interests and most
Congressmen to support draconian land regulations, radical revisions in the
FHA or national highway programs, or government-constructed new
towns.

The year 1968 marked the beginning of the first large-scale programs
under what was known as Title IV, part of the Housing and Urban
Development Act of 1968. Democratic senators pushed for $500 million
in support of new town projects, but opponents succeeded in reducing the
amount of aid, in part by citing problems at Reston, to $250 million. The
hopes of Title IV's framers also remained largely unmet. Although
Jonathan, Minnesota, and Park Forest South, Illinois, started under provisions of this bill, most developers remained unimpressed by the financial incentives, and the Nixon administration did not act aggressively to
expand the program.

In 1970 Title VII emerged, under the guidance of Congressman
Thomas Ashley (D) from Ohio, as a more substantive program of reform,
part of the much larger Urban Growth and New Community
Development Act of 1970. A new corporation was created within HUD,
the New Community Development Corporation (NCDC), to manage the
program and force executive action. A total of $500 million was appor-
tioned in bond guarantees with a maximum set at $50 million for each devel-
opment. Infrastructure and service grants as well as supplemental loans were
also promised for new communities.[30]

Ashley, the leading congressional sponsor, had visited the European new
towns during the 1960s and came back impressed by what he had seen. He
knew, however, that it would be difficult to duplicate European experiences
here. "Success in this kind of effort," Ashley admitted, "could not be obtained
by any kind of frontal assault on the established development process."[31]
Instead he explained that "the idea would be to pose an alternative form
of development that, on the basis of sheer competition, would be so much
superior to the living opportunities to the extent they exist at all for people of lesser means, that this form of development would begin to enjoy a
considerable reputation."[32] This sounds a great deal like James Rouse's stated
goals for Columbia. In fact, the goal of what became the federal new town
program was to encourage more Columbias and avoid more Restons by leveraging government money behind private developers. As Ashley himself said,
"I wish that Reston and Columbia were Title VII undertakings because even
the severest critics of new communities would have to say that, on balance,
they have been remarkably successful." He did point out, however, "Both

of these communities have been enormously successful in terms of lessons learned. Simon learned a hell of a lot, and some of it not very pleasantly, as far as Reston is concerned," referring to the fact that Simon had lost control of the project.[33]

The legislation provided for more than new towns, and reflects the indirect influence of European planning initiatives and Columbia. Title VII ambitiously proposed "the development of a national urban growth policy and to encourage the rational, orderly, efficient, and economic growth" of cities, suburbs, and rural areas.[34] The plan had three main elements: the creation of a national urban growth policy; the subsidy of state planning initiatives; and the underwriting of large-scale planned new towns. Only the last of the three received attention, because the bill's framers underestimated American discomfort, at all levels of government, with national planning schemes. The enthusiasm for new town projects among planners and many private developers, and the bill's reliance on decentralization and private action, made the specific new town provisions of the program much more popular.

Federal guidelines for the privately developed new towns included basic requirements that the new towns assist with orderly physical and economic growth in their regions; be part of regional and local plans if they existed; be economically feasible; and seek a balance in residential, commercial, and public facilities. These provisions were unremarkable yet did reflect in some small measure the policies of European governments vis-à-vis national new town planning. The last requirements mentioned reflected the more ambitious goals of congressional supporters. They required that the individual:

> (7) [new town] makes substantial provision for housing within the means of persons of low and moderate income and that such housing will constitute an appropriate proportion of the community's housing supply; and (8) will make significant use of advances in design and technology with respect to land utilization, materials and methods of construction, and the provision of community facilities and services.[35]

In these last provisions, Ashley and his supporters imitated European new town developments that pioneered social and design innovations but, as at Columbia, laid the burden of social and design innovations squarely on private developers to arrange these elements. Title VII also called openly for "the increase for all persons, particularly members of minority groups, the available choices of location for living and working, thereby encouraging a more just economic and social environment."[36] Ashley reminded his colleagues in the House during debate on the legislation, "[W]e are not going to be creating new lily-white suburbs."[37] The program did not set specific targets, but new town proposals were to be evaluated on their commitment to meeting these goals through either subsidized housing or affirmative marketing programs. During the operation of Title VII, proposals were indeed assessed on their commitment to these provisions.[38]

Congressmen admired the products of European planning, but they did not adopt the British system of new town sponsorship that created separate government agencies responsible for community development. Nor did the government propose to undertake direct construction of communities as had been done during the New Deal and in much of Western and Eastern Europe after World War II. Title VII stated instead that the government would "rely to the maximum extent on private enterprise" in the creation of new towns.[39] At heart, congressmen sought to harness the power of private enterprise for public policy, believing that they could save the government money by recruiting developers who would, through their plans, attract homebuyers and their mortgage money. Title VII thus relied on the individual choices of thousands of homeowners who would, in theory, buy homes in these towns and thus subsidize the high development costs of these communities, much as had happened at Columbia. Title VII looked to mint many more Columbias.

The New Community Development Corporation created to manage the program within HUD was not directly building new communities or even closely overseeing them. It was primarily a means to force the Nixon administration to speed up its efforts on behalf of new town development. That this was not as powerful an agency as one might find in Europe is clear from the activities of NCDC. The corporation oversaw a decentralized planning process designed to match the market orientation of the program. The government did not design or mandate a single model of the rational, orderly suburb it envisioned. The central office of NCDC in Washington, D.C., had only financial and administrative roles, evaluating programs and arranging financing. There was no high-profile national plan nor were famous planners involved in the federal office. Instead, each new town had to hire its own planning and administrative staff to develop unique plans. Congress believed that developers under this system would be more likely to create communities that, while innovative, would be commercially successful.

What the supporters of Title VII did not take into account was the enormous power of the new town concept at the time. Instead of underwriting different models of development, they gave their blessing to a group of remarkably similar projects. Much as had occurred at Columbia, developers proposed a mixture of elements from both European new towns and conventional suburban communities. The dominant new town ideal affirmed in the legislation guided the planning to such a great extent that the well-intentioned goal of decentralized planning only raised the costs and complexity for developers without adding significantly to the degree of originality, marketability, or fit to local areas. The towns varied more in scale than in style.

Between 1970 and 1973, NCDC approved and funded fifteen towns. Combined population goals of the towns neared 800,000 residents. Accepted proposals came from ten states and ranged from approximately 2,000 to 17,000 acres in size. By 1973 almost $325 million had been committed in bond guarantees, with individual towns receiving between $7 million and $50 million each, as well as some direct grants for infrastructure and services. Twelve of the fifteen projects were in metropolitan areas with population growth higher than the national average between 1960 and 1970, and four of the new towns were located in areas with almost three times the national average growth rate. The goal of organizing fast-growing sprawl thus seemed possible. Reflecting the program's popularity with developers, almost fifty more projects were on application at the national office.

Most developers approved for guarantees seemed genuinely committed to meeting the spirit of the statutory requirements. Although these plans were remarkably similar in their approach to planning, they were convincing realizations of the general goals of the new town supporters and shared much with Columbia. The numerous plans mixed standard, single-family suburban housing and cul-de-sacs with a wide range of housing types (including high-rise apartments and contemporary, experimental buildings), residential villages with the separation of pedestrians and vehicles, urbanistic town center plans, attractive industrial parks, public transportation plans, significant open space preservation, subsidized housing, and racial integration.[40] Developers planned communities of thousands of acres of land each and target populations numbering between 30,000 and 150,000 residents. Most of the new town bells and whistles appeared in these projects.

Examples included Soul City in North Carolina, founded by civil rights leader Floyd McKissick in 1972, designed as a means to black empowerment in the rural south. At Jonathan, Minnesota, unconventional apartment houses and single-family homes nestled among the former farm fields. Racial integration at Jonathan was the norm, and activities of the few residents included a summer theater festival, a child care center, teen center, art center, and a Renaissance fair.[41] Park Forest South in Illinois seemed well on its way to success by the early 1970s and quickly attracted thousands of residents. A mixture of apartment complexes, townhouses, and single-family homes characterized the new landscape. Affirmative action brought a mix of white and black residents to the community, a public art program received a boost from the National Endowment for the Arts, an open-classroom elementary school offered the latest innovations in education, industrial parks proved popular with many businesses, open spaces and a lake softened the landscape, and an incorporated town government gave residents a strong voice in local issues. An idealistic developer, Lewis Manilow, seemed to have it all together.

The Title VII program began on an idealistic note, and towns like these were ready to grow. The program, however, began to collapse at the very point it should have reached maturity. The towns proved difficult to market and grew more slowly than predicted. The recession of 1974 slowed housing construction on a national level but delivered a blow to the new towns from which most never recovered. Soul City, for instance, designed to house 46,000 residents, had only 160 by 1980. Jonathan, Minnesota, designed to house 50,000 residents, had only 3,000 in 1982. Riverton, New York, even after $24 million of government investment, housed only 1,200 residents in 1980, and the development company had declared bankruptcy. Even Park Forest South, with nearly 6,900 residents, was bankrupt by 1976.

Most developers, although well-meaning and idealistic, faced financial ruin during the 1970s economic downturn. Even Rouse had to fire half his staff and secure additional financing from his main investor. But problems at Title VII new towns had started even before the recession. Some developers lacked experience; others failed to find sufficient financial backing or projected unrealistic growth rates. Many of the new towns were, at that time, on the outer edge of suburban development and so less attractive to many commuters. Extra amenities and services, in combination with high costs for planning, taxed developers' limited resources. Above all, the mixture of market-rate single-family homes with unconventional architecture, high-density housing, industrial parks, racial integration, and subsidized housing that had proved successful at Columbia and given it much fame alienated many potential builders and residents in a less sensational context.

American homebuilders, the group most sensitive to public taste, were slow to show interest in these communities: "Either developers could not find builders interested in buying lots, or they were not building, themselves, because of a lack of money to do so and/or because of insufficient demand." Those builders who took the risk, or developers who built their own housing, found that new towns "were not as attractive to most homebuyers as might have been expected."[42] Popular rejection and indifference is evident in a NCDC marketing report from 1979 that found, among the many reasons for failure at Park Forest South, Illinois, for instance, that "the relatively high densities located near the core have created an environment perceived as urban and therefore undesirable by a large proportion of prospective residents." Other factors that contributed to Park Forest South's poor reputation among potential white, middle-class buyers, although not necessarily black buyers and renters, included "the involvement of the federal government" and "a growing minority presence among the project's residents."[43] Soul City not only was too far from Raleigh to attract commuters, but also had "a minority image." Shenandoah, Georgia, also "suffered from a marketing problem . . . the lot sizes may be too small to attract many potential home buyers; county officials and residents also perceive it to be a 'low-income project,' since almost one-half of its units constitute some form of assisted housing."[44] At Jonathan, Minnesota, the marketing director admitted that the developer had stressed architectural innovation in a community where "95 percent of the people wanted traditional housing."[45]

These were not isolated examples. According to a summary report from 1983, innovative housing types and technological innovations were pioneered at many new towns, only to be later abandoned because of popular rejection or poor design. Racial integration was also the norm in these new towns, and they did attract a small group of idealistic black and white buyers. By December of 1983 "nearly half of the Title VII communities have minority populations equal to or greater than are found in their market areas," a strong showing for new suburban developments. Other new towns in the program were not as successful, but they were all integrated. Plans for subsidized housing in six of the towns either met or exceeded projections and in six towns constituted half or more of the total housing units built by the 1980s. Almost all of the new towns, whether they met goals or not, included subsidized housing units. In addition, "the majority of the Title VII communities have achieved a higher residential density than that found in conventional development patterns." Rental housing and attached housing thus occupied an important place in all of the towns, and even single-family homes were reasonably priced. The report noted that "by developing communities which are more economically and racially diverse than other types of development, Title VII developers were being innovative within their market areas."[46]

These reports, usually conducted by independent experts, revealed what developers understandably tried to conceal. Innovation had not packed in suburban buyers and over time alienated not only white suburban buyers, but also almost all potential buyers. The few new towns that did survive the 1970s, like the Woodlands, Texas (supported by an oil company), and St. Charles, Maryland, abandoned alternative social and design aspects and became more conventional "community builder" developments.[47]

Discomfort with the mandates of the program, in an era that turned its back on many of the ideals of the 1960s, extended to the highest levels of government. The Nixon administration's unwillingness to provide promised grants for public facilities made these towns even more difficult to market to wary consumers. A study by an independent auditing firm found that initial savings gained from government subsidy of 1.5 to 2 percent per project decreased to only .2 percent in practice because of the failure to receive promised grants and extra administrative costs engendered by dealing with NCDC.[48] The central office of NCDC processed applications slowly, and rapid staff turnover (perhaps intentional on the part of the Nixon administration) made program continuity difficult. Efforts were made to save a few of the new towns, but most towns were terminated as Title VII projects by the Carter and Reagan administrations. A majority of the new towns were sold off in pieces, and development of unified plans generally ceased. Government officials of the 1970s and 1980s, when confronted with popular indifference and the financial problems of developers, did not pursue the program.

The new town suspects were gathered in 1975 before the House Committee on Housing and Community Development (of which Thomas Ashley was a member). Private developers recommended changes in the program, congressmen grilled HUD officials on their management of the program, and new community developers offered their own reasons for the sad state of the program. James Rouse "declared that large-scale planned developments offered the *only* possible solution to the problems of preserving resources, dealing with social needs and concerns, using tax money efficiently, etc." (italics mine)—a bold but not necessarily true assertion; there were, of course, other possible solutions. Private sector new town construction was the path favored by Rouse, but hardly the only solution to suburban sprawl. Rouse lamented that "the government seems to be satisfied with the view that Title VII is a 'disaster' and rather than encourage or assist it properly, the mechanisms of government have in fact impeded and frustrated new town development." He focused not on difficulties of marketing or developer missteps but on the fact that "all real estate developers are in some trouble these days." He came out for more generous underwriting of communities and improvements in national administration of the program.[49]

Lester Gross, developer of Harbison, a Title VII new town in South Carolina, and president of the League of New Community Developers, gave the consensus statement on behalf of the Title VII developers (paraphrased in the minutes): "He outlined problems caused new communities by the economic downturn, cutbacks in Federal program expenditures, the cancellation of subprograms of the Title VII program, the moratorium on new applications and consequent adverse publicity and the rapid turnover in the leadership of the program."[50] Although the reasons for failure given by Rouse and others were true, they all concealed a disturbing and damning fact. Part of the formula that had made the private new town projects attractive to the federal government was the money the suburban public, rather than the government, would provide to each town in the form of mortgages. Conspicuous by its absence from the discussion at this hearing was the public, the silent majority who held back their money and watched while the towns floundered. Developers and supporters obscured the more problematic reason for failure: the uneasy relationship of Title VII to the wider public.

By the 1970s, Americans had become accommodated to a very different role for the federal government in suburbia. Undermining the suburban reform goals of Title VII were the more powerful FHA (Federal Housing Administration), federal highway programs, and mortgage interest tax deductions. Title VII legislation was notably silent on the billions of dollars that had been spent by the 1970s. This immense sum of money had helped maintain social and racial segregation and undermined traditional city centers without demanding a direct role for the government in planning the new residential and commercial areas it was pioneering. Although many of the Title VII new towns stood to benefit from nearby highways and federal mortgage financing, the majority of federal financing during this period continued to go to homogeneous suburban developments that lacked innovative planning and social integration and were more popular with the American mainstream. This river of government support flowed from a different ideological source. As Rouse himself pointed out in 1983, there existed throughout this period a "government bias towards suburban development, expressed positively in funds for new highways, sewers, and water systems and liberal government-supported mortgage programs."[51] Changing this bias might have been more effective than bankrolling experimental new towns.

FHA financing and federal highway spending, while mandating a tremendous, long-term role of the federal government in suburban development, did not appear as intrusive community planning to ordinary citizens. The FHA indirectly supported developers through mortgage bankers. FHA lending policies also enshrined the traditions of private development. Private developers had, in essence, written FHA rules that incorporated already popular suburban qualities like single-family homes and social exclusivity. Conventional ideas of race, class, and design canonized in mainstream attitudes found a home in new suburban developments. Informal and secretive regulation of the neighborhood by mortgage bankers and realtors did not feel like planning, although it was in reality a kind of conservative social planning. Federal mortgage underwriting, even after liberal reforms of the 1960s, supported the status quo, not an alternative.

Promoters of Title VII had mistaken elite desires, as embodied in the social justice movements of the 1960s and Columbia, as popular concerns. Social reforms and design mandates that flowed from these elite conceptions of the good society had been transferred to private developers, not eliminated. The order and predictability of standard suburbia had been disturbed at the new towns. For this reason white, middle-class Americans did not line up to live in these places. Such popularity, for instance, might well have eliminated many of the financial problems that eventually occurred. Few people discussed the dangers of trying to place a heavy social burden on private developers. One could have imagined, for instance, a new town program that did not demand so many diverse aspects of reform—design, society, and politics—but could have gone a long way toward community planning in new suburbs. The notion that businessman's expertise went beyond profit and construction to social and design experimentation had been written into the legislation with dire results.

When Title VII failed, so did any national effort to end suburban sprawl. The planning initiatives of the legislation had never received much attention, and the highly publicized debacle of the federal new towns undercut any support for the new town concept. The failure of private developers at the new towns was widely seen not as the failure of the *best* option, but as the failure of the *only* viable solution to sprawl. The adoption of Columbia, and private new towns, as a model of reform unintentionally proved to be the end of federal suburban planning as a whole. Although Rouse never lost faith that the development process of Columbia was "replicable over and over again in America under a variety of circumstances," the Title VII experience looked different.[52]

In the end, the conditions that made Columbia a success were not easily duplicated. National press coverage, good timing, deep pockets, liberal residents, and superb management all combined to make Columbia a truly impressive and successful place. Most Title VII communities, and most private towns like Reston, were unable to assemble such a delicate mixture of elements. Columbia was the new town mirage that happened to be real. Although more government sponsorship might have kept other towns alive longer, the failure of the private sector cannot be placed entirely on the government's shoulders or the recession. *The ambitious goals of the private new town had to be met by the talent of the private sector, deftly guiding projects through the ups and downs of financial cycles.* If businessmen truly wanted to assume the leading edge of idealism, not just profit, they had to show that they were up to the task under nearly any conditions. What better test of business talents than building idealistic communities under adverse conditions?

In Rouse's many speeches can be found a scathing critique of his own manner of working, American land policies, and the approach of the Title VII new towns. Again he was likely influenced by his contact with the social democratic new towns of Europe. As early as 1966 he had called for "community development corporations" within local government that could "assemble the land, produce a plan, and extend the sewer, water and roads. Instead of transferring the added value represented by the extension of sewer and water to the property owner whose farm land happens to be in the way, a development corporation could take the value increment and transfer it to the acquisition of the stream valleys and forests."[53] Even once, in a speech likely from the 1960s, he argued that private land planning "won't prevent Columbia from precipitating its own sprawl on its edges. This calls for regional planning and regional control, which must be the function of government. And I think ultimately we must look to the United States government to establish a land use policy and [a] mechanism for unfolding it, and [at] the same time, states and counties and townships must similarly accept a very high responsibility . . . for controlling the use of land." This is the only statement of Rouse's I have found that advocates a direct role for the federal government in local land issues; most often, when he was not promoting private new towns, he stood for an expansion of local public powers.[54]

These slightly more radical sentiments occasionally crept into Rouse's public statements.[55] In 1968, while testifying in favor of new towns, he admitted that in the face of suburban sprawl "there are so many circumstances in which it cannot be done by a private developer, that there is no infringement of any kind of any local property rights for local government, local county township government, to form a public development corporation and go out and do exactly what we have done in Howard County. The Howard County Government could have done that too, and in many cases the government ought to have done it." Sounding slightly pink, and openly critiquing the traditional system of land development in American cities, he argued, "It is ridiculous that we use public action in these communities to create values and that we don't use these values to pay the deficit cost of the things we can't afford for the quality of life in the community."[56] Rouse even praised Holland's strict land-use control that "confines city-to-city, town-to-town, country-to-country. We don't have to do what we are doing in the United States."[57] He proclaimed in 1973, "I don't think that, as a nation, we want to see billions of dollars flow in to pay off either developers or property owners who have gained some speculative expectancy and a piece of land. It seems to me it's a gross misuse of taxpayer's money to see that happen."[58]

Rouse was eloquent at some meetings, but the example of Columbia, and the siren song of for-profit idealism, had already charted the tragic course of American suburban reform.[59] His high-profile activities as America's leading new town developer spoke louder than his words.

CHAPTER 6

American Midas:
Rouse and Festival Marketplaces

From tangled woods, from brooks, from honied vale,
From the deep sea, from prairies rolling scope,
From cheerful farmhome, from the garden'd plain,
From varied scenes, features of Nature's face,
The gifts of the earth, of sea, join in a glowing train,
To find at last their best intended place.

Nathaniel Childs

I hold a view . . . that the greatest piece of urban design in the United
States today is Disneyland.

James Rouse

Stall markets, picturesque sheds filled with produce and independent merchants, can still be found in most American cities. Findlay Market in Cincinnati, Lexington Market in Baltimore, and the Reading Terminal in Philadelphia, to name just a few, are nevertheless mere vestiges of once thriving urban public market systems. City markets began in the colonial era as modest sheds where farmers and traders sold directly to small urban populations. During the nineteenth century, in step with the growing scale of American cities, the markets grew in size and multiplied in number; in time, they became more formal and included established stall merchants and even grander architecture. The notion that the government would play a role in organizing this commerce in order to guarantee affordability, merchandise quality, and public safety persisted over the course of the nineteenth century. In many American cities, stall markets remained important until the 1920s and 1930s.

The willingness of the American public to invest in home refrigeration and automobiles nevertheless nearly eliminated the role of urban public markets by the 1950s. No matter how lively or inexpensive, markets, crammed into traditional downtown environments, had trouble competing with glistening supermarkets on the urban fringe offering abundant parking, spot-less interiors, and prepackaged foods. Although many stands in markets featured refrigeration, many more lacked cold storage and rarely was food prepackaged. Skepticism concerning a public role in private selling, related to antisocialist ideals, also raised questions about subsidized food markets offering what was seen as unfair competition to private businesses. The shift to African American shoppers living in surrounding neighborhoods also troubled many city officials seeking a white, middle-class vision for city centers. In cities across America, market buildings were destroyed, sold, abandoned, and only a few preserved. City governments did not, in most cases, know what to do with these vestigial public spaces.

Rouse was the first developer to rediscover the picturesque potential of the city market. He came on strong promoting a renewed market space, what became known as a "festival marketplace," as part of renewed downtowns. Rouse believed that festival marketplaces could fill two different but equally important roles in modern cities. He promised that the festival marketplace would offer an alternative to both the ramshackle city markets of the past and the "cellophane wrapped" malls he was building in the countryside. These revived places would become lively marketplaces full of local/unique products for locals and tourists alike. Most important, relationships between seller and buyer would be restored, offering innumerable psychological and social benefits to urban dwellers and visitors. National development companies under this model would nurture small-scale capitalism as part of a version of urban social reform. Nurturing of entrepreneurs, and contact of the general public with them, might incidentally foster even greater respect for the American "free enterprise" system.

This idealistic side of the festival market formula has been an abject failure, notwithstanding Rouse's good intentions. He again proved naïve or overly optimistic about the capabilities of the private sector, particularly a national corporation such as The Rouse Company, in managing small-scale capitalism. His Midas touch nearly always transformed modest and flavorful stall-market environments (even ones he created from scratch) into upscale, chain-dominated selling environments.

More successful has been the festival marketplace as a catalyst by the private sector for old downtowns. Rouse desired to test theories he had been nurturing for some time after his experience with suburban malls. The festival marketplace reflected the centralized management of an urban district he thought could correct the problems of diffuse and uncoordinated management of downtown districts, "to create the opportunity and responsibility for central management ownership, operation, [and] merchandising."[1] Rouse sought to capitalize on the resurgence of urban populations following urban redevelopment projects, including "new access roads,

better parking, public squares, new or expanded institutions, new office buildings providing new jobs" paired with "new values and new lifestyles of young
people [that] have made the city a more rational place for many than the
suburbs."[2] Informal gentrification related to urban renewal had created untapped
upscale retail potential in the city center.

Rouse offered a vision of capitalism as a direct sponsor and developer
of the leading public gathering spaces in major cities. In the nineteenth
century, city governments created great public spaces such as New York's
Central Park or Boston's Public Garden in a grand expansion of urban power.
Private sector activity had, of course, played a central role in creating urban
amusement parks and exciting sidewalk cultures (such as that along
Broadway in New York) during the nineteenth and early twentieth centuries, but business interests, by the 1970s, were not known for self-consciously creating lively public places downtown; many of the public plazas
created as part of urban renewal during the 1950s and 1960s remained windswept
and attracted far fewer citizens than projected. Rouse sought to expand the
capabilities of private enterprise in quasi-public space creation and succeeded
brilliantly.

The model for the festival marketplace derived first from Ghiradelli Square
(1962) in San Francisco, "the modern-day pioneer of what one critic dis-
parages as 'the hanging plant—scented candle, boutique syndrome.'"[3]
Rouse also knew city markets in Baltimore but in large measure borrowed
the festival marketplace concept from a former dean of the Graduate School
of Design at Harvard, Ben Thompson, who had had his eye on the old market area of Boston for a number of years. Faneuil Hall, a lecture hall, was
only a small part of what was an extensive market complex that by the 1960s
had lost much of its luster. Faneuil Hall stood in line with famous Quincy
Market, a grand Greek revival affair in stone with two impressive temple
fronts. On either side of lengthwise streets were the old warehouse buildings, known as the North and South Buildings. Through the efforts of planners such as Edward Logue, the area surrounding Faneuil Hall and Quincy
Market had undergone extensive redevelopment and tens of thousands of
workers now filled the Government Center area around a new city hall,
an estimated increase of "60,000 [professionals] in the last ten years," most
of them relatively young and affluent.

Mayor Kevin White provided the official and selective view of the area
that became the Faneuil Hall complex: "My office in City Hall looked out
over a largely vacant and rodent-infested old public marketplace behind historic Faneuil Hall."[4] By the 1960s the city had already started the process of
acquiring and renovating the North and South Buildings. The first step the
Boston Redevelopment Authority (BRA) had taken in 1964 when it
received a federal grant for renovation was to move the wholesalers out of

1 **Coffee Connection**
International Coffees and Teas

2 **Egerman's Bakery**
Fresh Bread, Bagels, Baked
Goods

3 **Magliore Carne**
Meats and Meat Products

4 **United Provision**
Meats Poultry, Fruits, Vegetables

5 **Charcutrix**
Sausage, Specialty Meats, Paté

6 **Great American Lobster**
Company
Fresh and Cooked Lobsters

7 **Paul Marks**
Eggs and Cheese

8 **Ming Tree Restaurant**
Chinese Foods

9 **Aegean Fare Restaurant**
Greek Foods and Pastries

10 **Baby Watson Bakery**
Cheese Cake and Confections

11 **Regina II**
Pizza

12 **Jennetta's Italian Grocery**

13 **Dembro's Meats**
Prime Beef, Meat, Poultry, Fruits

14 **Doe Sullivan Co.**
International Cheeses

15 **Cardoos Spices**
Herbs, Spices, Condiments

16 **Freedman Bakery**
Breads and Bagels

17 **Au Bon Pain Bakery**
French Bakery

18 **Belgian Fudge**
Fudge in all Flavors

19 **Jelly Shack**
Cape Cod Jams and Preserves

21 **Brown Derby Deli**
Hot Dogs and Sausages

22 **Black Forest**
German Delicatessen

23 **Rebecca's**
Paté, Quiches, Salads

24 **Yogurt Shop**
Cones, Containers

25 **Aris Barbecued Beef**
And Chicken

26 **Walrus and the Carpenter**
Raw Bar
Fresh Oysters and Clams

27 **E.N. West Meats**
Steaks, Cutlets, Roasts

28 **(Sea Food)**

29 **Prime Shop**
Prime Beef, Meats

30 **Marion's Restaurant**
Luncheon and Coffee Shop

31 **Heidi's**
Poultry and Game

32 **Carol Ann Bakery**
Pastries, Pies, Breads

33 **G. C. Lawson Ice Cream**
Cones, Ice Cream, Molds

South Arcade--Sidewalk
34 **Lily's Café**
Sidewalk Café with Menu

35 **Lucy's Bags**
Original Canvas Bags

36 **Monograms**
Lucite Products

37 **Bookbinder Books**
Books

38 **Left Handed Complements**
Products for the Other Hand

39 **Poppy Shop**
Decorative Dried Flowers

40 **City Side Café**
Food and Drink

41 **Produce House**
Full Line of Fruits and Vegetables

North Arcade--Sidewalk

42N **Lorden Flowers**
Cut and Potted Flowers

42S **Lipinski Flowers**
Cut and Potted Flowers

43 **Lily's Bar**
Sidewalk Café

44 **Chipyard Cookies**
Homemade Cookies

45 **Juicerie**
Fresh Fruit Drinks

46 **Anna's Fried Dough**
Hot Pastry

47 **KarmelKorn**
Sweets and Popcorn

48 **Produce House Flowers**

Figure 21. This illustration and key (ca. 1976) show that when Quincy Market first reopened under Rouse management, the market flavor and sellers had been preserved and even augmented. This situation rapidly changed when the tourists arrived and demands for high returns accelerated. Illustration by Jillian Nevers.

the North and South Buildings to suburban Quincy, a questionable move for the market's survival, and begin renovation of the recently vacated buildings.[5]

Quincy Market was still operating as a public stall market during these renovations and after. Although it was not thriving and had no modern supermarket, it did contain many businesses of a traditional food type renting their spaces at low rents of three dollars a square foot. There were at least twenty-four existing merchants at Quincy Market in the year 1973 when the contract with Rouse was signed. Many of these businesses had a good reputation. West's meat store, for instance, had a "home trade" they could count on as well as lady shoppers who made a traditional pilgrimage on Thursdays to shop.[6] Although one leading meat seller explained that "the area has hit the bottom and the only way it can go is up," another merchant asserted, "I've got a good business now, but more people attracted to the area sure in hell isn't going to hurt it."[7] Remaining stands included meat, pasta, pastries, fruit, seafood, and flowers, but management was certainly lackluster. The BRA and market managers never devoted any energy to revitalizing the stall market for modern shoppers.

Thompson first won a BRA contest to redesign the area in the early 1970s. He originally arranged the Faneuil Hall project with Van Arkel and Moss developers in Philadelphia, but this project, initially given the go-ahead by BRA officials, fell through as the BRA realized that Van Arkel lacked adequate financing. It was then that Thompson and his wife, Jane, found Rouse through new town developer Robert Simon, for whom Thompson was designing a downtown for the Title VII new town of Riverton, New York.

Thompson proposed to Rouse the Faneuil Hall model that would in time become the festival marketplace *formula* of The Rouse Company (Thompson would also design both Harborplace and South Street Seaport for The Rouse Company). Thompson was something of a gourmand and a leading architect in the region. He proposed that Quincy Market could become a gourmet food center offering a mix of the fresh products it had always been known for, in addition to high-end fast food, cafés, and local restaurants. The adjoining market buildings would feature a variety of high-quality dry goods stores, galleries, crafts, antiques, and clothing stores. Above shops would be offices for artists, architects, and civic and cultural organizations. The Market Streets were to become closed pedestrian ways with cafés spilling out into them with a mix of pushcarts and "spontaneous" entertainment. "The new Faneuil Hall Marketplace, operated and maintained as an entity including streets and public services, would be carefully laid out as a downtown bazaar, to gain the variety, color, balance and constant change that is missing from today's piecemeal development of inner cities. There would be special emphasis on provision of fresh foods, meats, seafood, baked goods and delicacies to serve area residents on a daily basis. Once again people from the entire region would come to the nation's famous Boston market for food, enjoying the broadest selection of quality and price from dozens of individual merchants."[8] Thompson explained to his fellow architects, "Unlike most modern shopping centers with large department stores as financial anchors, our plan sees a major market of small merchants, with a colorful diversity of life and events competing on a day-to-day basis. . . . The crux of making this happen is economic—having the special economic freedom to cluster and locate hundreds of small shops and stands in appropriate places to create that intense chaotic mix of Les Halles, of the Farmer's Market in Los Angeles, of the Piazza Navona on market day."[9]

This all sounded very exciting at the time, and Thompson added a nearly spiritual zeal and philosophy to the market restoration. This is apparent in a memo from the mid-1970s: "In becoming the city market basket again,

Faneuil Hall Marketplace has the chance of regaining that genuine character of a city center. People need the variety and abundance the markets bring. Socially, they need the communal security of personal contact and mutual exchange. Psychologically, they hunger for the festive activity and action that markets add to the central city. The natural pageantry of crowds and goods, of meat, fish and crops, of things made and things grown all to be smelled, tasted, seen and touched, are the prime source of sensation and amusement in whole populations—in many nations except our own."[10] The festival marketplace, as conceived by Thompson, was a critique of American culture of the Cold War, based on his cultural preconceptions. Like many urban-based designers, Thompson took umbrage at the supermarket and the new suburban shopping districts resplendent in plastic, metal, and concrete, even if it was the modern consumer's paradise. The American public did not share his distaste for supermarkets or his fascination with city markets, but this mattered little to a romantic like Thompson.

On first glance it might be unclear how Thompson ever convinced James Rouse to get involved in such an avant-garde urban project. Even some within Rouse's company had reservations about getting involved. Jack Meyerhoff, a leading member of Rouse's board, wrote to Rouse in 1972 that "this project certainly does not meet the criteria that was established for The Rouse Company to follow in its projects, and it is my opinion that this project should be sponsored by either a civic or philanthropic organization." Rouse also faced a tough battle for financing from banks. He adopted Thompson's scheme for some clear, if rarely discussed, reasons. Thompson's plan, while in description quite different from the malls Rouse had built in the 1950s and 1960s, did closely parallel what Rouse, in some of his less critical moments, *believed* about the function of his suburban malls. As indicated above, in contrast to most suburban developments, Rouse at least publicly saw his malls as being attractive, lively pedestrian zones with great cultural potential. He also made much of having nurtured small businesses in his malls and considered himself something of an expert in managing complex retail environments with lively market spaces. Looking back in 1983 after a visit to the Los Angeles Farmer's Market, he described it as a "a mixture of market, eating places, and some junk shops. It used to [be] everybody's image of what ought to be done. Many have tried . . . We flopped at Plymouth Meeting [mall]. But that image, hanging with us over the years, finally generated gourmet fare at Sherway Gardens [mall] then Picnic at Woodbridge [mall]. It was those two experiences that gave us the nerve to undertake Faneuil Hall Marketplace—and all that has followed."[11] As early as 1960 Rouse had praised the Farmer's Market in Los Angeles for its "special warmth and charm" while criticizing his own malls for "imposing" a "project feeling" in the suburbs.[12] That Thompson was proposing control not only of the buildings but also of the spaces around them as a privately controlled, centrally managed environment—and a ninety-nine-year lease—perfectly matched Rouse's views on the superiority of the completely managed environment. As one Rouse Company document laid out in 1973, "during the public hearings that were held TRC [The Rouse Company] emphasized that the inclusion of the Quincy Market Building and Streets, the development of the entire marketplace as an integrated whole, was the essence of its proposal."[13]

Thompson's ideas were in all likelihood the most carefully conceived, the most impressive on first glance, and the most financially promising. But the Thompson project, with Rouse as development partner, was not the only viable option. There is a forgotten part of the story of Faneuil Hall that illustrates the road not taken in the privatization of this public space. There was a far more public-oriented proposal in the air in Boston, a project more sensitive to the traditions of the market and its delicate economics. This proposal came from Roger Webb, a well-connected developer with a small firm known as Architectural Heritage, who had led the renovation of the old city hall nearby.

Webb proposed not only a different vision, but an alternative management structure that was designed to preserve the unique flavor of Quincy Market: "The major feature of the plan is the central Quincy Building, which will retain its traditional character as *Boston's Public Market*, the food center for the region. All the local merchants now in the Quincy Building will be invited (and helped) to remain. . . . New merchants will be brought in to make this a major FOOD CENTER, featuring fresh produce, fruits, meats, poultry and seafood, baked goods, coffee, spices, cheese, and dairy items—the complete range of fresh foods to serve Boston residents and employees on a daily basis." Although Rouse and Thompson promised to preserve the food sellers, they did not much talk about augmenting them. Webb also proposed that even in dry goods the emphasis would be on "daily needs in food, clothes, furnishings, hardware, sporting goods, marine goods, personal services, eating and entertainment. Tourists will be welcome, but the prime customer will be the local one."[14] What made the creation of this local market possible was the structure of the development proposal; a striking contrast to the hard-driving system that Rouse would use to woo the city.

Webb proposed that not only would Quincy Market remain a public-owned market, but also that his company would essentially act as a nonprofit developer acting on behalf of the city. He promised to return "70 cents of every dollar increase per square foot of space, since his organization would be acting 'as an agent' for the city, rather than as a profit-making organization."[15] This situation would have been more like the redevelopment undertaken at Pike Street in Seattle (where fresh food stalls are still popular). Webb boldly addressed the Urban Affairs Committee of the Boston City

Council and reminded them that, unlike Rouse, "he was bidding on the North and South Market Buildings only because the Quincy Market had always been and rightly should remain city property. He wanted a contract only for fifty years in order to get financing, not a lease and thus the property would always be owned by the city."[16] Webb explained his approach carefully: "We feel the market building is different from the other two. This building is the first Greek revival building constructed in New England, and it has always been publicly owned. It has always been the scene of a subsidized retail food market. We feel it is not necessary for the city to give up complete control for 99 years."[17]

The Webb alternative possessed a fair amount of political support. At one point it was thought BRA director Robert Kenney (a classmate of Webb's at Harvard Business School and an old chum) would award Webb the contract. In fact, a great cry went up from leading architects and preservationists because of the perceived inside playing that would land Webb the contract without a fair hearing for the other project. "When Thompson's first developer was forced to drop out, the question was in effect reopened by the BRA, and now it is on the verge of selecting Webb but without the public examination of the issues deserved by the city's 99-year commitment."[18] In many ways Webb was not up to the job of turning the area around. He had only a very small firm, one staff architect, no clearly formulated plan, and was somewhat controversial around town. That he was not a perfect man, however, does not make his proposal or his commentary on the Rouse project less valid. His was one of the few voices questioning the deal that even Thompson would partly regret.

The Rouse proposal appeared significantly more promising to the city. Rouse was working with Ben Thompson, was a leading developer with demonstrated success in retail operations, was known for his bullish tone on city redevelopment, and offered an exceptional reward in exchange for his ninety-nine-year lease. Unlike Webb, Rouse promised that the city would receive either 20 percent of gross revenues or a minimum yearly payment of $600,000 by the third year. The city had much to gain under the deal, and it has been an unfair argument against the festival marketplaces that they have been bad deals for most cities in terms of financing. As Rouse explained in 1976, "It's much more of a civic enterprise than the standard regional commercial shopping center. Ultimately 25 percent of the gross rent collected goes to the city."[19]

The only problem with this particular deal was that the projections of future income, which in hindsight turned out to be modest, were based closely on Rouse's experience as a mall developer. As he explained in 1973: "Based on existing Rouse Company rent programs and records . . . the growing success of the market retailers will produce increasing payments to the city well in excess of the guaranteed sum." Rouse bragged that in his malls "the firm averages $16 rents [per square foot] in its centers and in a number of cases reaches the $24 level. The rents are based on percentage of gross income of tenants and, through the success of its tenants, it's reasonable to expect the city will receive over $1 million annually starting in the late 1970s from this program."[20] As he admitted, "The cost (of renovation) can only be justified by high rents from high productivity in sales and high pedestrian traffic."[21]

Rouse proposed to transfer the revenue levels of malls to merchants selling sides of beef, cheese, and bags of fresh parsley at subsidized monthly rents of three dollars per square foot. That Rouse was generous to older tenants at first, and made verbal promises that the market would preserve some genuine market function, served as merely a stay of execution rather than a pardon. The company admitted in internal documents that although they were working hard to find "'one of a kind' distinctive stores, shops and restaurants," "the security of the Project is fundamentally tied to the achievement of projected sales averaging $125 to $150 dollars per square foot" with rents in proportion. The vendors needed these high numbers because the new businesses would be responsible for paying "a percentage of sales commencing at sales of zero" as well as special service and tax charges of five dollars per square foot (a figure that alone was higher than the original rents). The company knew that it might have to "settle for a complete subsidy on the order of 360,000 dollars over the first three years" of older market tenants, but after that time it had no responsibility to them.[22] Rouse saw no reason why these food sellers could not, with proper management and promotion, achieve record sales, but this optimism was not justified in practice.

The festival marketplace thus became the Trojan horse of the suburban reentry into the center city. Not only because the marketplace was a completely controlled environment combining the privatization of formerly public spaces and streets, and not only because the familiar chains moved in by the 1980s, but because The Rouse Company brought its system of suburban mall management to the central city. Management reports of the market from the 1970s provide descriptions of sales at the individual merchants with notes such as "watch sales," or "recapture space," or "replace" based on sales. Some of the tenants noted with these terms were the older fresh food tenants. Faneuil Hall did not look like a mall, it was not marketed as a mall, but its fundamental system of operation was that of the suburban mall. Whatever negative things one can say about city market operations—and there is much—they have not generally been operated on such a careful and ruthless manner; they were subsidized food markets with modest returns expected.

Rouse was awarded the contract by the BRA, and Webb fell from view forever. Most of the older tenants welcomed The Rouse Company, too. In the contract signed with the BRA in 1973, The Rouse Company seemed genuinely committed to preserving the older market stalls: "Revitalization of the Quincy Market as the unique and historic meat/cheese/produce market of the City of Boston is of central importance in our program for the redevelopment of the Faneuil Hall Marketplace. In this regard, we view the market as being the merchants more than the building." The company promised that they would do everything possible for "the retention of those existing merchants who are essential to what the market has been, what it is now, and what it can be."[23] Existing merchants received three-year leases beginning in 1975 at their current rents and promises that they could renew their leases at fair market value after three years. As The Rouse Company planners discussed in 1973: "Quincy Market is a meat/cheese/produce market and the intention is to keep it the same but increase the number of stalls on the lower level." In the North and South Market Buildings the company also promised "a collection of 'one of a kind' shops plus a very large number of restaurants."[24] Roy Williams, the retail expert behind the marketplace, modeled part of his work on Baltimore's Lexington Market: "If we were guided by a precedent for Quincy Market, it would be Lexington Market . . . If it's as good as Lexington Market we'll congratulate ourselves."[25]

Thompson still believed his initial vision had survived Rouse management and proposed that Quincy Market "will be operated as a food bazaar, with the first floor kept open as a continuous 'indoor street.' Along this street, individual retail concessions will offer meat, fish, produce, dairy goods, specialty foods and wines . . . [while] a variety of ready food stalls . . . will create an enormous international buffet served by a central eating area." Early plans projected "produce vendors" along the North and South Market Streets interspersed with cafés. The plan also envisioned pedestrian streets facing the renovated Market Street buildings "with plantings, benches, kiosks, play areas, and mobile vendors" to create a European-flavored environment.[26] Initially much of this description was achieved.

In the early years Rouse aimed to create a unique market environment. Although he was worried about the success of the fresh food dealers, he was confidant that "conventional market business will flow strong and the merchants will do well." Rouse also sent a special memo to his employees in 1976, entitled "Faneuil Hall Marketplace: Its Special Meaning and Potential for The Rouse Company," in which he tried to chart the course of the market in the future: "The overwhelming feeling of the shopping goods stores should be small, special shops run by their owners. An occasional Ann Taylor is okay but, as a whole, it must be a marketplace with stores that shoppers don't find elsewhere even in Chestnut Hill or on Newbury Street." Although this might seem contradictory with the financial screws that tightened on most merchants, it should be noted that Rouse, perhaps naïvely, was always of the belief that individual merchants could do as well or better on a square-foot basis than could chains—even though in many cases the chains, by dint of their great power, forced out small stores at his malls. Rouse even went so far as to say that "Faneuil Hall is a marketplace—we cannot let it slip into being a shopping center." He also explained, "There is not much room for chain stores here. The branch manager of a distribution center is not in the same spirit with merchants who now give character to the colonnade. I am pleased that Hickory Farms dropped out . . . We must do everything we can to reinforce the intensely personal quality of the market." Rouse was buoyant about the project, as he rightly should have been, in the early years: "It is already apparent that Faneuil Hall uplifts those who come to use it. It is of the good city. The flower shops, the trees and benches, and public spaces, the openness through the canopies and the colonnade, the richness drawn from the heritage of old buildings, the little shops run by their owners and the personal exchanges across the counters between the owner-merchants and their customers, the smallness, intimacy, smells, sounds and sights that are uniquely those of a market have all served to tap some deep yearning that reside[s] among most of us."[27]

The Rouse Company also created the Bull Market on the edge of Quincy Market, filled with quaint pushcarts selling a wide variety of goods: "The emphasis was placed on unique, quality, earthy products sold by people who understood in-depth merchandising in small areas, had a flair for display and presentation and who felt a sensitivity toward the project . . . The range stretched from cider presses to kites, from handprints to cookies."[28] The Bull Market, reflecting a market feeling rarely found anymore in American cities, spread under the new glass canopies alongside Quincy Market. Most of the businesses in the complex were local or regional businesses, and most wares, according to The Rouse Company, "reflect their Boston and New England heritages."[29] Specialty merchandise included whimsical, kitschy additions such as "a place that makes photocopies on brass, an oriental theme shop called Dynasty and a shop of costume and practical hats."[30] Rouse executives eventually added pushcarts to their mall environments, providing a gentrified urban flavor to even the most luxurious suburban malls.

When Quincy Market opened, Rouse had created plenty for market lovers to appreciate amid the prepared foods such as fudge, pizza, hot dogs, deli sandwiches, and ice cream cones. If one entered on the Faneuil Hall side of Quincy Market, one was hit by a nice cluster of fresh food sellers, including Egerman's bakery, Magliore Carne, United Provision, Charcutriz, even an egg and cheese stand. These were just some of the fruit and vegetable sellers, bakers, and butchers. Thompson explained the meaning of the stalls: "The major emphasis on a *complete food market* is critical to making the market area an everyday place. Meats and poultry—offered by the well-known existing merchants in the Quincy Building—are now rounded out with other individual vendors selling fruits, vegetables, coffee, tea, spices, cheese, wine, dairy goods, baked goods, and delicacies. The experience is again one of direct relationship between buyer and seller."[31]

In the *New York Times Magazine*, Jane Davison described Thompson's plan in glowing terms: "As early as 1966, Thompson proposed mounting a real revival, not just refurbishing the theater. The sets he planned then and that now exist are lavish with heaped fruit, vegetables, meat, flowers and baskets, a sensuous still life reminiscent of Les Halles, Campo dei Fiori in Rome, and innumerable other traditional marketplaces throughout the world. People are back on the scene, in crowds that are, if anything, too enthusiastic." She praised the fact that "Thompson-Rouse's complex offers real food and services in profusion: seventeen eating places and eighteen food merchants." Davison lavished encomiums on the innovative design and the great risks involved in such an unorthodox project, but also saw that the challenges had just begun: "The Boston project depends on leasing many small spaces to independent retailers who specialize within a general category such as food. Individuals compete against each other . . . they support the Marketplace and pay the developer not only rent but also a percentage of their gross." As discussed in an earlier chapter, built into the very heart of every Rouse retail project was a hyper-competitive process that sped up the rate of change and competition by demanding higher rents and portions of sales. Davison reminded Rouse, "[T]he developer must stay on guard against compromises in quality and competence if the marketplace is to hold on to its originality. The eccentricity rate among self-employed entrepreneurs is high, and the best bagel maker may be the worst businessman." Davison divined a likely fate for the marketplace: "Fast-buck operators and tourist trappers are always eager to lease but care little for taste and continuity."[32]

Architectural critic Robert Campbell offered an alternative analysis of the market that placed less emphasis on the market stalls and more on the successful environment projected for the mass public: "The Marketplace is an impersonation of a kind of urban life that no longer exists in most of America. It's a theatrical representation of street life. It has to be this, because that is a stage we have to go through as we begin cautiously, self-consciously to re-enact the urban culture we abandoned."[33] Rouse, in a letter to Campbell, praised him for coming closest to understanding the function of the market as he saw it. Such a view depended more upon good urban design than small-scale capitalism and stall selling.[34]

One dissenting voice at the opening derided the effort: "I give it a year. You can get things cheaper at a supermarket."[35] Another commented, "I can't afford any of this stuff," as he headed off to nearby Haymarket, a little slice of market life, usually selling lower-quality merchandise, around the corner. Comparisons between Haymarket and Quincy in a 1976 article indicated, "Prices and styles compete. Apples selling for 25 cents a pound at the Haymarket sell for 25 cents apiece across the street at the new Quincy market."[36] A *Boston Globe* reporter noted on opening day "more rubber-necking than serious shopping. A butcher at United Provision Meat Co. sighed: 'It's not my day.'" The reporter found comfort from Julia and Paul Childs, who "thought the marketplace would catch on. People at the opening wanted to look things over first, then buy, Childs said."[37]

Rouse believed in 1976 that although the market was a great hit with the "quick lunch customer, to the family on a lark and to the couple out for dinner," because of the many food choices "somewhat overwhelmed by the opening crowds has been the shopper who wanted to buy the week's meat, fish, cheese or produce." Rouse pointed out that although some fresh food merchants were doing well, others were "having an uncertain early experience." Moreover, Rouse celebrated the tourist market the company had uncovered, and although he admitted, "we have been so determined not to build 'a tourist trap,'" yet "it is a huge potential for us and it is right that we serve it well." Rouse noted, "it is people from the Boston area itself, from New England and from elsewhere who are attracted to the uniqueness, the liveliness, the warmth, the beauty, the flair, the reputation of Faneuil Hall Marketplace." It was Rouse's belief that the tourist could be encouraged to purchase and patronage better quality goods of a variety of price ranges: "The problem is with promoters who make a low standard interpretation of their needs and wants. We can do here for the marketplace and the tourist what Disney did for the amusement park."[38]

Within a few years, despite the good intentions of designer and developer, the tone of the Faneuil Hall Marketplace had changed. The millions who came to visit made Faneuil Hall a great commercial success story. The design standards were high, and yet the crush of people and the temptations of tourism, coupled with the hard-driving management of The Rouse Company, began to compromise the initial vision created by Thompson and sold by Rouse as a renewed marketplace. In a speech from 1977 Rouse explained, "Quincy Market averages $300 in sales per square foot—double that of successful regional shopping centers. In its first year Quincy Market, with only 80,000 square feet, attracted about as many people as Disneyland—10 million."[39]

These record sales were not evenly distributed. Market stalls were failing or had turned to fast-food selling. MIT urbanist Bernard Frieden explains the process: "One day a produce dealer who had too many ripe pineapples on hand decided to sell them by the slice and found he did it much better that way . . . Within the first few years fast food took over most of the central arcade."[40]

Figure 22. Attractive "public" spaces entranced millions of visitors to the Fanueil Hall marketplace complex and set new, high standards of design and maintenance for urban redevelopment across America. Where once urban renewal had been cold and formal, architect Ben Thompson and developer Rouse showed that the human and historical side of urban life could be a profitable investment. G. E. Kidder Smith, courtesy of Kidder Smith Collection, Rotch Visual collections, MIT.

A remarkable 1978 memo to The Rouse Company from Ben and Jane Thompson outlined the crisis in the marketplace vision. They began by sternly reminding Rouse managers that the Faneuil Hall complex faced "problems different from those conventionally encountered in managing successful malls." They noted the "urban location, the size and number of individual merchants, the heavy food orientation, and the very special mix of ingredients" that made the project fragile. The Thompsons reminded the company, too, that "Commitments were made to the City of Boston regarding its character and environment that must be honored for years to come. Representations were made to incoming tenants as well." This was not an auspicious start to their letter.[41]

A searing litany of problems quickly followed from the Thompsons. They began with what they called IMAGE, and lamented, "The success of fast food and singles drinking operations tends to drive out serious shoppers for groceries, fashion, and durable goods. The present local image of the Marketplace is something like 'pizza, piano bars, no-park, push and shove.' The Go-Go aspects need no more promoting." They singled out a "visible 'drift' and deterioration of merchandise quality . . . as each merchant reaches for the quick sale to the crowds now being attracted there." They also disliked what they called "spin-off" because "more and more of the unique and success-ful tenants are being 'serialized' in other The Rouse Company centers," thus converting "the once highly individualized owner-operated business of Faneuil Hall Marketplace into chain-like businesses with absentee owners." They decried "HOMOGENIZATION," wherein "inexperienced merchants, slow to get established, will tend to get displaced under pressures for financial perfor-mance. It can be anticipated that larger chains and franchises, eager for this prime location, will make strong bids for space. Successful FHM [Faneuil Hall Marketplace] merchants will seek to expand and multiply, leading to a radical change of character." Tour buses were distasteful to them as well, and the mixing of retail food with fast-food stands seemed to dilute the appeal of real food shopping. The Thompsons also noted a growing problem with the tenants, who were suffering because of "high costs and unexpected back billings." With no force behind them, the Thompsons suggested that the company redirect its market from mass tourism, enforce policies that would preserve quality of merchandise for sale, create policies to keep out chain stores, and reorganize the fresh food sellers "to reassert the market's identity as a viable, convenient place to shop for groceries of an unusual and quality kind.[42]

Even those more closely associated with the developer listed similar prob-lems. A former Rouse and BRA employee, Carol Todreas, wrote Rouse in 1978 expressing her dismay at the direction of the marketplace: "I am dis-turbed because the Marketplace as it was planned and conceived is in jeop-ardy." She remembered, "Quincy Market began its new life as a specialty food and food related market geared to presenting a variety of quality foods, cooking utensils, and table service appointments. Food to eat on the premises, restaurants, and cafes were to be a pleasant amenity." She blasted managers because "Quincy Market has been transformed to a giant fast food opera-tion with even the meat and produce merchants emphasizing the sale of fast food items." The Bull Market, too, had become a "vehicle for any ordi-nary trinket or a display case of duplicate items sold elsewhere in the Marketplace." Todreas could "see why Quincy Market is now hailed as Boston's latest amuse-ment park and tourist trap with the latest fad foods to eat and souvenir-type of items to buy."[43]

The Rouse Company and Rouse took few steps to prevent any real drift pinpointed by the Thompsons or Todreas—they had an expensive reno-vation debt to repay (and had invested, by one estimate, $30 million in private capital for the project[44]), high standards of cleanliness to maintain, an ambitious payment scheme to the city, and demands from their own investors. Maintaining a genuine market remained low on their list of priorities. A 1978 Rouse marketing study found that although some shoppers were com-

ing for "the special, extra fresh, extra quality item," the groceries were increasingly marginal: "The meat, cheese and produce shops at the Marketplace are effectively serving as the *principal* food (grocery) market for a very limited segment of the Marketplace shoppers—probably not more than 10 percent. For the vast majority of shoppers, it is simply too far from home."[45]
A Rouse internal memo noted,

> In addition to original 16 fast-food merchants, another 13 Quincy merchants have added fast-food items. This is in response to obvious opportunity represented by crowds and, in some cases, a response to financial need. Fast food is now available up and down the complete center aisle and at both ends of glass canopies—a departure from the original plan to keep fast food in two distinct areas along [the] center aisle. By and large, the original "pure food" merchants which now sell fast food make a poor presentation—frontage devoted to original merchandise is reduced; frontage devoted to fast food is often third-rate in appearance.

He even admitted, "Image of Quincy Building is 'fast-food'—taking on a 'Coney Island' look in some areas." Although Rouse's employees offered potential solutions, including subsidizing pure food sellers, Rouse wrote in margin notes on a memo encouraging subsidy of market tenants, "I'm not sure"—surely enough to end that discussion. One of Rouse's employees worried that "Serious shopping in the Quincy Building is being made more difficult—the predominance of fast foods is growing, as are crowds, and declining attention is being given to 'pure foods' by the merchants. Quincy Building may be reaching the point where it is no longer a legitimate marketplace for groceries and specialty take-home foods." In a short response Rouse wrote, "But it may have another purpose," indicating that the market function of the Quincy Building came second to financial and tourist realities. Another Rouse executive noted that "the more expensive quality goods and crafts originally offered in the Bull Market have met with less success than lower-priced quick-sale items," and that "common ownership of multiple shops is expanding, raising fears of 'homogenization' of ownership and merchandise."[46]
Rouse was not immune to criticism and on paper urged reform, but the big-business, private sector model lacked the tools to deal with this kind of crisis. He, himself, reminded his managers in 1978 that "there is much evidence of creeping mediocrity in other aspects of Faneuil Hall: unattractive kiosks that have sneaked out on the square between Quincy Market and South Market; the gradual spread of fast foods into all the market stalls (only one market merchant remains who is not selling fast foods); I hear that Friedman's Bakery is now selling soft drinks in cans. This seems very wrong

to me, not compatible with a bakery and a dangerous precedent which can soon lead to everybody selling soft drinks in cans—vending machines next?"[47] The demand for high returns from all merchants made the balance too precarious. As late as 1984, Rouse sent a letter to Rouse Company managers— he had retired—with some revealing notes: "I was surprised by the turnover—and improvement. Jim McLean said overall turnover now about 30% since beginning. My bet is that it is close to 40–50%." In addition, he reiterated the tough management that made the festival marketplace so profitable. Rouse approved of "weeding out weak tenants" and made "an interesting note—Crabtree and Evelyn now 4 times larger—doing over 1600/square feet."[48] In 2002 there are approximately twenty obvious chain stores, twenty-five specialty retail stores (some of which are spin-offs from other festival marketplaces), and a few local restaurants like Durgin Park. There are no fresh food market vendors at all. Architectural critic Robert Campbell made a recent visit (1996) and found that "the stores are bigger now, and more of them are national chains. Much of the flavor of Boston has disappeared. Things are more tourist-oriented, although it is a mystery why tourists travel to Boston for the same T-shirts and movieland mementos they can find anywhere."[49]

The victims of the management scheme were not just the market vendors, but also half of the festival marketplace concept. If in fact the role of the marketplace was in part to restore face-to-face contact between owner and seller and encourage a new kind of urban society by enlightened capitalism (and celebrate the American entrepreneurial spirit), the replacement of market stands with fast-food franchise-type operations or large stores with clerks and other low-level service workers represented more than just a change of scenery at the market. Relationships tied to market stalls selling real provisions were not secondary aspects of the festival marketplaces, and the loss of this element under the regime of the privatized public marketplace cannot be understated. That the small but vibrant Haymarket district survives nearby indicates that there remains interest in inexpensive stall-market vending, an opportunity ultimately lost at Quincy Market. The Faneuil Hall complex is still an important quasi-public space in Boston, a real gem in many respects. But it is, unfortunately, flawed.

Coda: The Harborplace Experience

> I have never seen capitalism look more attractive than it does right now at Harborplace.
>
> Matt Seiden, "Harborplace: A Lesson in Healthy Capitalism"

Harborplace! Harborplace! Harborplace!
God has blessed your birth
In a city's dawning.

Baari Abdul Akbar Shabazz, 1979 for opening of Harborplace

The selling of Harborplace in the late 1970s offered a new twist on the process of the Faneuil Hall Marketplace experience. Partnering with Thompson, no doubt sadder but also wiser for the Faneuil Hall experience, Rouse promised that he would create an attraction uniquely suited to the diverse character of Baltimore, particularly its vibrant market buildings. Baltimore still had a number of thriving public markets, including Lexington Market (which in 1979 had sales of $24 million a year), but Thompson & Rouse designed the new Harborplace market to fit comfortably alongside the recently renewed edge of Baltimore's waterfront, already a popular spot for ethnic festivals and community events. Since 1964 the waterfront had been reinvented by talented planners integrating an impressive mix of local, state, and federal money. Rouse's project fit comfortably into the master plan for the waterfront, but as at Faneuil Hall, the creation of the marketplace was hotly contested on the local scene. In this case, the competitor to the Rouse project was "open space" and concern for the Lexington Market area, promoted by a dedicated and nearly successful group of city activists and politicians.

The famed Inner Harbor of Baltimore well known today was an unsightly mess in the 1960s. Although once a place of bustling warehouses and ferries, its role as a port had slipped away (and the modernized port moved to larger facilities farther out), leaving a number of decaying piers, heavy auto traffic, and urban pests. According to one Baltimorean, Ellen Kelly, the harbor was a funky place in the 1960s. She and her husband kept "a crazy old stinkpot in 1964–1965 which we tied up to a couple of old barges decaying under Federal Hill." They reported, "the sounds consisted of traffic rumble and sirens all night long reverberating across the harbor. The smells were mixed; a lull in the wind gave off a gasping acrid smoke mixed with the rancid smell of rendered fish oil. (Some of the smoke was from the morgue [and crematoria] which moved in the 1970s, mercifully, and the other came from heavy industry.)"[50]

It was David Wallace and Tom Todd, lead planners on the Charles Center project, who were called into Baltimore in the 1960s to create a new master plan for the harbor. Johns Hopkins University professor Abel Wolman "returned from Europe with glowing tales of Stockholm's harbor" and convinced Mayor Theodore McKeldin to work with the Greater Baltimore Committee to assemble money for a comprehensive plan in 1964. As at Charles Center, Rouse catalyzed the plan's support with civic and business leaders. At one meeting, David Wallace recalled, "James W. Rouse played the crucial role, as he had in the earlier Charles Center days. He admitted that he was skeptical about the numbers, but then he said 'Gentlemen, we must not fail to do this!' Heads nodded and belief in the plan spread like wildfire."[51]

This plan established the key elements of the harbor area, including an emphasis on pedestrian access to the water, boulevards separating shoreline parks and facilities from the business district, and new buildings of consistent height lining the edge of these boulevards. Included from the beginning was a mixture of public and private buildings along this edge that would help pay for the improvements and make the most of the renewed settings. In terms of management, the continuation of quasi-private management of the whole project, known as Charles Center–Inner Harbor Development Corporation, placed the project in line with urban renewal projects everywhere. Tens of millions of dollars poured into the area, a mix of federal and local funds. The public end of the project came to fruition under the leadership of flamboyant Mayor William Donald Schaefer, whose political career from that moment forward was firmly hitched to the harbor's international fame.

Rouse reentered the scene in the late 1970s by proposing to develop the commercial component of the harbor redevelopment. Martin Millspaugh, head of Charles Center–Inner Harbor Development Corporation, invited Rouse to take a look at the renovated harbor in 1977. The city's progress impressed Rouse.[52] Millspaugh's offering of this opportunity to Rouse was not as strange or corrupt as it sounds. Certainly Rouse had been one of the original backers of the waterfront, but by the 1970s he was one of the few developers anywhere with the guts to invest in Baltimore's waterfront. Nor does there appear to have been a Baltimore version of Roger Webb as a competitor. Rouse, a local and trusted favorite among city elites, fresh from his Faneuil Hall triumph, was most likely to help reinvent the harbor. In 1977 The Rouse Company asked for commercial development rights of the harbor, and the city planning commission approved the Harborplace plans. The city council promptly gave its approval in 1978.

However, in that same year a petition drive by citizens was made with the goal of stopping the plan, and a battle raged over the relative merits of the proposal. Remarkably, the issue did not center on what was apparently a sweetheart deal for Rouse and his rather close relationship to the whole harbor project, but on the proper use of such renewed public space. Even without Harborplace, the waterfront had been steadily gaining popularity over the years. A variety of ethnic festivals filled the harbor on a regular basis, as did the very popular Baltimore City Fair. According to Martin Millspaugh, "the shoreline of the Inner Harbor has become the scene of a broad spectrum of assemblies and attractions for Baltimore families and groups, including City Fairs, Sunny Sundays, sailboat regattas, antique boat rendezvous, ethnic festivals, Greek, Italian, Lithuanian, and many more—jousting tournaments, kite-flying contests, skipjack appreciation days, Marine Corps ceremonies, Easter sunrise services, etc. etc.—the list is growing all the time, in both numbers and variety."[53]

Many opponents, led by market vendors at the Cross Street Market in nearby Federal Hill and restaurant owners in Little Italy (near the harbor), believed that Harborplace would hurt business in the surrounding neighborhoods of Baltimore and would cut into the popularity of the ethnic festivals and city fairs (which is likely true but not demonstrable). The old market area around Howard Street and the Lexington Market also seemed threatened. As it turned out, however, the commercial trajectory of Harborplace likely helped almost every business in the city or did not significantly affect the general trend one way or another. Cross Street Market remains one of Baltimore's more popular city markets. Howard Street and Lexington Market had already changed constituencies over the years to primarily African American shoppers and so remained remarkably similar over the twenty years of Harborplace (which appealed more to white, upper-class shoppers from the edge of the city or suburbs). As one Rouse Company marketing report pointed out, although the traditional large department stores were faltering in the late 1970s, "small merchants are holding their own," particularly along a pedestrian mall created between Howard and Liberty Streets. This area is still (2003) a vibrant shopping district for poor, African American people, a fact that city planning officials have consistently tried to ignore as part of recent redevelopment projects.[54]

The question of suitability, however, was a bit more complex, and opponents, and many liberals, including the ambitious president of the city council, Walter Orlinsky, did not believe that upscale shopping in the heart of Baltimore—even a marketplace with market stalls—suited the essentially working-class, poor constituency of the city. In this, of course, they were absolutely right, and over the years even Rouse officials boasted that the draw of Harborplace was primarily from wealthier neighborhoods in the city and the surrounding region rather than from the nearby lower-income areas. According to Brendan Walsh of *The Catholic Worker*, "the central issue is based on the conflict between the 'haves' and the 'have nots' . . . Baltimore, particularly its Inner Harbor, is fast becoming a place for those who 'have.' It is losing its 'charm'; it is playing homage to plastic, to red brick sidewalks, to Boston fern." Rejecting the dominant consumer ideology, Walsh encouraged citizens to realize that "we can entertain ourselves at the harbor. We are not wedded to what is chic and fashionable. We do not need more stores to encourage the wasting of our hard-earned dollars.

We can enjoy ourselves without money." He noted, "Harborplace and the entire Inner Harbor will be geared toward tourists and those Baltimoreans who 'have.'"[55]

The Rouse Company had some fairly strong arguments on its side. Not only was the money of wealthy suburbanites needed in city coffers (and the traditional shopping districts of downtowns had been supported by many suburban shoppers), but also Harborplace structures filled only three out of approximately twenty-nine acres of harbor waterfront. The area designated for Harborplace at that time was largely paved in concrete, and the concept was public-oriented if not perfectly public. The idea of Harborplace had also been on the books for a long time. As one supporter of the plan, David Barton, chairman of the city planning commission noted, "For some reason, they (the opponents) have forgotten we never intended to build a new park, but a new commercial living center."[56] As Rouse explained to the main opponent, Walter Orlinsky, "Harborplace will consist of two bright, colorful pavilions separated by a public plaza. They will contain sidewalk cafes, dozens of eating places, large and small, many fronting on terraces overlooking the harbor . . . It will not be like stores or restaurants that people only enter for the purpose of doing business— but a very public place open day and night where people will stroll, sit, watch, eat, and shop." Comparing the project to Ghiradelli Square and Faneuil Hall Marketplace, Rouse promised, "Harborplace will be uniquely 'Baltimore' in its feeling and function."[57] In answer to the argument that "commercial development is obviously contrary to public recreational, educational, and cultural uses," Rouse official Scott Ditch answered, "we are not causing the loss of any open space whatsoever to nonpublic uses. As a matter of fact, what we will do on this land will expand and enhance the usefulness to the public, thus making possible recreational, educational and cultural uses over weeks, months and hours when they would otherwise not be possible."[58] Indeed, for much of the year the waterfront typically remained barren and windswept.

Both of the city's newspapers, leading professional organizations like the American Institute of Architects and CPHA, and many average citizens saw much to be gained from the project. With support of many leading and wealthy citizens organized in the Citizens for Harborplace committee, Rouse succeeded in winning support for the plan in a November 1978 referendum. The city signed a seventy-five-year lease, and Rouse promised $105,000 in yearly ground rent and 25 percent of net profits yearly. During the final hearing before the signing, opponents wondered, humorously, if "it is unimaginative to tie the city down like that. If the mayor of 75 years ago had done this, Mayor Schaefer might be strapped with 700 hitching posts."[59] The marketplace nevertheless opened in 1980.

Essential to the selling of Harborplace from the beginning was a mix of local elements: local goods, local merchants, and local shoppers. Each of these received a great deal of attention before opening, but as a vision these elements have been neglected during the past twenty years. Martin Millspaugh believes even today that Harborplace's success is the result of its being "sold to people as their place."[60] Not only did the company promise to do a great deal to encourage minority ownership (which started well but failed miserably), but also Rouse promised all who would listen that the market would be a Baltimore place rather than a national chain store location. He wrote to the mayor of Baltimore in 1978 that Harborplace "must be a democratic, embracing, comfortable place for all people—rich and poor, young and old, of all races—a place which the diverse people of Baltimore can be proud to share." He also promised that "in recruiting tenants for the space in Harborplace, we will give special emphasis to 'local tenants'—meaning independent non-chain merchants with their only or principal place of business in the Baltimore area—preferably Harborplace. To the fullest extent possible, we want owners on the other side of the counter serving customers. We believe this to be important to the spirit of Harborplace."[61] Rouse also wondered, "How should Baltimore's heritage, personality, needs, yearning be expressed and served through Harborplace?"[62] According to the *Baltimore Sun,* "Rouse hopes to recapture a turn-of-the-century market in the interior where meats, cheeses and dairy products will be sold. Another section will have a bakery and wine, coffee and health food stores. There will be a crafts area and a number of small pavilions where various kinds of food will be for sale."[63] These promises smelled strongly like the faltering small-scale capitalistic vision of Faneuil Hall.

Early promotional materials made much of the city market characteristics of Harborplace: "The Light Street Pavilion includes at ground level a Colonnade Market featuring purveyors of produce, fish, meat, and dairy foods, and a two-story skylit Trading Hall for baked goods, gourmet foods, candies, coffee, tea and other specialties. On the second level a Food Hall . . . offers a variety of small eating places serving international foods. The adjoining Sam Smith Market . . . is a colorful bazaar for a changing array of crafts and gift items." According to these materials, "approximately 120 to 150 businesses, primarily local and owner operated, reflect the character and life styles of Baltimore and the Chesapeake Bay region."[64] Mathias Devito of The Rouse Company bragged in 1981 that 90 percent of the businesses were Baltimore-Washington businesses.[65]

Rouse Company officials were not above soliciting Lexington Market retailers, either, as indicated by a letter from the Lexington Market Authority to DeVito: "To my dismay, I learned that your leasing people at Harborplace are approaching clients of the Lexington Market Authority."

DeVito explained logically that although Harborplace was an addition to existing districts, "we have made the equally strong commitment that, to the fullest extent possible, Harborplace will be a largely local enterprise, with a wide representation of local merchants." It appears that the market merchants may have been seeking out Rouse officials, not the other way around.[66] In the early years, too, the fresh food market area seemed to be catching on at Harborplace. According to a marketing study from 1981, "The fresh food markets at Harborplace appear to have been accepted by shoppers in that 40 percent of respondents have made purchases there."[67]

The Rouse Company carried out an impressive job at first of finding local tenants or nurturing new ones that would create the local, market feeling. In the Light Street Pavilion, focused on food (the other, the Pratt Street Pavilion, focused upon dry goods), the Colonnade Market included A. B. Cheese, Inc., Bayside Fruit and Nut, the French Bread Factory, Herbs Unlimited, Light Street Bakery, Homemade Polish Kielbasa, Philips Seafood, Vincenzo's Produce Company, Harvest Fare, a flower shop, and a few dessert places that were mostly local businesses. The Food Hall, however, featured fairly conventional fast food including Haagen Daz ice cream, but also Thrasher's French Fries (a regional favorite), Little Greece, some African food, and Southern Barbecue. Cafés included branches of successful upscale eateries from the region, the American Café and Philips (specializing in seafood), but also gourmet restaurants such as Jean Claude's Café and the Soup Kitchen. Harborplace opened with a financial bang in its first year: 42 million dollars in taxes for the city, 2,300 new jobs, and 18,000 visitors.[68]

The *Baltimore Sun*, ever a Rouse supporter, buttressed these claims to regional uniqueness, particularly in 1980 as the market first opened: "This is a big day for the Baltimore region and for all of Maryland as once again at Pratt and Light streets as in days of yore, commercial activity will bring together Chesapeake Bay seafood, Eastern Shore poultry and melons, dairy products and vegetables from Western Maryland and all kinds of native craftsmanship and retail ingenuity." Another gem in the *Sun* explained that Harborplace "is 'ours,' with all its jobs, new business ventures, supply orders, tax revenue and year-round vitality. And also, we discovered, with its marvelous smells of chocolate, spices, flowers, French fries, cheeses, crabs and new-car interior." Harborplace was also a democratic space according to the *Sun* "But we hope that always at the Inner Harbor, efforts will be made to bring old and new Baltimore together, that those who voted for Harborplace or sweated to build it will feel at ease to shop and drink there, and that floppy-shoed urchins will continue to catch crabs as part of Baltimore's enduring charm."[69] Rouse explained his success in 1983 when he claimed, "it is in the marketplace that all people come together—rich and poor, old and young, black and white. It is the democratic, unifying, universal place."[70]

Figure 23. At the Harborplace project (1980) Rouse promised the City of Baltimore that he would make a new marketplace that reflected Baltimore's unique sense of place and history. Although it remains an attractively designed set of buildings, and has been financially successful, it has become an upscale, homogenized selling environment little different from the many malls and festival marketplaces managed by The Rouse Company. Photo by the Author.

As a piece of urban design Harborplace remains one of the leading sets of commercial buildings created in America during the postwar period, and the pavilions remain underappreciated in the architectural community in light of, and perhaps because of, their tremendous popularity with the public. Harborplace's two pavilions created a corner to the harbor and buffered promenades and public spaces along the waterfront from the busy boulevards. The development also added public value to the surrounding area.

Jane and Ben Thompson sought out prototypes "related to this dual setting of harbor and park where land and water meet" and borrowed from "the tradition of commercial waterfront construction," including warehouses, boathouses, and ferry terminals as well as "pleasure pavilions" found in urban parks.[71] Rouse explained that "over 60% visit Harborplace with no intention of eating or buying but simply for the delight of being there; for the festival provided by thousands of people sitting, standing or walking slowly along the harbor promenade."[72]

Thompson Associates again showed that it had the vision to make a truly inspiring addition to a city's fabric. As Mary Griffin of the *Baltimore News American* wrote in 1980: "Now, when you promenade along the water, it is against a backdrop of people and activity, of outdoor cafes and brightly

colored awnings, of glass and lights, rather than trucks and cars." She carefully noted the marked contrast between the old city markets and
Harborplace: whereas the inside of Lexington Market "is full of colorful
foods and tantalizing smells," from the outside it is "as blank and uninvit-
ing as a suburban shopping center." "Harborplace rejects this low-profile
approach" and "is dazzling, particularly at night . . . the bands of tiny bright
lights and dramatic merchandising displays continue to draw passers-by."[73]
The festival marketplace was slick inside and out, better drawing in visitors. Lexington Market, a less attractive and lavish set of buildings, however, still includes tantalizing smells and market stalls and serves the actual
residents of the city of Baltimore. Asian grocers sell vegetables, meats, and
prepared foods to African Americans and a few white tourists and businesspeople.
Located at a major transit stop on the subway and near a thriving low-cost
shopping area, Lexington Market isn't slick and it is no great piece of urban
design, but it still reflects the majority experience in Baltimore.

National press for Harborplace overflowed with praise from the first day.
The finest analysis of the complex urban experiment in process came from
Wolf Von Eckardt, architecture critic for the *Washington Post*. Eckardt believed
that the new marketplaces being created by Rouse promised a renewed "heart"
in center cities. They did this by creating unique spaces found nowhere else
in America. Cities had grown up around markets, and without them they
were perishing, citing for proof that "Paris has never been the same after
Les Halles were demolished." "A real marketplace reaffirms our humanity,"
opined Eckardt. "It is not just a place to trade. It is a place *to be,* a place
where lovers can meet, a place for spontaneous encounters, a place where
buyers are not just consumers and sellers are not just sales personnel, but
where people are dealing with people." He praised market halls, including
Faneuil Hall and Harborplace, for their "fragrant mix of butcher's sausage,
bakers' bread and candlestick makers' wares, of freshly caught seafood and
freshly picked produce, of restaurants and eateries for all tastes and persua-
sions, of pushcarts and stores that are not in chains—the hustle and bustle
of a real market, in short—is an irresistible attraction for almost everyone."
The Harborplace market halls "are exactly as market halls ought to be, simple, dignified structures of concrete beams and columns, with pleasantly pitched
green aluminum roofs," and "The west pavilion features restaurants, cafes,
and the market. The meats, poultry, cheese, baked goods, seafood, and produce—all of it local—are sold from a white tile platform." Eckardt noted
that proper administration would be essential to maintaining the mix or "the
market will succumb to tackyness, T-shirts and trinkets." "But James Rouse
denies that this could happen to Harborplace," Eckardt reported that
Rouse promised, "We will maintain complete quality control."[74]

The built-in problems that plagued Faneuil Hall eventually affected

Harborplace and have diminished respect for the design as a whole in crit-ical circles. First to fail to appear was a genuine reflection of the city's pop-ulation. At least part of the appeal of Harborplace was the diverse citizenry that was to fill its halls. Certainly they could be found out on the waterfront, but it was less likely that they would be found in the market of expensive fresh foods, restaurants and shops. By 1981 a Rouse market-ing study recorded that "Harborplace is attracting a clientele which is afflu-ent and proportionately more white than metropolitan Baltimore patterns. It draws more shoppers from the suburbs than from the city, and there is a distinct dependence on areas to the north which are suburban in nature . . . Additionally, Harborplace does not penetrate city or subur-ban blue-collar neighborhoods particularly well. High prices (or perceived high prices) may be responsible for this in large measure."[75] How much the market actually reflected Baltimore when it attracted primarily affluent con-sumers never really entered the discussion beyond the opponents of the mar-ketplace. It is fair to say that the people who fill a marketplace are as important a part of its composition as its sellers. As Faneuil Hall was flooded by tourists, so too was Harborplace flooded by upscale white shoppers. That Harborplace was full of white suburbanites made it a financially success-ful place, but far more uniform in tastes and daily appearance than origi-nally planned.

The fresh food sellers fell by the wayside during the 1980s until there was not much left of this part of the market. The Colonnade Market area used to be vibrant but now nearly echoes except for Philips, an Italian bak-ery, and a few fast-food operators. Regional favorite Philips Seafood remains a major part of the Light Street Pavilion, but dominating Harborplace are chains like Sbarro, California Pizza Kitchen, Pizzeria Uno, Planet Hollywood, Hooters, and the Cheesecake Factory. The food court area is entirely taken up with mall food court fare for the conven-tion crowd. In addition, the unique stores have nearly all been replaced by national retailers like the Discovery Channel Store and Sunglass Hut or small retailers selling national goods or tourist junk. The ethos of the mar-ket is of national goods rather than the quirky soul of Baltimore.

Current Rouse Company materials make clear the transition: "Located at the center of Baltimore's Inner Harbor, Harborplace is an urban market packed with the most popular retail shops in the USA."[76] Jacques Kelly, a local food critic, writing in 2002, remembered twenty years back when Rouse promised "to take the charm of the city's public markets and replicate it by the harbor." Kelly described the original market flavor: "the original 1980 Harborplace had butchers, baskets of potatoes and onions and stands of flow-ers—the things that Jim Rouse knew and loved in the Baltimore markets of his youth. With many small merchants lined up displaying their wares,

the 1980 festival marketplace was not a bad imitation." He had less praise
for the contemporary manifestation: "The Light Street Pavilion has been
reconfigured, and much of that original recipe has been altered. The small
shopkeepers were often replaced by chain restaurants. So much for the charm
of city markets."[77]

"Harbor Place [*sic*] is a busy place, Harbor Place [sic] is a noisy place,
Harborplace is an expensive place. But I love Harborplace," explained fifth-
grader Gardiner Offutt near opening day. Harborplace remains an
impressive quasi-public environment with attractive views over the harbor and delightful outdoor chain restaurants; there is still much to love.
It has helped catalyze extensive downtown renovation, but as at Fanueil
Hall, the marketplace reflects only half of the ambitious promise on which
it was based.[78] National companies like The Rouse Company built
delightful urban spaces, but proved ham-handed when it came to restoring small-scale capitalism and the intimacy and character of actual city
marketplaces.

For Rouse, even in its tourist market form the festival marketplace always
remained a crucial piece of the businessman's utopia. Against growing evidence of homogenization in the 1980s, he still believed that visitors
responded "to the color, fragrance, noises, texture of the marketplace, to
small merchants, mostly independents . . . to the diversity of the shops,
market, eating places, to the humanity, personality of the place. An unex-
pressed yearning was being satisfied."[79] Rouse defended the marketplaces
in 1981 by appealing to qualities quickly slipping away: "There is a yearning for participation, for real merchants and real owners on the other side
of the counter, for the informality, diversity, color, texture, fragrances."[80]
Anyone who has had the pleasure of dealing with small businesspeople knows
that there is an important qualitative difference between poorly paid service workers and dedicated, often charismatic, owners.

In 1987, as part of his activities with the Enterprise Foundation, Rouse
developed new ideas about the possibilities of stall markets, particularly in
low-income areas. He visited and was excited by Pike Place Market in Seattle
and its "fifty stalls selling fish, meat, fruit and produce, etc., a farmers market with seasonal tables, a craft area of fifty spaces." He noted that it was
"Very, very busy—any time . . . probably 50% tourist but stall market mainly
local." He proposed that the foundation consider creating markets with real
stalls, tables for farmers, small shops with crafts and antiques, street musi-
cians, and so forth, and he pointedly noted, "It should not be formal, slick
like a H'Place, FHM or Waterside. But seem 'public'—belonging to the people—simple, unfancy design—perhaps asphalt floors, wooden or tin
pitched roof, open sides in spring, summer, fall . . . clean, neat, well-managed and promoted." He thought of certain towns like Norfolk, San

Antonio, Baltimore, or Long Beach as potential sites (and the Enterprise Foundation has renovated one city market in the Sandtown area).[81]

Rouse, the Midas of marketplaces, did have some sense that his own work had been slick, but he never entirely understood the reasons for his failure to capture that market feeling; his success in first-class management had made him a fortune, but was ill suited to the quirkier goals of the festival marketplaces. In 1983, for instance, he wrote to Mayor William H. Hudnut of Indianapolis after visiting the Indianapolis City Market, praising "the charm of a fine old building," and he suggested that the City Market could be valuable to the city "if it is leased, merchandized, managed, promoted with the sensitivity, taste and vigor to match its opportunity. We are uniquely equipped to develop this opportunity with the city."[82] Luckily, the city turned down his offer and the City Market remains a vibrant public stall market.

Rouse had entirely overlooked the salient elements that distinguished Pike Place and Indianapolis City Market from his festival marketplaces. Bernard Frieden and Lynn Sagalyn offer a succinct portrait of Pike Place in their book *Downtown, Inc.* that points up these differences. They found that the Pike Place merchants benefited from below-market rents, simple renovation standards kept rents low, and management had decided to reject chain businesses. In addition, "housekeeping standards are casual. This is no sanitized Disneyworld. It is a busy, littered market, kept tolerably clean, but showing all the signs of hard use." Even more important was that Pike Place is not only "public" in appearance, but also in operation. The public agencies that oversee Pike Place "use their control for the sake of helping merchants start businesses, preserve traditional retailing, and bringing in businesses to serve the poor." This approach could not be more different from Rouse Company policies.[83]

Most of the arguments made against the festival marketplaces over the last twenty years, those showing little economic spillover from the marketplaces (particularly for low-income citizens) in the rest of the city, are important but have partly missed the mark. The simple fact is that the festival marketplaces that have survived—Faneuil Hall, South Street Seaport (New York City), Harborplace, and Riverwalk (New Orleans), to name a few—have made money not only for Rouse but for the cities in which they are located. Those that failed were largely those created by the Enterprise Foundation as charitable works and were placed in metropolitan areas, such as Flint and Toledo, that were too small and poor to support them.

What I believe is a far more relevant critique of the festival marketplace is that they have failed in spirit. Rouse did not propose chain malls when asking for choice urban spaces and market buildings—he promised renewed marketplaces with a strong community sense and daily shopping functions closely linked to local urban character and life. Although The Rouse Company made reasonable efforts to preserve or enhance a market feeling in the first years, the company proved insensitive to the needs of market sellers and so lost this important part of the marketplace formula. In their rush for profits and cutting-edge management, Rouse and his managers lost sight of half of their vision. Big business was simply not up to the challenge of urban "character" development. Rather than being a cynical ploy—Margaret Crawford believes that festival marketplaces "use cultural attractions such as museums and historic ships to enliven predictable shopping experiences"—we see a truncated historical process where excessive idealism about private sector capabilities failed to generate alternative values. It was too much to expect the private sector to generate its own critique. This, then, was the Midas story reinvented for postwar America.[84]

At first glance, the festival marketplace and the malls, their close cousins, were convincing pieces of the businessman's utopia. They were two different but similar expressions of Rouse's private sector vision wherein the businessman demonstrated competency in ever expanding arenas of human activity. The mall offered the vision of a renewed civic life in suburbia, a luxurious type of Main Street by private interests. Rouse projected the festival marketplace as the private sector's catalyst for renewed local character, vibrant public space, and small-scale capitalism in older city centers. But the devil was in the details for both institutions, as Rouse himself at times admitted. How did one create genuine cultural and civic life in a mall when a private company controlled every aspect of the development? How did one preserve a genuine, small-scale market feeling in a festival marketplace after demands for profits squeezed out the real stall merchants? Both the malls and the festival marketplaces reflected a comparatively high level of design for their respective environments and continue to do so today. But the heart of each has been lost.

Private sector management on a national level creates select values well—cleanliness, slickness, quality design, and profit—but could not produce unique textures, diversity, spontaneity, individualism, informality, or local sensations, not even with the best of intentions. Although the public plays a major role in creating conditions for both types of institutions, rarely are public rights, or a broader notion of the public beyond a focus upon upscale consumers and vendors, factored into the ongoing management of malls or festival marketplaces. Much the same way leftists overplayed the role of the public sector, so businessmen like Rouse overplayed private sector talents.

Both malls and festival marketplaces today seem strangely out of place in their respective environments, and both are stamped with a model of urban culture that may have been cutting-edge in the 1960s and 1970s but now feels antiquated. These pieces of the businessman's utopia—the malls and festival marketplaces—still look good, but they smell funny and they pinch at the corners of the postmodern American.

Epilogue

Capitalism, whose practices government is asked to imitate, has not always been internally healthy and without sin, and it has even been whispered among the unregenerate that great corporations have their own diseases paralleling those of government, including politics, deadheads, nepotism, illusions of grandeur, hardening of the arteries, gout, and the Chinese rot.

Robert Moses, "The Budget Must Go Up"

Rouse's life is an extraordinary record of both the moving powers and the limits of that [American] spirit to deal with urban ills that worsened, rather than improved in his lifetime. Urban ills in America evidently cannot fundamentally be cured, by even an honest partnership between the public and private sectors.

David Harvey, "Builder of a Flawed Utopia"

The corruption, crumbling housing projects, and crushing unemployment now revealed in Soviet cities has made American cities, even with their massive slum districts, look better. America's diverse private sector efforts—urban renewal, shopping malls, suburban subdivisions, community development corporations, and many festival marketplaces—have better stood the test of time. In much the same way that the military overestimated the Soviet threat, so Rouse and others overstated the threat of communist progress in urban affairs.

During much of the Cold War it was easy to be fooled by Soviet claims. The communists had lavished money on cities, probably more than the USSR could reasonably support, to make them appear to be the leading edge of a fully modernized, socialist society. Communist leaders also limited access to much of the country and projected an unrealistic, glossy image. Was the crumbling of the Soviet Union (beyond failed military adventures) a complete rejection of urban social welfare or an acknowledgement that the Soviet regime did not have the talent or resources to create the ideal society it had promised? We will never know, but the Soviet threat has obviously dwindled.

Social democratic Europe remains a better example of the potential for urban social welfare. Most Europeans, living under diverse forms of "sewer socialism," have by no means jettisoned the urban social welfare systems they created during the last century. The social democratic countries such as Sweden and Britain *have* watched their stock partly slide. The new towns, housing estates, massive urban reconstruction, and universal health care systems may have eliminated the worst slums and pacified urban populations, but they have also revealed serious flaws. Many of the public housing estates have become quasi-slums, government spending has taxed diminishing revenues, racial tensions have grown, and unemployment has remained stubbornly high.

Even these cracks in social democratic policies have not catalyzed a wholesale abandonment of urban social welfare systems. "The cold war and the Atlantic alliance concealed for half a century deep differences between two sharply contrasting sorts of society," writes Tony Judt, a leading analyst of European history and affairs. Europeans, during even the last twenty-five years of uneven economic growth, have chosen "to devote a lot of money to expensive (and very popular) public services. The result is that in many crucial respects Europe and the US are actually less alike than they were fifty years ago."[1]

A casual visit to European cities reveals the influence of social democratic policies that have mitigated some of the most dramatic urban contrasts of the capitalist city, differences in urban life Rouse himself always noted but never attributed to the positive side of massive European social spending. Many of the worst state housing projects are being renovated or rebuilt, and some have been sold in part to poor residents; many of the better-designed estates that antedate the 1960s tower-block style are still in fine, if not stellar, condition. Extensive transit systems still provide access across vast urban regions to all segments of the population. The national health care systems, child care networks, a large public sector, and family allowance programs, while trimmed over the decades, still mitigate the worst aspects of urban life. Europeans have not created a Socialist utopia, but it now appears that in most cases European leaders pursued a moderate, pragmatic path mixing democracy, statism, and private sector growth. Peter Dreier finds that "even today, Europeans and Canadians expect more from their national government—in terms of economic security, health insurance, child care, and housing assistance—than Americans do."[2]

The celebratory mood that followed the collapse of communism has allowed Americans to overlook the evident limitations of private sector urban solutions here at home. American cities—where great resources have been devoted to shopping centers, highways, suburban subdivisions, prisons, office towers, and downtown luxury housing—are better in terms of consumption and comfort than most Soviet cities. In some cases they are also more attractively and thoughtfully designed than their social democratic and Soviet counterparts.

The standards of living within American cities, however, are so unequally weighted that too many city residents live unspeakably mean lives in the very shadow of breathtaking luxury. It is this shocking inequality in urban conditions that continues to distinguish the United States from other industrialized nations. A majority may be miserable in the Soviet Union, and quality of life is comparatively lower for many Europeans (in terms of consumer goods and square feet of living space), but the contrast in urban conditions in the United States, in light of national prosperity, remains an American specialty.

The American urban landscape looks the way it does because it has been shaped most to suit the interests of business elites and the prosperous suburban middle classes. Cultural and intellectual propaganda, as in communist nations, too often substituted for substantive change in slums and left many problems untouched. Just as the central planner's utopia made little room for private enterprise, the businessman's utopia found too few resources for urban social welfare. Businessmen succeeded in creating and reshaping whole cities, but they failed to address the scale of human suffering, the need for environmental regulation, uneven metropolitan tax systems, or the genuine need for public space and local character in modern cities and suburbs. Winning the Cold War and the retreat of world socialism does not mean that a true capitalist utopia in the United States has been achieved.

Nearly full employment, waves of new immigration, and well-publicized community development success in the 1990s contributed to improvements in crime and fiscal health in some large American cities and made some people believe America had solved its urban problems, but these improvements did remarkably little to solve many of the enduring urban problems pinpointed by Rouse as early as the 1950s. A drop in criminal activity and the rise of new immigration to cities overshadowed the relatively high crime rates that remain (and packed prisons), failing schools, blighted housing, loss of affordable rentals, growing inequality, and flight of the affluent. Cities have not faced these problems alone. Traditional urban problems have become part of the aging suburban fringe as old garden apartments and cheaply constructed subdivisions and strip malls decline. The preservation of important natural areas around cities only rarely has been achieved, and the average suburban environment remains unsatisfying to many suburbanites. The bad news, according to Dreier, is that "in no metropolitan area in the nation can a family earning the minimum wage afford fair market rents."[3]

The call for further privatization of city services, reduced social spending, and limits on regulation nevertheless continues, because many Americans still distrust public power. The most powerful voices, including many leading urban politicians, claim that only further shrinking of

Figure 24. A photograph of some of the vast districts of declining neighborhoods in Baltimore. These troubled neighborhoods are a common sight in cities across America and have been little touched by decades of reform. The complex problems of these spreading zones of decay, now reaching across city lines in many cases, far exceed the limited resources of the private sector solutions Rouse proposed throughout his life. Photo by the author.

the government can save cities. That James Rouse found support from both Republican and Democratic politicians primarily reflects the minor differences between the major parties in the United States. The pressure from the left in Europe—that made even many conservative parties tolerate national health care systems and housing programs, for instance—never coalesced in the United States. Minor political differences between parties, from the local to the national level, masked unanimity on antistatist solutions in the United States throughout the postwar period.

Americans such as Rouse successfully attacked "big" urban social spending in America as if the United States had developed a comparably large social welfare state to Europe. This argument, what Peter Marcuse calls the "Myth of the Meddling State,"[4] served political and philanthropic goals but misrepresented the situation in the United States. With the support of a willing public, Rouse and like-minded allies had successfully prevented the creation of generous urban policy in the United States after the Second World War. Private sector policy worked admirably in building affordable suburbs and center city redevelopment, but has never yielded the desired impact in poor neighborhoods or suburban regulation.[5]

The city in which Rouse had the most powerful impact, Baltimore, for instance, has suffered worse than most cities and tops most lists in terms of crime, teenage pregnancy, sprawling suburbs, educational failure, and housing decline and abandonment. Baltimore as a region may have Charles Center, Columbia, numerous attractive Rouse malls both in the city and suburbs, Harborplace, and Sandtown, but it looks best from a distance. Remarkably few benefits have reached the poor residents of the city, and Baltimore continues to hemorrhage population. Since 1950, the city's population has declined by a third, even suffering 10 percent of this loss during the booming 1990s. Now Baltimore is spreading its problems and angry, poor people across the region—stimulating ever more distant sprawl. The many business-friendly redevelopment projects have failed by any standard to live up to their promise to stem either inner-city decline or to tame sprawling urbanization.

Rouse became so influential because, unlike many conservatives, he not only attacked state action, but he offered the mainstream American public a promising dream—a vision of capitalism and capitalists with a wide-ranging capacity for urban management, for creating public life and public spaces, and even for pursuing the goals of social justice on a large-scale, for-profit basis. This vision of a capitalist utopia, with all of the benefits of private enterprise and no negative side effects, has not been realized. The public side of the public/private partnership has been slighted over the years, leaving government, and particularly urban mayors, the questionable role of subsidizing business interests.

Investments in education, housing, mass transit, environmental regulation, employment, child care, and health care are needed at all levels of government that will never yield profits but are not of themselves reflective of a true socialist mentality. A broader commitment to alternative forms of public action—beyond massive military spending, mortgage insurance, prisons, and highway programs—would address the notable defects in urban policy without seriously compromising the free market traditions of the United States. An American liberal tradition, before the era of virulent anticommunism, once vigorously pursued state solutions as important ingredients in the solution of complex social problems. The fall of communism at last offers the moment for revisiting a broader approach to state action in the United States. Liberals can reclaim urban social welfare platforms with less fear of socialist and communist labels.

There could be some simple first steps to achieving a more just urban order in the United States. We can demand, first, that cities, states, and the national government slow down on business subsidies and policies designed to benefit the middle and wealthier classes—corporate tax breaks, home mortgage interest tax deductions, professional sports stadiums, massive new prisons, and highway expansions—and use these resources to build cities that work for the majority poor populations that inhabit their borders. Curtailing these types of government subsidies would free funds for creative action. America now stands to learn a great deal from long-term experiments in social policy around the world. Social welfare of all kinds *will* have to be better managed in the future, including stricter rules for clients and general fiscal discipline, in order to avoid mistakes of the past, but it is likely the only route for addressing the *actual scale* of urban needs.

Housing is a clear example where a great deal of experimentation has finally yielded hard lessons, partly thanks to James Rouse. Community development corporations would build affordable housing on a more impressive scale if they were more generously supported by public money (rather than just getting by on private funds and tax credits). New York has been the leading city in CDC activity in large measure because the Koch administration committed five billion dollars in housing funds. This major source of funding allowed the CDCs to operate on a vast scale and physically transform many neighborhoods.[6] New and existing public housing could occasionally be sold to poor residents or managed cooperatively. Income ceilings should also be revised to avoid poverty concentration that plagued so many housing projects. Strict rules of conduct should also be reintroduced in order to maintain order and maintenance. In the future, contextual and small-scale public housing projects could be built in many more communities of this country, including affluent suburbs that have so far avoided housing poor people. That our version of public housing, and even that in Europe, has not worked as envisioned does not mean that public housing cannot by its nature work.

Inspiring examples of well-designed or at least well-managed public housing prosper both in the United States and Europe. New York City, for instance, has preserved a remarkable public housing system that may not be beautiful, or acceptable to middle-class citizens, but is a major source of low-cost housing for over 500 thousand people in that very expensive city. The degree to which Hope VI rebuilding has not been a part of most of New York public housing redevelopment is striking. Even the massive towers that were a complete failure in other cities remain full in most of New York. By no means the ideal manner of low-income housing, the towers are nevertheless decently managed compared to projects in other cities. The "working poor" people of New York remain the bedrock constituency of public housing, and management has not allowed projects to decline beyond repair. Decisive application of state power, as seen in the best examples of social housing, will prove just as important as funding.

Affordable and public housing expansion is necessary, but more important to improving urban conditions is questioning the excessive faith of reformers such as Rouse in the ability of a renewed physical environment to alter social behavior. This faith, far from confirmed in practice, still motivates an impressive amount of social policy in this country. Stickier issues, such as access to decent jobs, educational opportunities, health care, and child care, are talked about frequently but have not received actual funding in proportion to political rhetoric.

The potential support for social action has been underestimated in the Unites States. Americans may respond negatively to welfare as a general concept, but a majority, in surveys, also "want to strengthen social security, spend more on the poor and the unemployed, guarantee universal access to medical care . . . have more governmental help with child care, and simultaneously increase taxes on the rich." The tax cutting and budget trimming now underway, from the local to the national level, is out of step with majority concerns. Savvy politicians, however, will only capitalize on the latent generosity of the American people with creative new approaches and programs. The business classes could well serve as a model to liberal politicians; after all, they showed a true talent for generating government support of their activities (while shamelessly attacking that same government for being too generous in social policy).[7]

Part of the secret of New York's public housing may lie in the fact that tenants of public housing have access, through a famous system of mass transit, to a wide range of job and educational opportunities that poor people in other cities do not have; in addition, New York has for a hundred years pursued its own unique, local version of fairly generous social welfare in health care, welfare, and nonprofit services. Americans elsewhere will likely have to commit themselves to far more generous social programs if they are serious about eliminating the worst aspects of urban poverty on a grand scale. Such a growth in social spending will have to be sold to the public in an entirely new way, stressing the desire to create disciplined, basic universal systems on a professional basis. The patchwork social welfare systems developed in this country are dreadful precedents for future policy.

As dismal as the urban situation is, suburban regulation on a wider scale has appeared. Although New Urbanist new towns such as Seaside, Florida, and Kentlands, Maryland, are the most fashionable showcases of suburban planning, the slow but steady growth in Smart Growth legislation is a more important effort to extend state power to suburban land regulation. Initiatives by states such as Maryland to concentrate development in existing urban places and set restrictions on new subdivisions in rural areas might make a difference. That such efforts are still weak and subject to legal challenge does not make them any less important. A serious examination of European land planning and controls might also help politicians develop realistic scenarios for large-scale planning.

Over the decades, too, a few activist city governments—in cities such as Albuquerque, Indianapolis, and Houston—have quietly responded to suburban growth by annexing territory; these "elastic" cities are generally considered the most successful in maintaining public confidence and dealing fairly with education, housing, and transit.[8] Where cities are hemmed in by affluent suburbs that resist annexation, dynamic city government, extending over a regional scale, such as the relatively successful METRO regional government in Portland, Oregon, could also be politically practical, might attract a new generation of highly skilled people to its ranks, and would likely help mitigate some of the inequalities and environmental problems that plague many metropolitan areas. These are examples of reorganized public powers—Smart Growth, annexation, and regional government—that are likely to have a more dramatic impact upon urban conditions than the private sector solutions proposed by Rouse.

Citizens of the United States also need to consider the broader potential of local government, particularly urban governments that extend over a regional scale. Forgotten by many are the accomplishments of city governments over the preceding centuries; municipalities that once controlled nearly all the urbanized areas surrounding them were once quite creative and effective in terms of providing social goods even in the face of hostile, rural-dominated state legislatures and often corrupt machine politicians. Urban governments of the nineteenth and twentieth centuries proved remarkably able in addressing the challenges of massive urbanization, creating functional systems of education, transportation, water, sanitation, and parks at a scale never before witnessed and rarely equaled outside of the industrialized world to this day: "By century's close, American city dwellers enjoyed, on the average, as high a standard of public services as any urban residents in the world."[9] Many of these improvements were in partnerships with private enterprise, and many businessmen crossed into government or manipulated government programs to their benefit, but over time wider civic ideals set the broader course of urban public policy. The aggressive nature of urban growth through annexation made possible economies of scale and greater equity on a regional basis.

Even up until the 1960s many cities made strides in sewage treatment, city rebuilding, transportation, planning, and health care. The growing migration to suburbia and the Sunbelt, rather than just egregious urban corruption or bureaucratic torpor, ultimately undercut municipal efficiency. Left with declining resources, battles began between city departments and unions for remaining resources. It was precisely at this time that the business model, as promoted by Rouse and others, began to replace a broader vision of urban public power. Leading mayors and city councils, too timid to challenge suburban isolationism, also jumped on board the private/public bandwagon. The private sector model, and the private/public partnership, when compared to struggling, capital-starved city governments, inevitably looked to be superior in almost all cases. Corruption and mismanagement in government, not suburban and Sunbelt flight, became the perceived urban problems, as if corruption and mismanagement did not color life in private industry, too. City government might have become a force for social change and equity, but through urban renewal, highway programs, and temerity, magnified inequality by ignoring social needs.

The American Cold War skepticism of public power is long overdue for a critique. Corporations have shown a unique talent for generating impressive profits and new technologies, but even the most successful and well-intentioned proponent of for-profit social policy, James Rouse, rarely demonstrated the ability to translate these management abilities into successful urban social policy. Nor did even his more successful examples generate the scale of imitation for which he hoped. At times, too, he occasionally advocated for extensions of state power (in suburban planning, for instance) when it became apparent that his preferred solutions had faltered in practice, but these ideas were overshadowed by his more popular private enterprise efforts.

Nevertheless, we live so deeply within the more familiar ideas of business leaders like Rouse that we can hardly imagine alternative urban visions that do not involve further reliance on private sector abilities. Dynamic public sector leadership, offering creative, disciplined, and nondoctrinaire approaches to long-standing urban problems, must retake the initiative in public policy from the local to the national level. Would investing in the poor and their neighborhoods or creating new systems of suburban regulation really pay less to cities in the long term than the massive financial commitments now made to stadiums, prisons, suburbs, highways, and fancy downtowns?

In partnership with a great many different allies, James Rouse spent fifty years carefully working to make private sector projects and ideals appear to be not only the most logical answers to urban needs, but also the best solutions conceivable. Access to the mass media and the most powerful people in the county made his preferred urban solutions the most popular with both elected leaders and the general public. Alternatives melted away not because they lacked any merit, but because his powerful cultural and intellectual program crowded out other visions. Rouse and his allies even successfully cast most of their failures as reflective of a crisis so deep that both private and governmental interests could have little effect. The enduring and massive problems of the American city are unlikely to be solved through such a narrow vision of social possibility. Our cities, and particularly their impoverished citizens, deserve better.

Acknowledgments

I would like to thank Barbara Kellner and Robin Emrich at the Columbia Archive for allowing me early access to the James Wilson Rouse papers. Rouse, self-conscious of his historical importance, did all researchers a great favor by collecting an impressive range of materials related to urban affairs during the past half-century. His longtime assistant, Nancy Allison, superbly organized and preserved these materials for future generations. I also drew upon material at the Tulane University Libraries, Loyola University Library, Enoch Pratt Free Library, and National Archives II. Tulane University has been my academic home during the writing of this book, and I owe a great debt to the university's administration and faculty. My officemates Penny Wyatt and Nicole Learson, in particular, have provided delightful company during the past year. I would like to thank one of Tulane's brightest students, Seth Knudsen, who proved to be a first-rate research assistant. Peter Marcuse, Howard Gillette, Peter Hall, Joseph Arnold, Martin Meyerson, and Jon Teaford made many helpful suggestions after reading drafts of the manuscript. Heather Lee Miller at The Ohio State University Press smoothly guided the book through the lengthy review and production process. Zane Miller offered excellent suggestions, many of which I adopted, for improving the manuscript. Stephen Johanson and Pam Weller in Baltimore again generously invited me into their home during my research. My parents, Ronald L. Bloom and Naomi Dagen Bloom, have continued to show great faith in my unconventional academic career. Leanne Whitford has tried, on a day-to-day basis, to make sure that I lead a more balanced life.

Notes

The Columbia Archive (CA) is located in Columbia, Maryland, and includes documents relating to the creation of Columbia, Maryland, by The Rouse Company and the extensive James W. Rouse papers. Comprehensive location information is given in the endnotes for letters and other hard-to-find documents from the collection. Other documents cited in the endnotes, including speeches and related ephemera, can be found with relative ease in the fourteen series into which the Rouse papers have been divided.

Notes to Introduction

1. I use the term "social democracy" in this book to describe the various forms of socialist-inspired planning in Western Europe. Conservative Americans during the 1950s made few distinctions between democratic forms of socialism and communists, although they were really entirely different systems of government and economics. Stephen Padgett provides a helpful definition of the term: "Social democracy is inspired by socialist ideals, but is heavily conditioned by its political environment, and it incorporates liberal values. The social democratic project may be defined as the attempt to reconcile socialism with liberal politics and capitalist society" (Stephen Padgett and William E. Paterson, *A History of Social Democracy in Postwar Europe* [New York: Longman, 1991], 1). The most comprehensive treatment of social democracy in Europe can be found in Donald Sassoon's *One Hundred Years of Socialism: The West European Left in the Twentieth Century* (New York: New Press, 1996). The origins of social democratic thought and policy can be found in James T. Kloppenberg, *Uncertain Victory: Social Democracy and Progressivism in European and American Thought, 1870–1920* (New York: Oxford UP, 1986).

2. Other books exploring the nonmilitary aspects of the Cold War period include Thomas Borstelmann, *The Cold War and the Color Line: American Race Relations in the Global Arena* (Cambridge, Mass.: Harvard UP, 2001); Noam Chomsky, et al., *The Cold War and the University: Toward an Intellectual History of the Postwar Years* (New York: New Press, 1998); Mary L. Dudziak, *Cold War Civil Rights: Race and the Image of American Democracy* (Princeton, N.J.: Princeton UP, 2000); Margot A. Henriksen, *Dr. Strangelove's America: Society and Culture in the Atomic Age* (Berkeley and Los Angeles: U of California P, 1997); Elaine Tyler May, *Homeward Bound: American Families in the Cold War Era* (New York: Basic Books, 1988); Karal Ann Marling, *As Seen on TV: The Visual Culture of Everyday Life in the 1950s* (Cambridge, Mass.: Harvard UP, 1994); Lisle Rose, *The Cold War Comes to Main Street: America in 1950* (Lawrence: UP of Kansas, 1996); Annabel Jane Wharton, *Building the Cold War: Hilton International Hotels and Modern Architecture* (Chicago: U of Chicago P, 2001); Jane C. Loeffler, *The Architecture of Diplomacy: Building America's Embassies* (Princeton, N.J.: Princeton Architectural Press, 1998).

3. Alvin A. Snyder, *Warriors of Disinformation: American Propaganda, Soviet Lies, and*

the Winning of the Cold War (New York: Arcade, 1995), 20.

4. James Rouse, Speech to the International Council of Shopping Centers, San Francisco, 3 May 1960, 5. CA.

5. James Rouse, "Free Enterprise in a Free America," Speech given 13 February 1985, Engineering News-Record Man-of-the-Year Dinner, New York, 14, CA.

6. Quoted in Richard O. Davies, Housing Reform during the Truman Administration (Columbia: U of Missouri Press, 1966), 96.

7. Adlai Stevenson, "The American City—A Cause for Statesmanship," Speech given at ACTION's Newark Conference, May 1959, CA.

8. See, for instance, Michael Curtin, Redeeming the Wasteland: Television Documentary and Cold War Politics (New Brunswick, N.J.: Rutgers UP, 1995), 152–76, as well as Dudziak and Borstelmann.

9. Henry Hazlitt, "Who Is Misleading What?" Newsweek, 19 November 1951, 81.

10. Rose, The Cold War Comes to Main Street, 8, 47.

11. Edwin Amenta, Bold Relief: Institutional Politics and the Origins of Modern American Social Policy (Princeton, N.J.: Princeton UP, 2000), 4–5.

12. See Aaron L. Friedberg, In the Shadow of the Garrison State: America's Antistatism and Its Cold War Grand Strategy (Princeton, N.J.: Princeton UP, 2000); Seymour Lipset and Gary Marks, "It Didn't Happen Here": Why Socialism Failed in the United States (New York: Norton, 2000); Brian Weddell, The War against the New Deal: World War II and American Democracy Dekalb: Northern Illinois UP, 2001). Peter Dreier, for instance, notes that the National Assocation of Manufacturers "launched a major public relations campaign, to which business groups contributed $37 million, to sell free enterprise. They opposed federal intervention in health care, education, civil rights, labor relations, housing, antitrust activities, progressive taxation, and other policy areas." During the late 1940s. Peter Dreier, "Labor's Love Lost? Rebuilding Unions' Involvement in Federal Housing Policy," Housing Policy Debate 11, no. 2 (Fannie Mae, 2000): 334.

13. See, for instance, Mark I. Gelfand, A Nation of Cities: The Federal Government and Urban America, 1933–1965 (New York: Oxford UP, 1975); Bernard J. Frieden and Lynne B. Sagalyn, Downtown, Inc.: How America Rebuilds Its Inner Cities (Cambridge, Mass.: MIT Press, 1991); Robert M. Fogelson, Downtown: Its Rise and Fall, 1880–1950 (New Haven, Conn.: Yale UP, 2001); Jon C. Teaford, The Rough Road to Renaissance: Urban Revitalization in America, 1940–1985 (Baltimore: Johns Hopkins UP, 1994); Alexander Garvin, The American City: What Works, What Doesn't (New York: McGraw-Hill, 1995); Howard Gillette Jr., Between Justice and Beauty: Race, Planning, and the Failure of Urban Policy in Washington, D.C. (Baltimore: Johns Hopkins UP, 1995); Donald A. Krueckeberg, Introduction to Planning History in the United States (Camden, N.J.: Center for Urban Policy Research, 1983); Mel Scott, American City Planning since 1890: A History Commemorating the Fiftieth Anniversary of the American Institute of Planners (Berkeley and Los Angeles: U of California P, 1969); and Planning the Twentieth-Century American City, ed. Mary Corbin Sies and Christopher Silver (Baltimore: Johns Hopkins UP, 1996).

14. William Zeckendorf, "Cities vs. Suburbs," Atlantic Monthly, January 1952, 28.

15. Howard Gillette Jr.'s article "Assessing James Rouse's Role in American City Planning," Journal of the American Planning Association, 15 April 1999, is the best short introduction to the life and times of James Rouse. This article alerted me to Rouse's long-term record in urban affairs.

16. Malcolm Jones Jr., "James Rouse Sparked New Life in Old Cities," Newsweek, 22 April 1996, 76.

17. Daniel T. Rodgers, Atlantic Crossings: Social Politics in a Progressive Age (Cambridge, Mass.: Harvard UP, 1998), 173.

18. James Rouse, Speech to the Real Estate Board of Baltimore, 1 February 1964, 12. CA.

19. James Rouse, Speech to the National Retail Dry Goods Association, New York, 8 January 1957, 2–3. CA.

Notes to Chapter 1

1. Frank Fisher, "Rebuilding Our Cities," *The Nation*, 8 August 1945, vol. 161, no. 6, 130.

2. Alexander Budaev, "15 Million Apartments in Cities and Towns," *Soviet Life*, ca. 1959, 18–25.

3. "Soviet Exhibit in New York," *Soviet Life*, ca. 1958, 6–9.

4. Budaev, 18–25. See also Mikhail Heller and Aleksandr Nekrich, *Utopia in Power: The History of the Soviet Union from 1917 to the Present* (New York: Summit Books, 1986).

5. Blair Ruble, "From Krushceby to Korobki," in *Russian Housing in the Modern Age: Design and Social History*, ed. William Craft Brumfield and Blair A. Ruble (New York: Cambridge UP, 1993), 232.

6. Ibid., 256.

7. Derek Diamond, "New Towns in Their Regional Context," *New Towns: The British Experience*, ed. Hazel/Evans (New York: Wiley, 1972), 54–56.

8. Lady Sharp, "The Government's Role," in *New Towns: The British Experience*, 40.

9. See Miles Glendinning and Stefan Muthesius, *Tower Block: Modern Public Housing in England, Scotland, Wales, and Northern Ireland* (New Haven, Conn.: Yale UP, 1994).

10. Peter Hall, *Cities in Civilization* (New York: Fromm International, 1998), 843–57.

11. "At the Stiff Oak," *Time* 47, no. 20 (May 1946): 26; "Basic Revolution," *Time* 49, no. 3 (20 January 1947): 30.

12. Dorothy Baruch, "Sleep Comes Hard," *The Nation*, 27 January 1945, vol. 160, no.4, 95–96.

13. James Rouse to Hunter Moss, 26 October 1945, CA, 4.

14. "Mr. Wyatt's Shortage," *Fortune*, April 1946, 105.

15. Editorial, "Let's Have Ourselves a Housing Industry," *Fortune*, ca. September 1947, 12.

16. Wendy Kozol, *Life's America: Family and Nation in Postwar Photojournalism* (Philadelphia: Temple University Press, 1994), 79, 80.

17. "The Industry Capitalism Forgot," *Fortune* 36, no. 2 (August 1947): 61–67, 167–70; see also "Miami Worries about Another Boom," *Life*, 12 February 1945, 63–69; and "Rush for Houses," *Life*, 4 June 1945, 30.

18. See Thomas Hanchett, "Roots of the Renaissance," in *Planning the Twentieth-Century American City*, 283–304.

19. "The Promise of the Shortage," *Fortune* 33, no. 4 (April 1946): 101–103.

20. "The Housing Mess," January 1947, 81–85, 216–21.

21. From extension of remarks by Congressman Melvin Price, 5 April 1954. *Congressional Record*, page and further details unavailable. Quotation from an article titled "Growth of FHA," *Trainman News*, 5 April 1954.

22. See Kenneth T. Jackson, *Crabgrass Frontier: The Suburbanization of the United States* (New York: Oxford UP, 1985); Thomas J. Sugrue, *The Origins of the Urban Crisis: Race and Inequality in Postwar Detroit* (Princeton, N.J.: Princeton UP, 1996).

23. See *Public Housing Design: A Review of Experience in Low-Rent Housing* (Washington, D.C.: National Housing Agency, Federal Public Housing Authority, 1946).

24. Charles Abrams, "Homeless America," *The Nation*, 4 January 1947, vol. 164, no.

1, 16. See also Nathan Strauss, "These Men Block Housing," *The Nation* 160, no. 5 (January 1946): 6–8; Maurice Rosenblatt, "Haunted Housing," *The Nation* 162, no. 6 (9 February 1946): 161–63; I. F. Stone, "Some News to Cheer," *The Nation* 162, no. 7 (16 February 1946): 186–87; and Charles Abrams, "We Need a Better Housing Bill," *The Nation* 164, no. 20 (17 May 1947): 562–63.

25. John Bauman notes that opposition to public housing could be noted as early as 1944 in "Visions of a Post-War City," in *Introduction to Planning History in the United States*, 148.

26. James Rouse to Kramer, 29 September 1981. CA. Series 4, Box 20, folder: Mail by month, September 1981.

27. Daniel Seligman, "The Enduring Slums," *Fortune*, December 1957, 216.

28. Congressman John Philips, "Political Hysteria versus the Cold Facts about Government Housing." Appendix to the *Congressional Record*, 19 June 1948, A4480.

29. Congressman Ralph Gwinn, *Congressional Record*, 14 April 1948, 4440–41.

30. Congressman E. E. Cox, *Congressional Record*, 22 June 1949, 8131.

31. Statement by Senator Scott Lucas, *Congressional Record*, 20 April 1948, 4614.

32. Congressman Ray Madden, *Congressional Record*, 22 June 1949, 8134.

33. Statement by Senator Robert Taft, *Congressional Record*, 20 April 1948, 4600–01.

34. Robert Taft quoted in Arthur M. Schlesinger Jr., *A Life in the Twentieth Century* (Boston: Houghton Mifflin, 2000), 427.

35. Roger Biles, "Public Housing and the Postwar Urban Renaissance," in *From Tenements to the Taylor Homes: In Search of an Urban Housing Policy in Twentieth-Century America*, ed. John F. Bauman, Roger Biles, and Kristin M. Szylvian, (University Park: Pennsylvania State UP, 2000), 144–59. R. Allen Hays, *The Federal Government and Urban Housing: Ideology and Change in Public Policy* (Albany: State University of New York Press, 1995) provides an excellent overview of the strengths and weakness of the federal housing programs.

36. Hays, 166.

37. Peter Dreier, "Labor's Love Lost? Rebuilding Unions' Involvement in Federal Housing Policy," *Housing Policy Debate* 11, no. 2 (Fannie Mae Foundation, 2000): 351.

38. Seligman, "The Enduring Slums," 145.

39. Biles, "Public Housing and the Postwar Urban Renaissance," 144.

40. Teaford, *Rough Road*, 145–47.

41. Cathy D. Knepper, *Greenbelt, Maryland: A Living Legacy of the New Deal* (Baltimore: John Hopkins UP, 2001); Joseph L. Arnold, *The New Deal in the Suburbs: A History of the Greenbelt Town Program, 1935–1954* (Columbus: Ohio State UP, 1971).

42. James Lash for Central File re: New Image Project, 24 August 1960. Series 2, Box 103, Folder; General Correspondence (2 of 3), January–June 1960.

43. Rouse, "Free Enterprise in a Free America," 14.

44. James Rouse, Report from his trip to Russia, 1979, New Town Working Group of the Joint USA-USSR Commission on Housing and Other Construction, CA, 45.

45. Ibid.

46. Sassoon, "One Hundred Years of Socialism," 84.

47. "Life of the Soviet People," *Soviet Life*, ca. September 1959, 35–37.

48. David Childs, *The Two Red Flags: European Social Democracy and Soviet Communism since 1945* (London: Routledge, 2000), 51.

49. Mark Kesselman, "Prospects for Democratic Socialism in Advanced Capitalism: Class Struggle and Compromise in Sweden and France," *Politics and Society* 11, no. 4, 402.

50. Christopher Pierson, *Hard Choices: Social Democracy in the Twenty-first Century* (Cambridge, Eng.: Polity, 2001), 42–43.

51. John Logue, "Scandinavian Welfare States between Solidarity and Self-Interest," in *Futures for the Welfare State*, ed. Norman Furniss (Bloomington: Indiana UP, 1986), 266.

52. Hall, *Cities in Civilization*, 851.

53. "Sweden: Eighth Straight Victory," *Time* 7, no. 14 (30 October 1960): 24.

54. Logue, *Futures for the Welfare State*, 266.

55. "Sewer Socialist," *Time* 60, no. 1 (7 July 1952): 28.

56. Childs, *The Two Red Flags*, 28.

57. Nicholas Barr, *The Economics of the Welfare State* (London: Weidenfeld and Nicolson, 1993, 33, see also 31–39.

58. Henry Hazlitt, editorial, *Newsweek* 48, no. 14 (1 November 1956): 76.

59. "The Doctor's Bill," *Time* 53, no. 9 (28 February 1949): 33. See also "The Winning Issue Was Not Churchill but New Homes and Jobs for Britons," *Newsweek* 26, no. 6 (August 1945): 23–26; "Britain: Labor Looks Back," *Newsweek* 27, no. 25 (24 June 1946): 44–45; "John Bull's Medical Binge," *Newsweek* 33 (10 January 1949): 44–45; "An American Guide to the British Election Vote . . ." *Newsweek* 35, no. 9 (27 February 1950): 26–27; "Perspective: The Men and Issues in the Tory Campaign," *Newsweek* 35, no. 9 (27 February 1950): 28–29; "Britons OK Health Plan Despite Beefs," *Newsweek* 36, no. 6 (7 August 1950): 46–49; and "Budget 'Without Malice or Hatred,'" *Newsweek* 37, no. 17 (23 April 1951): 42–43.

60. "Foreign News," *Time* 63, no. 13 (28 March 1949): 27.

61. Robert Kuttner, "The Erosion of the Welfare State," *Transatlantic Perspectives*, Publication of the German Marshall Fund, September 1984, 10.

62. Amenta, *Bold Relief*, 12.

63. Rose, *The Cold War Comes to Main Street*, 48.

64. "The Price of Health: Two Ways to Pay It," *Time* 55, no. 8 (20 February 1950): 19–21.

65. "The Moon and Sixpence," *Time* 53, no. 18 (2 May 1949): 18.

66. Michael B. Katz, *The Undeserving Poor: From the War on Poverty to the War on Welfare* (New York: Pantheon, 1989).

67. Barr, *The Economics of the Welfare State*, 36.

68. Katz, *The Undeserving Poor*, 112–13.

69. Lois Bryson, *Welfare and the State: Who Benefits?* (New York: St. Martin's, 1992), 99.

70. Rodgers, *Atlantic Crossings*, 505.

71. James Rouse to Jack Clarke, 25 August 1989. CA. Series 4, Box 34, folder; August 1989 (1).

Notes to Chapter 2

1. "Boston: An Old City Looks Ahead," *Life* 18, no. 3 (15 January 1945): 65.

2. See Karl Schriftgiesser, "The Pittsburgh Story," *Atlantic Monthly* 187, no. 5 (May 1951): 66–69; Robert Lasch, "Chicago Unfreezes Its Building Code," *Atlantic Monthly* 106, no. 2 (February 1950): 62–64; William Zeckendorf, "Baked Buildings," *Atlantic Monthly* 188, no. 6 (May 1951): 46–49; idem, "Cities vs. Suburbs," *The Atlantic Monthly* 190, no. 1 (Jnaury 1952): 25; idem, "New Cities for Old," *Atlantic Monthly* 188, no. 5 (November 1951): 31–35, and also Ray Runnion, "Chicago the Beautiful," *The Nation*, 161, no. 3 (July 1945): 61–62; "New York City's Dream Airport," *Life* 20, no. 11 (18 March 1946): 76–80; "New Hearts for Our Cities," *Newsweek* 43, no. 13 (29 March 1954): 74–75; "This Is the New New York," *Newsweek* 48, no. 2 (9 July 1956): 87–92; "Success Story of a Street,"

Newsweek 48, no. 14 (1 October 1956): 71–74; and "Our Changing Cities," *Newsweek* 50, no. 10 (2 September 1957): 61–68.

3. Fisher, "Rebuilding Our Cities," 130.

4. Fogelson, *Downtown*, 392.

5. "Parking Problem," *Life* 21, no. 14 (30 September 1946): 73–79.

6. James Rouse, "Plan Big, Plan Wide, Plan Deep," Speech in Charlotte, North Carolina, 9 January 1963. CA.

7. Zeckendorf, "Cities vs. Suburbs," 25.

8. Rouse Speech, National Retail Dry Goods Association, 12. CA.

9. Rouse Speech, Real Estate Board of Baltimore, 1 February 1964, 12. CA.

10. Schriftgiesser, "The Pittsburgh Story," 69. See also Robert Moses, "Slums and City Planning," *Atlantic Monthly* 175, no. 1 (January 1945): 63–68.

11. Thomas Hanchett, "The Other 'Subsidized Housing,'" in *From Tenements to the Taylor Homes*, 169. See also Raymond Mohl, "Planned Destruction: The Interstates and Central City Housing," in *From Tenements to the Taylor Homes*, 226–45.

12. Rouse Speech, National Retail Dry Goods Association, 11. CA.

13. Rouse Speech, International Council of Shopping Centers, 5. CA.

14. Ibid.

15. James Rouse, Speech to the Baltimore Real Estate Banguet Board, 2 February 1964, 3. CA.

16. "People: Mortage Banker Jim Rouse . . . Named President of ACTION," publication unclear, November 1958, 63, CA.

17. "'Urban Genius' Dead at 81," *Baltimore Sun*, 10 April 1996.

18. James Rouse, "The New Highways: Challenge to the Metropolitan Region," Speech given at Connecticut General, 9–12 September 1957, 5, CA.

19. Ibid., 6.

20. Ibid., 6–7.

21. See Sies and Silver, *Planning the Twentieth-Century American City*; Krueckeberg, *Introduction to Planning History*; Scott, *American City Planning*; and William H. Wilson, *The City Beautiful Movement* (Baltimore: Johns Hopkins UP, 1989).

22. Alan Gowans, *Styles and Types of North American Architecture: Social Function and Cultural Expression* (New York: Harper Collins, 1992), 271–317.

23. Schriftgiesser, "The Pittsburgh Story," 65–69.

24. James Rouse, "Baltimore Speech," ca. 1950s. CA.

25. Rouse Speech, "New Highways," 4. CA.

26. Thomas Winship, "Exploiters Claim Safe Profits from Urban Land Redevelopment," *Washington Post*, 12 October 1951, 25.

27. Rouse Speech, "Plan Big, Plan Wide, Plan Deep." CA.

28. Minutes from a Businessman's Committee, Marling House, Baltimore, 18 December 1952, 1–4. Series 1.1, Box 402, folder: Levi, Robert—Businessmen's Committee 1952–1954. CA.

29. Memo to Levi, Kohn, Moss, and Hollyday from James Rouse, 18 December 1952. Series 1.1, Box 402, folder: Levi, Robert—Businessmen's Commmittee, 1952–1954. CA.

30. A. J. Field, "Citizen Participation in City Planning: Preliminary Report on Baltimore, Maryland," as part of the Providence Master Plan Project, 1959. CA.

31. Ibid., 5.

32. Ibid., 6.

33. "James Rouse, Profile of a Believer," *Planning*, September 1979, 34.

34. James Rouse to Richard Schubert, 18 January 1960. CA.

35. Greater Baltimore Committee, Inc., Annual Report, 1959 Projects. CA.

36. Martin Millspaugh, "Charles Center–Inner Harbor Fact Sheet," January 1977. CA.

37. "James Rouse, Profile of a Believer," 34. CA.

38. James Rouse to Richard Schubert, 18 January 1960. CA.

39. Field, "Citizen Participation in City Planning," 11.

40. James Rouse to David Rockefeller, 25 September 1958. Series 2, Box 108, folder; Greater Baltimore Committee: Charles Center Proposal, 1958–1960. CA.

41. Jane Jacobs, "New Heart for Baltimore," *Architectural Forum*, ca. 1958.

42. "James Rouse, Profile of a Believer," 34.

43. "Summary of Progress: Charles Center–Inner Harbor Redevelopment Program," November 1976. CA.

44. Ibid.

45. "The History of a Bold Adventure in Community Betterment," ACTION, ca. 1961. CA.

46. Ibid.

47. James Rouse to Arthur Goldman, 2 December 1958, 1–2. Series 2, Box 101, folder; ACTION—General Correspondence (2 of 2), September 1958–January 1959. CA.

48. ACTION, "Agenda for a Good City," Presented at the Newark Conference on the ACTION Program for the American City, 4–6 May 1959. CA.

49. James Rouse to Norman Mason, Administrator of the Housing and Home Finance Agency, 30 October 1959. CA.

50. James Rouse, "The New Image Project," Draft, 1960. CA.

51. James Rouse to Norman Mason, 30 October 1959. Series 2, Box 102, folder: Ford Motor Company, 1959–1967. CA.

52. James Rouse to Thomas Reid, Ford Motor Company, Civic and Governmental Affairs Manager, 9 September 1960. Series 2, Box 102, folder: folder: Ford Motor Company, 1959–1967. CA.

53. Jack Rosenthal, "Hartford Region Gets Growth Plan," *New York Times*, 7 May 1972, 42.

54. Allan R. Talbot, "Processing Hartford: An Idea-Laden Interim Report," *City* (summer 1972), 1.

55. "Mayor Backs Moynihan's Criticism of City," *Hartford Courant*, 2 October 1969, 1A.

56. Viola P. Willson, "Why Business Backs Process," *Hartford Business Times*, 14 October 1971, 9-D.

57. Donald Canty, "What Could Make Hartford Tick?" *City* (summer 1971), 31–35.

58. Talbot, "Processing Hartford," 1.

59. Janet Anderson, "Hartford Process, Inc., Mum on Plans," *Hartford Courant*, 8 August 1971, 15.

60. Lead Editorial, "Vista of a Better Community," *Hartford Courant*, 6 April 1969, 2-B.

61. Donald Canty, "What Could Make Hartford Tick?" 31–35.

62. Press Release, American City Corporation, 11 May 1972, 1, 6. CA.

63. Leo Molinaro, "Presentation to the Greater Hartford Corporation," 5 November 1969, 16–17.

64. Brian Walsh to Mike Spear, American City Corporation, 6 December 1969. Series 1.5, Box 424, folder: ACC-GHP: Greater Hartford Process (3 of 3), 1969. CA.

65. Citations from Christopher Feise and Peter Friedland, "Hartford Process and Citizen Participation, March 1973, 1–16.

66. Talbot, "Processing Hartford," 1.

67. Donald Canty, "What Could Make Hartford Tick?" 31–35.

68. Monroe Karmin, "Greater Hartford: Businessmen, Politicians Seek to Renew a City and Help Suburbs, Too," *Wall Street Journal*, 26 July 1972.

69. James Rouse to Mrs. Miles Pennybacker, 10 December 1975. Series 1.5, Box 425, folder: ACC-GHP: Greater Hartford Process, 1973–1976. CA.

70. John Lacy, "Behind the Skyline . . . A City in Serious Trouble," *Hartford Courant*, 23 August 1970.

71. John Sherman, "Private Enterprise Joins Region Planning Effort," *Hartford Courant*, 6 April 1969.

72. Lacy, "Behind the Skyline."

73. "Hartford Sets Pace of U.S. in Model Plan," *Hartford Times*, 20 May 1970.

74. Monroe Karmin, "Romney Readies a Secret, Supposedly Cheap Plan to Attack Social Ills—and Help Nixon Win Votes," *Wall Street Journal*, 30 December 1971.

75. Teaford, *Rough Road*, 153–54.

76. Roy Lubove, *Twentieth-Century Pittsburgh* (New York: Wiley, 1969), 139–40.

77. James Rouse, Speech, Boston, ca. 1978. CA.

78. James Rouse, Speech, ca. 1980s. CA.

Notes to Chapter 3

1. "Slum Clearance: A Way to a Permanent Housing Boom," *Time* 65, no. 6 (7 February 1955): 74.

2. Sassoon, *One Hundred Years of Socialism*.

3. P. Stewart Macaulay, "A Basis for a Baltimore City Plan: Recentralization of Population and Elimination of Blighted Areas," *Baltimore Sun*, 6 January 1935.

4. "City's Blighted Areas Found Divided between Races," *Baltimore Sun*, 8 May 1950.

5. James Rouse, Speech to Urban Renewal Conference, Baltimore, Maryland, 27 March 1961.

6. Arnold Hirsch, "Searching for a 'Sound Negro Policy': A Racial Agenda for the Housing Acts of 1949 and 1954. *Housing Policy Debate issue* 2 (Fannie Mae Foundation): 410.

7. Greater Baltimore Committee, Inc., Annual Report, 1959 Projects.

8. James Rouse, "It Can Happen Here: A Paper on Metropolitan Growth," 23 September 1963.

9. Fisher, "Rebuilding Our Cities," 131. See also Greg Hise, *Magnetic Los Angeles: Planning the Twentieth-century Metropolis* (Baltimore: Johns Hopkins UP, 1997), and Marc A. Weiss, *The Rise of the Community Builders: The American Real Estate Industry and Urban Land Planning* (New York: Columbia UP, 1987).

10. Rouse Speech, "The New Highways," 3. CA.

11. Rouse Speech, National Retail Dry Goods Association, 10. CA.

12. Moses, "Slums and City Planning," 65.

13. Rouse Speech, "The New Highways," 2. CA.

14. See Cliff Ellis, "Professional Conflict over Urban Form" in *Planning the Twentieth-Century City*; Mark S. Foster, *From Streetcar to Superhighway: American City Planners and Urban Transportation, 1900–1940* (Philadelphia: Temple UP, 1981); Mark Rose, *Interstate: Express Highway Politics, 1939–1989* (Knoxville: U of Tennessee P, 1990); and Bruce E. Seely, *Building the American Highway System: Engineers as Policy Makers* (Philadelphia: Temple UP, 1987).

15. Jack Star, "The All-American Cities . . . " *Look*, 10 February 1953, 42.

16. "Housing Code Enforcement and Urban Renewal," Greater Baltimore Committee, Planning Council, 21 November 1960.

17. Ibid. See also Martin Millspaugh, "Baltimore's Unique Experiment: A Report on the Baltimore Plan and Its Effect on Our Slums," *Baltimore Sun*, 4 January 1954, 17.

18. ACTION Research Memorandum, "Case Study: Baltimore Fight Blight Fund," 1956.

19. Edgar Jones and Burke Davis, "The Baltimore Plan," *Atlantic Monthly*, May 1949, 35–38.

20. Congressman Joseph W. Martin, *Congressional Record*, 22 June 1949, 8130.

21. "These Slum Landlords Got Smart," *Saturday Evening Post*, 31 January 1953.

22. Star, "The All-American Cities," 42.

23. Encyclopedia Britannica Films, "*The Baltimore Plan* Script," ca. 1952. CA.

24. *The Baltimore Plan*, from the collection of the Iowa State University Instructional Technology Center, 16 mm film transfer, ca. 1953.

25. "Memorandum on the Encyclopedia Britannica Fight Blight Movie," *CPHA*, 28 October 1952. Series 2, Box 107, folder: Fight Blight Fund. CA.

26. "Visiting Mayor Unimpressed by Slum Job," *Baltimore Sun*, 4 September 1953; "Untitled," *Baltimore Sun*, 5 September 1953.

27. "Baltimore Plan Urged for Nation," *Baltimore News American*, 30 March 1952.

28. Garland A. Ruark, "Beware! The Baltimore Plan," *Federationist*, 4 September 1953, 20.

29. "Mayor Zeidler Confirms Baltimore Plan Failures," *Federationist*, 11 September 1953.

30. "The Baltimore Plan Is Ready for Appraisal," *Baltimore Sun*, 31 January 1953.

31. Martin Millspaugh, "Tentacles of Blight Still Evident," *Baltimore Sun*, 7 January 1954.

32. "Mayor Zeidler Confirms Baltimore Plan Failures," CA.

33. James Rouse, Speech, "The Baltimore Plan," *Baltimore Sun*, 10 April 1953. CA.

34. James Rouse, "The Impact of Housing Improvement on the Community," Massachusetts Institute of Technology, 1954, 5. CA.

35. James Rouse to G. H. Griffith, The Fund for Adult Education, 17 August 1953. Series 2, Box 107, folder: Fight Blight Fund, 1951–198. CA.

36. Dwight D. Eisenhower to James W. Rouse, 22 September 1953. Series 7.5, Box 5, folder: Correspondence. CA.

37. James Rouse to Ferd Kramer, 29 September 1981. Series 4, Box 103, folder: mail by month, September 1981. CA.

38. Ibid.

39. James Rouse, "The Impact of Housing Improvement on the Community," MIT, 1954. 7. CA.

40. Dwight D. Eisenhower, "Housing Program—Message from the President of the United States," *Congressional Record*, 25 January 1954, 737–38.

41. Harry Bates, "The Administration's Housing Program—It Bears Little Relation to the Nation's Need," *American Federationist*, March 1954, reprinted in *Congressional Record*, Appendix, 1954, A2382–83.

42. Patrick Malone, "8600 Dollar Housing Program But No 8600 Dollar Housing," *Work*, Catholic Labor Alliance, January 1954.

43. Gurney Breckenfeld, Speech to the Symposium on Urban Renewal, Time and Life Building, New York, 7 May 1964, 7–19. CA.

44. "People: Mortgage Banker Jim Rouse, Long a Crusader against Slums, Named President of ACTION," publication unclear, November 1958, 63. CA.

45. Charles Abrams, "The Walls of Stuyvesant Town," *The Nation*, 24 March 1945, vol. 160, no. 1, 328–30.

46. Eisenhower, "Housing Program," 737–38.

47. Albert Cole, Administrator of the Housing and Home Finance Agency, Remarks to the Economic Club of Detroit, 8 February 1954, "Role of the Federal Government in Housing," printed in the *Congressional Record*, 17 February 1954, A1289.

48. Albert Cole, quoted in the *Congressional Record*, 2 April 1954, 4468.

49. Charles Slusser, Commissioner of the Public Housing Administration, address printed in *Congressional Record*, 6 April 1954, A2640.

50. Congressman Harold Donohue, *Congressional Record*, 2 April 1954, 4448. See also Congressman Harold Donahue, "The Public Housing Program Should Be Continued in the National Interest and Welfare," *Congressional Record*, speech given 30 March 1954, Appendix, 1954, A2471.

51. Joseph P. McMurray, Speech to the Potomac Chapter of the National Association of Housing Officials, Washington, D.C., 1 December 1954, *Congressional Record*, 2 December 1954, A6922.

52. Comments by Congressman William Widnall, *Congressional Record*, 2 April 1954, 4461.

53. Congressman Martin Dies, *Congressional Record*, 2 April 1954, 4465.

54. Ibid., 4466.

55. Congressman Don Wheeler, ibid., 4473.

56. Congressman Ralph Gwinn, ibid., 4478–79.

57. Congressman Joe Evins, *Congressional Record-House*, 8 April 1954, 4928.

58. Congressman William Colmer, ibid., 4464.

59. "New Housing Law Called Major Gain by President," *(Camden) Editorial, Courier Post*, 4 August 1954.

60. Roger Biles, "Housing Policy in Postwar America," in *From Tenements to the Taylor Homes*, 140. See also 144–45.

61. Congressman Vito Marcantonio, *Congressional Record*, 22 June 1949, 8137.

62. "New 'Hearts' for Our Cities," *Newsweek* 43, no. 13 (29 March 1954): 74.

63. "2 Experts Lined Up to Map D.C. Program for Slum Clearance," *Washington Star*, 12 September 1954.

64. "No Slums in Ten Years: A Workable Program for Urban Renewal," Report to the Commissioners of the District of Columbia, James Rouse and Nathaniel Keith, January 1955, 3–4.

65. Ibid, 14, 18, 28, 29, 31.

66. "The New Washington," Editorial, *Washington Post*, 15 January 1955, 6. See also Robert Albrook, "All-Out War is Mapped to Rid D.C. of Slums, *Washington Post*, undated.

67. Seligman, "The Enduring Slums," 148.

68. Harry S. Jaffe and Tom Sherwood, *Dream City: Race, Power, and the Decline of Washington, D.C.* (New York: Simon & Schuster, 1994), 29.

69. Gillette, *Between Justice and Beauty*, 151–69.

70. James Rouse to Norman Mason, Housing and Home Finance Agency, 30 October 1959. Series 2, Box 102, folder; Ford Motor Company, 1954–1964. CA.

71. ACTION, Board of Directors, 14 October 1955. CA.

72. ACTION, Urban Renewal Reports Research Program for ACTION, 1954. CA.

73. ACTION Research Memorandum, April 1955, 1–9. CA.

74. Milton Vieser, Vice Chair ACTION, The Maryland Club, Baltimore, 16 February 1960. CA.

75. ACTION *Reporter* 4, no. 4 (Feb.–March 1960). CA.

76. ACTION Chairman, Roy Johnson, quoted in ACTION *Reporter* 4, no. 4 (Feb.–March 1960). CA.

77. "ACTION's Rouse Urges Cities to Fight Blight," Convention Daily, United States Savings and Loan League, Miami Beach, 16 November 1960. CA.

78. From "The History of Bold Adventure in Community Betterment," ACTION, ca. 1961. CA.

79. First Year Report, ACTION, 1956. CA.

80. *The Man of ACTION,* Iowa State University, Instructional Technology Center, 16 mm transfer.

81. "ACTION to Date," 1 September 1962, 13. CA.

82. A. E. Hotchner, "Is Your Neighborhood Going to Seed?" *Baltimore Sun,* 9 October 1955, 7+.

83. "ACTION to Date," 5–8. CA.

84. Leo Molinari to James Rouse, Internal ACTION Report, 1969. Series 1.5, Box 424, folder; Feb. 6, 1970 Presentation 1969. CA.

85. James Lash to Ladd Plumley, 6 April 1961. Series 2, Box 103, folder: General Correspondence, April 1961. CA.

86. "A Proposal by ACTION," 1961. CA.

87. James Rouse, Executive Committee Meeting, 28 March 1961, 7A. CA.

88. James Rouse, "Utopia: Limited or Unlimited," National Housing Conference, Inter-Religious Coalition for Housing, Interchurch Center, 14 November 1979. CA.

89. James Rouse, Speech at Massachusetts Institute of Technology, ca. 1984. CA.

90. Mark Cohen, "Captain Enterprise," *Baltimore Magazine,* April 1987, 80, 83.

91. James Rouse to Nestor Weigant, 17 June 1987. Series 4, Box 27, folder: June 1987. CA.

92. "Harborplace Brings Project Expertise to Japan," *Washington Post,* 23 July 1990.

93. Ibid.

94. James Rouse, Testimony before the Subcommittee on Housing and Urban Affairs of the Committee on Banking, Housing and Urban Affairs of the United States Senate, 20 April 1989, 1. CA.

95. James Rouse to Hugh Carey, 19 December 1990. Series 4, box 37, folder: December 1990 (1). CA.

96. Testimony of James Rouse, Hearings before Ways and Means Committee of the U.S. House of Representatives on Rehabilitation of Low-Income Housing, 9 July 1985. CA.

97. Mina Wright, "Untitled," *Blueprints* 6, no. 2, spring 1988, 4.

98. James Rouse and Elizabeth Rouse, "Wage Peace, Mr. President," paid advertisement, *Washington Post,* 7 May 1970.

99. James Rouse to Ferd Kramer, 1 May 1984, 2. Series 4, Box 23, folder: May 1984. CA.

100. James Rouse to Nancy Allison, 11 August 1983. CA. Series 4, Box 22, folder: August 1983.

101. James Rouse to Robert Smith, 7 December 1988. Series 4, Box 32, folder: December 1988 (2). CA.

102. James Rouse, Speech at the Four Seasons Hotel, ca. 1985. CA.

103. James Rouse, Speech at the Charlotte Housing Symposium, 20 November 1986, 23. CA.

104. Musgrove Housing Policy Retreat, Center for Community Change, 30 October 1987, 2. CA.

105. Testimony of James Rouse, Hearings before Ways and Means Committee of the U.S. House of Representatives on Rehabilitation of Low-Income Housing, 9 July 1985.

106. James Rouse to Bruce Smart, 20 July 1982. Series 4, Box 21, folder: July 1982. CA.

107. James Rouse to Jay Moorhead, Special Assistant to the President, Private Sector Initiatives, The White House, 11 November 1982. Series 4, Box 21, folder: November 1982. CA.

108. James Rouse to Douglas and Susan [last name unknown], Fund-raising letter, 20 March 1991. CA.

109. Kuttner, "The Erosion of the Welfare State," 8–10.

110. "Special Report: The Future of Social Insurance and Welfare," Ford Foundation Letter, 1 February 1985.

111. "Special Report: The Future of Social Insurance and Welfare."

112. James Rouse, Presentation to Cities' Congress on Roads to Recovery, Cleveland, Ohio, 9 June 1982, 22. CA.

113. James Rouse, Statement before Senate Subcommittee on Housing, 29 March 1968, 1247–48. CA.

114. James Rouse to John Sawyer, 27 July 1983, 2. Series 4, Box 22, folder: July 1983 (2). CA.

115. Rouse Presentation, Cities' Congress on Roads to Recovery, 22.

116. Paul Engelmayer, "Developer of Festival Marketplaces Sets Up Foundation to Renovate Inner City Homes," Wall Street Journal, 29 December 1983.

117. Rouse Speech, "Free Enterprise in a New America," 14.

118. James Rouse to Aaron Gural, 22 August 1989. Series 4, Box 34, folder: August 1984 (1). CA.

119. Rouse Speech, Four Seasons Hotel. CA.

120. James Rouse, Testimony before the Subcommittee on Housing and Urban Affairs of the Committee on Banking, Housing and Urban Affairs of the United States Senate, 20 April 1989. 1. CA.

121. James Rouse to Warren Buffet, 25 September 1984. CA. Series 4, Box 23, folder: September 1984. CA.

122. James Rouse to Raymond Chambers, 8 November 1989, 2. Series 4, Box 35, folder: November 1989 (2). CA.

123. James Rouse, "Make No Little Plans," Speech at International New Towns Association Conference, Barcelona, Spain, 3 October 1983, 26, 28. CA.

124. Testimony of James Rouse, 1982 National Urban Policy Report, Hearings before the Joint Economic Committee, Congress of the United States, 11 July 1982. CA.

125. James Rouse, Testimony before the Subcommittee on Housing and Urban Affairs of the Committee on Banking, Housing and Urban Affairs of the United States Senate, 20 April 1989.

126. Donald Riegle, People for the American Way publication, 14 October 1993.

127. David Schwartz, Editorial, Journal of Commerce, 30 March 1988, 8A.

128. James Rouse to Jack Kemp, 30 November 1989. Series 4, Box 34, folder: Nov. 1989 (1).

129. Editorial, "Redeeming HUD," Baltimore Sun, 5 October 1989, A-26.

130. "And the . . . Great Hope," Business Week, 10 July 1989, 74.

131. Michael Seipp to James Rouse, 22 June 1990. Series 4, Box 36, folder: June 1990 (1). CA.

132. Keynote address of Henry Cisneros, 2000 Annual James W. Rouse Forum, 25 September 2000, 1.

133. Anna Borgman, "Jim Rouse's Plan to Save the Slums," Washington Post, 14 April 1996, C-1.

134. Cohen, "Captain Enterprise," 80.

135. James Rouse to Andy Sigler, 27 December 1990. Series 4, box 37, folder: December 1990 (1). CA.

136. Ralph Smith, quoted in Joan Walsh, "Stories of Renewal: Community Building and the Future of Urban America," Rockefeller Foundation, January 1997.

137. James Rouse to Paul Brophy, 1 November 1989. Series 4, Box 34, folder: Nov. 1989 (2). CA.

138. James Rouse to Jim [last name unknown], 13 June 1990. Series 4, Box 36, folder: June 1990 (2). CA.

139. Kristen Bradfield, "Project Case Study," Affordable Housing Finance, October 2001.

140. James R. Cohen, "Abandoned Housing: Implications for Federal Policy and Local Action," Urban Studies and Planning Program, University of Maryland, College Park, 13, 23.

141. Dreier, "Labor's Love Lost?" 365.

142. George Will, "The Free Citizens of Sandtown," *Baltimore Sun*, 2 January 1996. See also Claire Carter, "Yes, It Can Be Done," *Parade*, 12 May 1991, 4–5.

Notes to Chapter 4

1. James Rouse, AMC meeting, The Greenbriar, "The New American Marketplace: A Challenge to Department Store Leadership," 27 April 1976. CA.

2. Kozol, 183.

3. Marling, 283.

4. Kenneth T. Jackson, "Memphis," in *American Places: Encounters with History: A Celebration of Sheldon Meyer*, ed. William E. Leuchtenburg (New York: Oxford UP, 2000).

5. Robert Wood, *Suburbia: Its People and Their Politics* (New York: Houghton Mifflin, 1959), 163.

6. James Rouse to Arthur Goldman, 2 December 1958. Series 2, Box 101, folder: ACTION—General Correspondence (2 of 2), September 1958–Jan. 1959. CA.

7. Ibid.

8. "Urban Genius Dead at 81."

9. Rouse Speech, International Council of Shopping Centers, 2–3. CA.

10. James Rouse to Harvey Moger, Connecticut General Life Insurance Company, 4 February 1960. Series 1.4, Box 421, Folder: Cherry Hil 1957–1960. CA.

11. James Rouse to Stockton Strawbridge, 30 December 1960. CA.

12. James Rouse, Speech to the American Institute of Planners, October 1977. CA. Untitled transcript of speech with April Young introduction for JWR.

13. James Rouse, "Proceedings," ca. 1978. Series 5, Box 216, folder: American Institute of Planners, October 10–12, 1977. CA.

14. James Rouse to Arthur Goldman, 2 December 1958. CA.

15. Margaret Crawford. "The World in a Shopping Mall," in *Variations on a Theme Park: The New American City and the End of Public Space*, ed. Michael Sorkin (New York: Farrar, Straus & Giroux, 1991), 22.

16. Frieden and Sagalyn, *Downtown Inc.*, 65.

17. James Rouse, "The New American Marketplace: A Challenge to Department Store Leadership," Speech at AMC meeting, The Greenbriar, 27 April 1976. CA.

18. See, for instance, Richard Longstreth, *City Center to Regional Mall: Architecture, the Automobile, and Retailing in Los Angeles, 1920–1950* (Cambridge, Mass.: MIT Press, 1998); William S. Worley, *J. C. Nichols and the Shaping of Kansas City: Innovation in Planned Residential Communities* (Columbia: U of Missouri P, 1993); William Severini

Kowinski, *The Malling of America: An Inside Look at the Great Consumer Paradise* (New York: Morrow, 1985); Ira G. Zepp, *The New Religious Image of Urban America: The Shopping Mall as Ceremonial Center* (Niwot: UP of Colorado, 1997); Harvey M. Rubenstein, *Pedestrian Malls, Streetscapes, and Urban Spaces* (New York: Wiley, 1992); Barry Maitland, *Shopping Malls: Planning and Design* (New York: Nichols, 1985); and Ann Satterthwaite, *Going Shopping: Consumer Choices and Community Consequences* (New Haven, Conn.: Yale UP, 2001).

19. Victor Gruen, *The Heart of Our Cities; The Urban Crisis: Diagnosis and Cure* (New York: Simon & Schuster, 1964), 190–98.

20. "Mid-City Shopping Center," *Architectural Forum*, March 1953, 134.

21. Rouse Speech, International Council of Shopping Centers, 2. CA.

22. Rouse Speech, "The New American Marketplace," 4. CA.

23. James Rouse, "The Regional Shopping Center: Its Role in the Community It Serves," 7th Urban Design Conference, Harvard University, 26 April 1963. CA.

24. James Rouse, Memo to Peyton Cochran, 11 October 1966. Series 4, Box 6, folder; Mail by Month, October 1966. CA.

25. Rouse Speech, "The New American Marketplace," 4. CA.

26. James Rouse, Memo, 12 February 1976. CA.

27. Rouse Speech, "The New American Marketplace," 2–3.

28. Rouse Speech, International Council of Shopping Centers, 3.

29. "The Future of the American Out-of-Town Shopping Center," Harvard Graduate School of Design, Seventh Urban Design Conference, *Ekistics*, Doxiadis Associates, vol. 16, no. 93, August 1963, 99.

30. Josh Olsen interview with Ned Daniels, 5 July 2000, 113–14.

31. Eastfield Promotional Materials, 29 November 1966, Rouse Company. CA.

32. "The Future of the American Out-of-Town Shopping Center," 99. CA.

33. Rouse Speech, "The Regional Shopping Center," 6. CA.

34. Stephanie Dyer, "Designing 'Community' in the Cherry Hill Mall: The Social Value of Consumer Spaces, 1961–1973," draft manuscript, 12. CA.

35. James Rouse to Larry Wolf, 20 October 1967.

36. Ned Daniels to James Rouse, 14 September 1979.. Series 1.5, Box 437, folder: Harborplace, Baltimore, 1979–1981. CA

37. "Promotion," Pamphlet, CRD, ca. 1960. CA.

38. Rouse Speech, International Council of Shopping Centers, 2.

39. Gurney Breckenfeld, *Columbia and the New Cities* (New York: I. Washburn, 1971), 214.

40. Don Wharton, "Those Amazing Shopping Centers," *Reader's Digest*, May 1962. Reprint.

41. Jean Holmes, "Checking Rouse Company's Cherry Hill Center," *Howard County Times*, 14 October 1964.

42. Seth King, "Supermarkets Hub of Suburbs," *New York Times*, February 1971, 58.

43. Rouse, "Proceedings," ca. 1978, 20. CA.

44. Rouse Speech, "The Regional Shopping Center," 8. CA.

45. "The Future of the American Out-of-Town Shopping Center," 96–103.

46. Rouse Speech, Real Estate Board of Baltimore, 1 February 1964, 11. CA.

47. Rouse Speech, "The New American Marketplace," 10. CA.

48. "Columbia: A New City," Promotional Brochure, The Rouse Company, 1966, 12. CA.

49. "Soviet Experts See a 'New Town,'" *New York Times*, 26 April 1973.

50. For a short summary of court decisions related to free speech in malls, see Lizabeth Cohen, "From Town Center to Shopping Center: The Reconfiguration of Community

Marketplaces in Postwar America," *American Historical Review* 101, no. 4 (October 1996): 1068–71.

51. Ibid., 1080–81.

Notes to Chapter 5

1. Robert Owen, quoted in Edward K. Spann, *Brotherly Tomorrows: Movements for a Cooperative Society in America, 1820–1920* (New York: Columbia UP, 1989), 25.

2. Fisher, "Rebuilding Our Cities," 131.

3. Ada Louise Huxtable, "'Cluster Instead of 'Slurbs," *New York Times Magazine*, 9 February 1964, 37; and Marya Mannes, "How Do You Want to Live?" *McCall's*, June 1966.

4. Wolfgang Langewiesche, "Look at America's 'New Towns,'" *Reader's Digest*, March 1967, 4.

5. Breckenfeld, 222.

6. Heikki von Hertzen and Paul D. Spreiregen, *Building a New Town: Finland's New Garden City, Tapiola* (Cambridge, Mass.: MIT Press, 1971); Pierre Merlin, *New Towns: Regional Planning and Development* (London: Methuen, 1971); and Ann Louise Strong, *Planned Urban Environments: Sweden, Finland, Israel, the Netherlands, France* (Baltimore: Johns Hopkins UP, 1971).

7. Langewiesche, "Look at America's 'New Towns,'" 6.

8. The 1950s and 1960s critics included Lewis Mumford, *The City in History: Its Origins, Its Transformations, and Its Prospects* (New York: Harcourt, 1961); Richard E. Gordon, Katherine K. Gordon, and Max Gunther, *The Split-Level Trap* (New York: Random House, 1964); John Keats, *The Crack in the Picture Window* (Boston: Houghton Mifflin, 1956); John R. Seeley, R. Alexander Sim, and Elizabeth W. Loosely, *Crestwood Heights: A Study of the Culture of Suburban Life* (New York: Basic Books, 1956); William Whyte, *The Organization Man* (New York: Simon & Schuster, 1956); David Reisman, *The Lonely Crowd: A Study of the Changing American Character* (New Haven, Conn.: Yale UP, 1950); and Betty Friedan, *The Feminine Mystique* (New York: Norton, 1963).

9. Josh Olsen, Appendix, Interview Transcripts, Robert Tennenbaum, 80. CA.

10. Breckenfeld, 257.

11. Columbia, 1966, Rouse Company, 3. CA.

12. Wallace Hamilton, "Interim Memo: The Presentation of the Plan," 30 November 1964. CA.

13. James Rouse, "Great Cities for a Great Society," Chicago Chamber of Commerce and AIA, 8 April 1965. CA.

14. "Columbia Voyage: Discovering Columbia's Tomorrows," 14 October 1989. CA.

15. "Welcome to Columbia," Columbia, spring 1968. CA.

16. Jeanne Lamb O'Neill, "Columbia: Gem of America's 'New Towns,'" *American Home*, May 1970; and Wilmon White, "He's Building a New City," *Together*, December 1968.

17. W. B. Ragsdale, "A Prophet in the Marketplace," *Home Missions*, ca. 1960s. CA.

18. Wolf Von Eckardt, "Prophet of the Urban Eden," *Washington Post*, 7 July 1979, 4.

19. Adam Sachs, "More Is at Stake than Just Sandtown, Rouse Says," *Baltimore Sun*, 23 July 1995, 1-E.

20. Robert Tennenbaum, ed., *Creating a New City: Columbia, Maryland* (Columbia, MO: Perry, 1996), 81.

21. "The First Settlers," Editorial, *Washington Post*, 5 July 1967.

22. Gelfand, 357–58.

23. John McEwan to James Rouse, 3 March 1966. Series 5, Box 203, folder: Weaver Testimony HR 12946 (1 of 2), 1966. CA.

24. James Rouse, Testimony before the Housing Sub-Committee, House Banking and Currency Committee, 25 March 1966. CA.

25. George T. Morgan Jr. and John O. King, *The Woodlands: New Community Development, 1964–1983* (College Station: Texas A and M UP, 1987), 15–16.

26. "James W. Rouse, The City Builder," *Baltimore Magazine*, June 1970, 40.

27. Nancy Allison Memo to Rouse, 8 November 1971. Series 5, Box 212, folder: 17th Housing Industry . . . , November 10–14, 1971. CA.

28. Miles Colean to James Rouse, 25 April 1966. Series 5, Box 203, folder: Weaver Testimony MR 12946 (2 of 2), March 25, 1966. CA.

29. The President's National Advisory Commission on Rural Poverty, the National Commission on Urban Problems, the Advisory Commission on Intergovernmental Relations, the American Institute of Planners, and the National Committee on Urban Growth Policy all issued reports demanding a federal role in planning for a better urban future. Most recommended some form of planned new towns to shape future urban growth.

30. Title X of the Housing and Urban Development Act, approved in 1965, led to about twenty-five projects involving ten thousand acres and $50 million in support receiving approval. Title IV of 1968 was slow to start, the first communities not receiving approval until 1970. Projects started under Title IV (Park Forest South, Illinois, and Jonathan, Minnesota) were integrated into the Title VII program passed in 1970. Title VII also included grants to states and regions for planning and opened the possibility of creating a demonstration project, but the record indicates little interest in these provisions. For details on debates and the progress of the legislation see *Congressional Record*, 90th Congress, 2nd Session (1968), 20562, 20597, 15266–71, 20087, 23682–89, 23691; *Congressional Record*, 91st Congress, 2nd Session, (1970), 39461–62, 39465, 39479–99, 39831, 40916, 41339, 42299–42314, 42316, 42438, 42442, 42629–31, 42635.

31. Carlos C. Campbell, *New Towns: Another Way to Live,* (Reston, Va.: Reston Publishing Company, 1976), 196.

32. Ibid., 196.

33. Ibid., 201.

34. *United States at Large,* 91st Congress, 1970–1971, 1791–1794 (Washington, D.C.: U.S. Government Printing Office, 1971).

35. *Congressional Record,* 17 December 1970, 42307.

36. *United States at Large,* 91st Congress, 1970–1971, 1790–92.

37. *Congressional Record,* 26 July 1968, 23689.

38. Department of Housing and Urban Development, "An Evaluation of the Federal New Communities Program," Division of Policy Studies, Office of Policy Development, 1983, 1.6. National Archives II.

39. Ibid.

40. See, for instance, "HUD Issues Commitment for First New Community," *HUD News,* 13 February 1970; United States Department of Housing and Urban Development, Office of New Communities Development, "Report on Riverton, A New Community Proposal," July 1971; William J. Nicoson, "Interim Economic and Financial Report-Soul City," 15 September 1971; HUD, Office of New Communities Development, "Report on Cedar-Riverside, A New Community Proposal," March 1971. National Archives II.

41. See "Report on Riverton." The legislation also allowed for smaller new-towns-in-town within existing urban areas, a measure demanded by urban mayors. Two projects received

approval, Cedar Riverside, Minnesota, and Park Central, Houston. See NCDC, "Report on Cedar-Riverside." See also Editorial, "The New Town for Cedar-Riverside," *Minneapolis Tribune*, 15 April 1970. National Archives II.

42. Department of Housing and Urban Development, "An Evaluation of the Federal New Communities Program," 3.8, 4.22. National Archives II.

43. NCDC, "Report on Park Forest South: Disposition Alternative," Park Forest South Interdisciplinary Team, 16 October 1979. National Archives II.

44. "An Evaluation of the Federal New Communities Program," 4.3.

45. Thomas Lippman and Bill Richards, "New Towns: Realities Dim Dreams," *Washington Post*, 12 January 1975, A-1, A-12.

46. "An Evaluation of The Federal New Communities Program," 5.8–5.15, 5.24.

47. The following documents at the National Archives II offer details on the problems in new towns and the dissolution of the program: "NCDC: Redirection Study Working Paper," 4 April 1980; NCDC Board of Directors, Minutes of Meeting, 7 April 1982; NCDC, "Confidential Memo, Program Highlight," 1982; "Testimony before the Subcommittee on Housing and Community Development, Committee on Banking and Currency," Jonathan Howes, AIP, Director, Center for Urban and Regional Studies, 23 September 1975.

Press coverage of the demise was extensive, particularly in the *Washington Post*, where it was particularly damaging. Those in the Washington area were understandably interested in the fate of this federal program. See Thomas Lippman, "U.S. Aided New Towns Face Crisis," *Washington Post*, 15 November 1974, A-1; Thomas Lippman, "HUD Ends New Town Program," *Washington Post*, 11 January 1975, A-1; Thomas Lippman, "Minnesota Dream Now Up for Sale," *Washington Post*, 15 January 1975, A-1; Bill Richards, "Developers Seek Alternatives to New Towns," *Washington Post*, 17 January 1975, A-7; Thomas Lippman and Bill Richards, "New Towns: Realities Dim Dreams," 12 January 1975, A-1; "Soul City, N.C.: High Risk Experiment, *Washington Post*, 15 January 1975; "U.S. New Towns Plan Facing Huge Loss," *New York Times*, 12 December 1976, 1.

48. Thomas Lippman, "HUD Retreats from New Town Idea," *Washington Post*, 14 January 1975, A-1.

49. Ibid., 2.

50. Summary of New Community Oversight Hearings, 29 September 1975, Department of Housing and Urban Development, 5. National Archives II.

51. Rouse Speech, "Make No Little Plans," 6–7.

52. James Rouse, Speech to Urban Land Institute, Atlanta, 30 May 1977. CA.

53. James Rouse, "How to Build a Whole New City from Scratch," *Savings Bank Journal*, October 1966, 32. CA.

54. James Rouse interview in the American Issues Forum, Voice of America, n.d., 115. CA.

55. As part of the Hartford Process in the early 1970s, Rouse planners proposed to create a nonprofit development corporation to develop a new town that reflected more closely planning designs from Europe, but this idealistic plan failed due to a combination of excessive idealism, insufficient public support, and the national recession. See for instance, Press Release, American City Corporation, 11 May 1972, 3. CA.

56. James Rouse, Statement before the Senate Subcommittee on Housing, 29 March 1968, 1232–33. Rouse made a similar proposal in 1972 in front of the Banking and Currency Committee of the United States House of Representative, 29 September 1972, and in 1975 before the House of Representatives; see "Report of Proceedings," House of Representatives, Subcommittee on Housing and Community Development, 8 October 1975. CA.

57. James Rouse, Testimony before the Subcommittee on Housing, United States House of Representatives, March 29, 1968, 1217, CA.

58. James Rouse, Speech to the International Council of Shopping Centers, 4 June 1973. CA.

59. New Urbanism reinvented the new town tradition in the 1980s but did not significantly alter the formula that Rouse had promoted. Most New Urbanist towns such as Celebration, Florida, and Kentlands, Maryland, as the new towns before them, have been created as a private sector solution to the deficiencies of suburban regions, but remain limited in their regional impact and scale, although they are media darlings. More promising has been the growing popularity of smart growth planning in states such as Maryland and New Jersey, beginning in the 1990s, that has for the first time proposed a more aggressive state role in land planning and direction. The leverage of state contracts and road programs, in tandem with conservation, has finally proved acceptable to the general public, who are increasingly frustrated with overdevelopment.

Notes to Chapter 6

1. Rouse, "Proceedings," ca. 1978, 19. CA.

2. James Rouse to Ann Satterthwaite, July 21, 1983. CA. Series 4, Box 22, folder, Mail by Month—EOC, July 1983.

3. Neal Peirce, "Dazzling Baltimore," *Baltimore Sun*, 30 June 1980.

4. Kevin White, "Fanueil Hall and Quincy Marketplace," in People for the American Way publication, 1993, Honoring Rouse, 14 October 1993. CA.

5. Anthony Yuddis, "Not JUST an Opening," *Boston Globe*, 22 August 1976, 4.

6. Margo Miller, "The Day the Marketplace Opened," *Boston Globe*, 27 August 1976, 1.

7. "Untitled," *Boston Herald American*, 1973. CA.

8. "What Will the New Faneuil Hall Marketplace Be?" Description of the Plan by Benjamin Thompson and Associates, n.d.. Series 1.5, Box 435, folder: Fanueil Hall Marketplace (FHM), 1972. CA

9. Benjamin Thompson to John Harkness, Board of Directors of Boston Society of Architects, 9 January 1973. Series 1.5, Box 435, folder: FHM. CA.

10. Benjamin Thompson and Jane M. Thompson, "Restoration of Faneuil Hall Marketplace: Comments on Historic, Architectural and Urban Issues," ca. 1976. CA.

11. Rouse Letter to "Bill [William White]" 27 July 1983. Series 4, Box 22, folder: Mail by Month—EOC, July 1983 (3). CA.

12. James Rouse, Speech to the International Council of Shopping Centers, 3 May 1960, 4.

13. "Faneuil Hall Marketplace," Rouse Company Internal Document, 10 July 1973. CA.

14. Webb Plan, Rouse Papers, undated, ca. 1973. Series 1.5, Box 435, golfrtz; FHM, October–December 1973. CA.

15. Anthony Yuddis, "Boston Market Plans Show Marked Differences," *Boston Globe*, 7 January 1973, A-49.

16. "Re: Faneuil Hall Marketplace," Rouse Company Intra-Office Memorandum, Peyton Cochran to John Nuttle, 21 February 1973. Series 1.5, Box 435, folder: GHM, January–February 1973. CA.

17. Luix Overbea, "BRA Decision Awaited on Markets Project," *Christian Science Monitor*, 21 March 1973.

18. "Open the Market Window," *Boston Globe*, 8 January 1973.

19. Yuddis, "Not JUST an Opening," 1.

20. Yuddis, "Boston Market Plans," A-49.

21. James Rouse, "Are We Losing Our Downtowns by Default?" Speech to the Main Street Revitalization Conference, ca. 1977. CA.

22. Roy Williams, Faneuil Hall Marketplace Memorandum, 10 July 1973. Series 1.5, Box 435, FHM, May–September 1973. CA.

23. Intra-Office Memorandum, Rouse Company, 31 August 1973. Series 1.5, Box 435, folder: FHM, October–December 1973. CA.

24. "Minutes Design Review," Rouse Company, 31 October 1973. CA.

25. Tracie Rozhon, "Rouse Wins over Hesitant Boston," *Baltimore Sun*, 26 August 1977.

26. Joseph Tierney, Boston City Council, letter sent by Thompson to Rouse, 12 March 1973. CA.

27. James Rouse, Memo, "Faneuil Hall Marketplace: Its Special Meaning and Potential for the Rouse Company," September 1976. Series 1.5, Box 435, folder: FHM, 1976–1977. CA.

28. "The Bull Market," Sharon Cavanaugh to Rouse and others, 12 September 1976. Series 1.5, Box 437, folder: Harborplace, Baltimore (1 of 2), 1978. CA.

29. "Faneuil Hall Marketplace," Rouse Company, promotional materials, 1976. CA.

30. Robert Campbell, "Evaluation: Boston's Upper of Urbanity," *AIA Journal*, June 1981, 29.

31. Thompson and Thompson, "Restoration of Faneuil Hall Marketplace." CA.

32. Jane Davison, "Bringing Life to Market," *New York Times Magazine*, 10 October 1976; reprint *Eastern Review*, February 1977, 14–19.

33. Campbell, 25.

34. James Rouse, Letter to Robert Campbell, 5 October 1981. Series 4, Box 20, folder: Mail by Month, October 1981. CA.

35. Yuddis, "Not JUST an Opening," 4.

36. "Boston Succeeds in Waterfront Urban Renewal," *Baltimore News American*, 12 September 1976.

37. Miller, "The Day the Marketplace Opened," 1.

38. James Rouse, "Faneuil Hall Marketplace: Its Special Meaning and Potential for the Rouse Company," September 1976. CA.

39. James Rouse, "Are We Losing Our Downtowns by Default?" Speech to the Main Street Revitalization Conference, ca. 1977. CA.

40. Frieden and Sagalyn, *Downtown, Inc.*, 175.

41. Benjamin and Jane Thompson to the Rouse Company, "Guiding the Future of Faneuil Hall Marketplace," 5 December 1978. Series 1.5, Box 435, folder FHM—Critiques 1978. CA.

42. Ibid.

43. Carol Todreas to James Rouse, 5 October 1978. Series 1.5, Box 435, folder: FHM—Critiques 1978. CA.

44. Davison, "Bringing Life to Market."

45. Faneuil Hall Marketplace Research Summary, Rouse Company, 28 November 1978. CA.

46. Woody [last name unknown] to James Rouse, 19 December 1978, CA. Series 1.5, Box 435, folder: FHM—Critiques 1978. CA.

47. James Rouse to Michael Spear, 4 October 1978, 2. CA. Series 1.5, Box 435, folder; FHM—Critiques, 1978.

48. James Rouse to K. A. Gorman and Vann Massey, 17 October 1984. Series 4, Box 32, folder: Mail by Month, EOC/EF, October 1984 (2). CA.

49. Robert Campbell, "The Man Behind Faneuil Hall," *Boston Globe*, 5 May 1996, A-3.

50. Ellen Kelly, "Reflections on Historical Ingredients of Baltimore's Inner Harbor," late 1970s. Report for The Rouse Company, unpublished. CA.

51. David A. Wallace, "An Insider's Story of the Inner Harbor," *Planning*, September 1979, 21.

52. Martin Millspaugh, Interview with the author, 17 December 2002.

53. Martin Millspaugh, "The Inner Harbor: A Progress Report," n.d. CA.

54. "Sales Potential Analysis," Rouse Company, January 1979. CA.

55. Brendan Walsh, "Harborplace and the Poor: Ripoff or Boon," *Baltimore Sun*, ca. 1978.

56. David W. Barton, "Stores in the Inner Harbor," *Baltimore Sun*, 8 October 1977, A-15.

57. James Rouse to Walter Orlinsky, 28 June 1978. Series 1.5, Box 437, Harborplace, Baltimore, 1978. CA.

58. Intra-Office Memo, Scott Ditch to Bruce Alexander, 11 May 1978. CA.

59. Michael Wentzel, "City Signs 75-year Harborplace Agreement," *Baltimore Sun*, 28 December 1978, C4.

60. Martin Millspaugh, Interview with the author, 17 December 2002.

61. James W. Rouse to William Donald Schaefer, 18 December 1978. Series 1.5, Box 437, Harborplace, Baltimore, 1979–1981. CA.

62. James Rouse to Henry Johnson, 18 April 1978. Series 1.5, Box 437, folder: Harborplace, Baltimore, 1978. CA.

63. "The Look of Harborplace," *Baltimore Sun*, n.d.

64. "Harborplace: Downtown Baltimore," Rouse Company, ca. 1981. CA.

65. James Rouse to William Donald Schaefer, 18 June 1981. CA.

66. Robert Levi to Mathias Devito, undated, and Mathias DeVito to Robert Levi, 23 July 1979. Series 1.5, Box 437, Harborplace, Baltimore, 1978. CA.

67. Consumer Research, Harborplace, Rouse Company, January 1981. CA.

68. "The Master Builder Who Rescues Dying Downtowns," *Reader's Digest*, December 1981, 156.

69. Editorial, "Year-Round at the Harbor," editorial, *Baltimore Sun*, 2 July 1980; "Jubilation Day at Harbor," *Baltimore Sun*, 3 July 1980; and "Baltimore Goes National" editorial, *Baltimore Sun*, 29 June 1980.

70. Rouse Speech, "Make No Little Plans," 18.

71. Donald Canty, "Baltimore's Lively Downtown," *AIA Journal*, June 1981, 36.

72. Ibid.

73. Mary Griffin, "Harborplace Succeeds as a 'People Place,'" *Baltimore News American*, 3 July 1980, 18-A.

74. Wolf Von Eckardt, "Welcoming Waterfront," *Washington Post*, 5 July 1980.

75. Consumer Research, Harborplace, Rouse Company, January 1981. CA.

76. Harborplace Pamphlet, Rouse Company, CA.

77. Jacques Kelly, "City Markets Remain Charming Treasures," *Baltimore Sun*, 16 February 2002, 8-D.

78. Eckardt, "Welcoming Waterfront."

79. James Rouse, Speech at the Real Estate Roundtable, Nantucket, 16–20 September 1987. CA.

80. James Rouse, Letter to Robert Campbell, 5 October 1981. CA.

81. Rouse Notes, "Conference on Public Markets," Seattle, Washington, 8 August 1987. CA.

82. James Rouse to William Hudnut, 8 July 1983. CA.

83. Frieden and Sagalyn, *Downtown, Inc.*, 180–81, 183.

84. Crawford, "The World in a Shopping Mall," 17.

Notes to Epilogue

1. Tony Judt, "Its Own Worst Enemy," *New York Review of Books*, 15 August 2002, 8.

2. Peter Dreier, "Labor's Love Lost/Rebuilding Unions' Involement in Federal Housing Policy," *Housing Policy Debate* 11, no. 3 (Fannie Mae Foundation): 361.

3. Ibid., 352.

4. "Housing Policy and the Myth of the Benevolent State," in *Critical Perspectives on Housing*, Rachel Brett, Chester Hartmann, and Ann Meyerson, eds. (Philadelphia: Temple UP, 1986).

5. Peter Hogan, *The Failure of Planning: Permitting Sprawl in San Diego Suburbs, 1970–1999* (Columbus: The Ohio State University Press, 2001), passim.

6. Paul Grogran and Tony Proscio, *Comeback Cities* (Boulder, Colo.: Westview Press, 2000), passim.

7. Charles Noble, *Welfare As We Knew It: The Political History of the American Welfare State* (New York: Oxford UP, 1997), 12.

8. David Rusk, *Cities without Suburbs* (Washington, D.C.: Woodrow Wilson Center, 1993); and Myron Orfield, *American Metropolitics: The New Suburban Reality* (Washington, D.C.: Brookings Institution, 2002).

9. Jon C. Teaford, *The Unheralded Triumph: City Government in America, 1870–1900* (Baltimore: Johns Hopkins UP, 1984), 6.

10. See Jon Teaford, *The Rough Road to Renaissance* (Baltimore: Johns Hopkins UP, 1990), and Teaford, *The Unheralded Triumph*.

Index

Urban Life and Urban Landscape Series
Zane L. Miller, General Editor

The series examines the history of urban life and the development of the urban landscape through works that place social, economic, and political issues in the intellectual and cultural context of their times.

Cincinnati, Queen City of the West, 1819–1838
Daniel Aaron

Domesticating the Streets: The Reform of Public Space in Hartford, 1850–1930
Peter C. Baldwin

Proportional Representation and Election Reform in Ohio
Kathleen L. Barber

Fragments of Cities: The New American Downtowns and Neighborhoods
Larry Bennett

The Lost Dream: Businessmen and City Planning on the Pacific Coast, 1890–1920
Mansel G. Blackford

Suburban Alchemy: 1960s New Towns and the Transformation of the American Dream
Nicholas Dagen Bloom

Planning for the Private Interest: Land Use Controls and Residential Patterns in Columbus, Ohio, 1900–1970
Patricia Burgess

Cincinnati Observed: Architecture and History
John Clubbe

Lancaster, Ohio, 1800–2000: Frontier Town to Edge City
David R. Contosta

Suburb in the City: Chestnut Hill, Philadelphia, 1850–1990
David R. Contosta

Main Street Blues: The Decline of Small-Town America
Richard O. Davies

For the City as a Whole: Planning, Politics, and the Public Interest in Dallas,
Texas, 1900–1965
Robert B. Fairbanks

Making Sense of the City: Local Government, Civic Culture, and
Community Life in Urban America
Edited by Robert B. Fairbanks and Patricia Mooney-Melvin

The Mysteries of the Great City: The Politics of Urban Design, 1877–1937
John D. Fairfield

Faith and Action: A History of the Catholic Archdiocese of Cincinnati,
1821–1996
Roger Fortin

Cincinnati in 1840: The Social and Functional Organization of an Urban
Community during the Pre–Civil War Period
Walter Stix Glazer

The Poetics of Cities: Designing Neighborhoods That Work
Mike Greenberg

History in Urban Places: The Historic Districts of the United States
David Hamer

The Failure of Planning: Permitting Sprawl in San Diego Suburbs,
1970–1999
Richard Hogan

Columbus, Ohio: A Personal Geography
Henry L. Hunker

Getting around Brown: *Desegregation, Development, and the Columbus*
Public Schools
Gregory S. Jacobs

Regionalism and Reform: Art and Class Formation in Antebellum Cincinnati
Wendy Katz

Building Chicago: Suburban Developers and the Creation of a Divided Metropolis
Ann Durkin Keating

Silent City on a Hill: Landscapes of Memory and Boston's Mount Auburn Cemetery
Blanche Linden-Ward

Plague of Strangers: Social Groups and the Origins of City Services in Cincinnati, 1819–1870
Alan I. Marcus

Visions of Place: The City, Neighborhoods, Suburbs, and Cincinnati's Clifton, 1850–2000
Zane L. Miller

Boss Cox's Cincinnati: Urban Politics in the Progressive Era
Zane L. Miller

Changing Plans for America's Inner Cities: Cincinnati's Over-the-Rhine and Twentieth-Century Urbanism
Zane L. Miller and Bruce Tucker

Polish Immigrants and Industrial Chicago: Workers on the South Side, 1880–1922
Dominic A. Pacyga

The Rise of the City, 1878–1898
Arthur Meier Schlesinger

The New York Approach: Robert Moses, Urban Liberals, and Redevelopment of the Inner City
Joel Schwartz

Designing Modern America: The Regional Planning Association and Its Members
Edward K. Spann

Hopedale: From Commune to Company Town, 1840–1920
Edward K. Spann

Visions of Eden: Environmentalism, Urban Planning, and City Building in St. Petersburg, Florida, 1900–1995
R. Bruce Stephenson

Welcome to Heights High: The Crippling Politics of Restructuring America's Public Schools
Diana Tittle

Washing "The Great Unwashed": Public Baths in Urban America, 1840–1920
Marilyn Thornton Williams